EARLY COMME

*Showing the Way: Peter Oberlander and
the Imperative of Global Citizenship*

As the consummate Canadian urbanist of the 20th century, Peter Oberlander's mark is all over Greater Vancouver and other pace-setting cities, not only through his own innovations but also through the work of so many of the students that he taught and mentored. Ken Cameron's superbly crafted book tells the story of this ever-forward man who set the foundation of the urban culture of our country.

**—Larry Beasley CM, Retired Co-Director of Planning, City of Vancouver, and
Distinguished Practice Professor of Planning, University of British Columbia**

Showing the Way is much more than a description of a life. This book teaches us that the value of life lies not in what you get but in what you give. Peter Oberlander had every reason to turn inward after being subjected to the horror of the Nazis. He had even more reason to turn bitter when he experienced the unexpected antisemitism of Canadians - Canadians who only very grudgingly provided him refuge. Instead Peter Oberlander dedicated his life to building the very containers needed for a true democracy, *i.e.* cities where all are valued and all can find their place. His optimism and generosity under the circumstances described in this book are breathtaking. His life and work are a beacon for young city builders to follow in these unsettled times.

**—Patrick Condon, Professor, Urban Design, School of Architecture
and Landscape Architecture, University of British Columbia**

While this book at one level tells the life story of a most remarkable man, it also offers great insight and perspective on the planning history of Vancouver and Canada. It will be of interest to not only those who knew or met Peter Oberlander, but also to others around the world who want to understand why cities and citizens in Canada, and especially Vancouver, have excelled at creating livable urban environments. It advances the powerful idea that one of the keys to the future of humanity is better cities, managed by their citizens.

**—Michael Geller, planner, developer and commentator on urban
affairs, former CEO of Simon Fraser University Trust**

In this book, Ken Cameron has produced a compelling story of the life and contributions of a legendary Canadian planner, educator, and humanist. Peter Oberlander is one of several immensely influential immigrants – including Thomas Adams, Humphrey Carver, Hans Blumenfeld, and Jane Jacobs-- who have shaped the way we imagine and plan Canadian cities. This book ably addresses a gap in the history of Canadian planning by documenting Oberlander's trajectory – from elder child of a middle-class Viennese Jewish family, to interned teenage refugee, to brilliant student at McGill and Harvard, to university professor and to leadership roles in government agencies and international commissions. Peter Oberlander's commitment to creating spaces for active, sustainable, and meaningful citizenship shines through on every page.

—Jill Grant, Professor Emeritus and former Director,
Dalhousie University School of Planning

Ken Cameron's great tribute to Peter Oberlander is terrifically written! Peter was the embodiment of an engaged citizen of the world, with a unique talent for turning ideas about cities and citizenship into action.

—Mike Harcourt CM, former Mayor of Vancouver and
former Premier of British Columbia

In his characteristically perceptive profile of Peter Oberlander as global citizen, Ken Cameron has opened a new window of understanding into the character of Canadian cities. Across Canada, and well beyond it, Oberlander's thinking has opened minds to creating the cities that we now depend on.

Many people wonder: What lies behind the particular look and feel of a Canadian city? Our urban communities often appear poised somewhere between the refined form and sophisticated function of the great Old World cities and America's expansive civic exuberance. Some marvel at how Canadian cities can offer up the best features of both old and new urbanism in one place, and Cameron has contributed an important piece of the explanation for what makes our cities stand apart from, and often above, their counterparts.

Cameron reveals in elegant prose how Peter Oberlander was uniquely situated to provoke, persuade and push others to embrace the best features of both European and American urban development. The arc of Peter Oberlander's trans-Atlantic life reveals how Canada began building its modern urban identity from the ashes of a war that transformed Europe and North America, building upon the gradual, yet resolute, rejection of prejudice and hatred by drawing on the insight of one of its survivors. Peter

Oberlander did much to advance urban practice, and this book explains both how and why with great insight.

Canadian cities have had an out-sized impact on the world - and the world of planning. Why? Who led, guided and imagined what our cities could be? What made it happen? Ken Cameron makes the case that many answers can be traced to one man: Peter Oberlander.

—Anthony Perl, Professor of Urban Studies and Political Science and former Director the Urban Studies Program, Simon Fraser University

In Canada we periodically get planners who are as much leaders and great teachers as politically astute bureaucrats. Some become celebrities. But they are among the many who were trained to lead, guide and imagine at a time when the issues of Canadian cities began to emerge, and we believed we could plan ourselves a better future.

Peter Oberlander came to Canada from Eastern Europe as a victim of the Second World War, but he was a global citizen. A student, a professor, a director. Competently trained and organizationally ambitious. Truly working at local, national and global scales - with a core belief in the possibility of creating beautiful, humane and democratic cities. Which Canada largely achieved.

This book is that story - of the man, his times and his achievements. Engaging, entertaining, with a message of hope.

—Gordon Price, former City of Vancouver councillor and Metro Vancouver director, former Director of Simon Fraser University's City Program and Co-editor of Price Tags (https://pricetags.ca/)

It is no understatement to say that Peter Oberlander is one of only a few people who can be credited with originating the distinctive approach taken by Vancouver and British Columbia to urban development and planning. He virtually invented the province's planning profession, he was the intellectual godfather of the Agricultural Land Reserve, and he played a crucial role in the development of Vancouver's citizen-based approach to planning. Ken Cameron does us a great service by connecting these dots. More importantly, however, he reveals the man in full and in his historical context. Self-assured, optimistic, and brilliant, Oberlander always seemed to be in the right place at the right time, soaking up the vital ideas of the times and building the networks and coalitions needed to put them into practice. Cameron presents Oberlander as a man whose appalling early experiences led him to confront a divided world with a generous humanism and, in so doing, showed us the way toward a global concept of citizenship.

This is what the book is really about: Oberlander's life as a model of the importance of individual action in bending a complex and conflict-filled world toward a better future.

— **Zack Taylor, Professor of Political Science, University of Western Ontario**

In *Showing the Way*, Ken Cameron weaves together three themes in a triple helix: the story of visionary Canadian planner Peter Oberlander; the development of community and regional planning as a profession in Canada; and the meaning of citizenship in a world of immigrants and refugees. Peter Oberlander's lifelong dedication to building community and a sense of place in his adopted country was forged by his early experiences in World War II as an Austrian-Jewish refugee, forcibly separated from family and interned in the UK and Canada. This compelling book draws on Cameron's personal knowledge of Oberlander, from student to colleague and friend. He offers warm and sometimes humorous accounts of their collaborative attempts to influence the federal and provincial governments to address Canada's challenges as an urban nation. Oberlander's brilliance, energy and stubbornness, along with his ability to find a way around problems (often through carefully cultivated personal relationships) contributed to his many accomplishments. These include the School of Regional and Community Planning at UBC, the development of regional governance in British Columbia, the establishment of a role for the federal government in urban affairs, and his ongoing contributions at the international level to UN Habitat and to the International Centre for Sustainable Cities. *Showing the Way* is a testament to the commitment both Cameron and Oberlander have demonstrated to urban sustainability, to citizen engagement in planning, and to bringing ideas into action.

— **Nola Kate Seymoar, CEO Emeritus, International Centre for Sustainable Cities and Co-Chair, Vancouver City Planning Commission**

Ken Cameron's book tells the story of Peter Oberlander, a remarkable world citizen. In a most enjoyable read, the book describes Peter's many international, Canadian and Vancouver achievements through his teaching, community service, consulting and planning practice.

— **Ray Spaxman, former Director of Planning, City of Vancouver**

SHOWING THE WAY

Tellwell Talent
www.tellwell.ca

ISBN
978-0-2288-0155-9 (Paperback)
978-0-2288-0157-3 (eBook)

SHOWING THE WAY

Peter Oberlander and the
Imperative of Global Citizenship

Peter Oberlander[1]

KEN CAMERON

Foreword by Penelope Gurstein

Table of Contents

PREFACE

This is not a biography of Peter Oberlander, but rather a story about how his life illustrated and informed the concept of global citizenship as it emerged during his lifetime.

"Citizenship" has two meanings that were equally important to him. First, it is a legal term to describe a person's status within a city or a country. Peter Oberlander was stripped of his native Austrian citizenship and endured some of the most trying years of his life as a stateless person before gaining Canadian citizenship and, ultimately, being named a Citizenship Court judge. Second, "citizenship" is a term that describes the spirit of a person who is aware of a set of rights and responsibilities as a member of a human community. Peter Oberlander's life showed the way in which, if humanity is to have a future, these rights and responsibilities must be seen at not just the local and national levels but at the global level.

The idea for the book came from a celebration of Peter Oberlander's life, moderated by Michael Geller, that was held at the Architectural Institute of British Columbia on March 25, 2009. It was an evening of mellow reflections by people with an amazing diversity of experiences set against a background of memorabilia assembled by his widow, Cornelia Hahn Oberlander, which included publications, photos and even a collection of Peter's bow ties.

In preparing my remarks for that evening, I thought of the many important influences Peter had had on my life. He helped me find my life's work and was a collaborator, mentor, and promoter of my achievements. As important as these influences were to me, they seemed to pale beside the scope of his activity and the passionate commitment he had to a better future for humanity. I said:

> Two of the things I admired most about Peter were his ability to act and think both locally and globally, and to move effortlessly between teaching, research, practice and public service. One of

the driving forces for these characteristics was his strong sense of citizenship, and his deep understanding of the multi-layered meaning of that term to the future of humanity at a time at which we must be responsible citizens not only of our communities and our country but of the world. As a planner and as an active citizen of Vancouver, of Canada and of the earth, Peter Oberlander has made an outstanding contribution.

A few months after that celebration, Cornelia contacted me and asked me to consider expanding on these themes in a book. Eight and a half years later, the project is done. That the job got done after all this time is a testament to the enduring meaning of Peter's legacy for me. That the legacy seems, if anything, more relevant than ever to humanity's continuing challenge to overcome tribalism, nativism, and protectionism is evidence of our need for more people like Peter Oberlander in our world.

Ken Cameron
Vancouver, British Columbia
March 2018

DEDICATION

Brahm Wiesman FCIP June 13, 1926 – July 20, 2003[2]

This book is dedicated to the late Brahm Wiesman, who was a Professor at UBC's School of Community and Regional Planning (SCARP) between 1967 and 1979. He served as Acting Director of the School from 1971 to 1977 and as Director from 1976 to 1979. He was later instrumental in securing a Centre for Excellence award from the Canadian International Development Agency to undertake capacity-building projects in China, Indonesia, and Thailand.

If SCARP were a ship, Brahm would have been the keel, providing the stability, continuity, and commitment to excellence that enabled the School, while many of the achievements recorded in this book were being pursued, to continue to produce graduates who would make outstanding and diverse contributions in all parts of the globe.

From the moment we met, Brahm took a personal interest in my success and guided me through a professional education that provided a solid platform for me to make a contribution, in my own small way, to a better future for humanity at the local, national and global levels. At critical moments throughout my career, Brahm would materialize with a suggestion, a contact or a piece of advice to help me find my way forward. I was not alone in this; many others enjoyed the benefits of the "lifetime warranty" that came from a planning education in which Brahm was involved.

Without Brahm Wiesman's dedication, support, and spirit of global citizenship, many of the successes described in this book, and perhaps the book itself, would not have been possible.

Ken Cameron FCIP RPP
M.A. (Community and Regional Planning)
University of British Columbia, 1970

ACKNOWLEDGMENTS

Much of the research for this book was done by Magdalena Urgarte and Benita Menezes who were retained as research assistants under the University of British Columbia's Work Study Program, with additional financial resources provided by the Oberlander family and the author. Penelope Gurstein, Director of the School of Community and Regional Planning, graciously agreed to serve as Principal Investigator for the project, and the School made a financial contribution to the book's publication costs.

I am grateful to Cornelia Oberlander for her co-operation and patience, for the many hours she spent providing me with insights that would not otherwise have been available, and for giving me access to a wealth of material related to Peter Oberlander and their life together.

My sincere thanks are also due to the people who reviewed and commented on all or part of the draft manuscript: Cornelia Oberlander, Penelope Gurstein, Angela Walkinshaw, Ira Nadel, Silver Donald Cameron, Zachary Taylor and Darshan Johal.

The 40+ people who gave their time and interest to participate in interviews are listed in Appendix A. Their insights, whether referenced in the book or not, provided the feedstock from which this story is derived. My discussions with them were the most satisfying aspects of the project, and I am deeply grateful.

Finally, I am grateful to my daughter Jen, my partner Angie Walkinshaw, and my brothers Silver Donald and David Cameron for their support and their faith in my ability to complete this project.

Ken Cameron, FCIP

FOREWORD

Dr. Penelope Gurstein MCIP, Director, School of Community
and Regional Planning, University of British Columbia

As this fascinating book shows, Peter Oberlander's contribution to planning in Canada was complex, many-faceted and multi-layered. He was a planner, a civil servant, a politician and a diplomat of sorts, but, above all, he was a teacher and an inspiration to the first generation of Canadian planners actually to have been born and educated in this country. Integral to Oberlander's philosophy was the concept of the planner as citizen, with rights and responsibilities at local, national and international levels.

In this book, Ken Cameron provides the first published account of the conditions of Peter Oberlander's early life that forged his beliefs on planning and citizenship. His comfortable youth in Vienna was shattered by World War II and the events leading up to it. His Austrian citizenship became worthless, and he was unjustly incarcerated by the Allies; he arrived in Canada as an internee. One cannot help but be touched by the story of his determination to overcome these challenges and establish himself as a citizen of Canada and a leader in the effort to build cities that would reflect the needs and aspirations of Canadians.

The book explains how, along the way, Peter Oberlander learned to cope with many of the core elements of Canada's existence as a nation and their influence on how planning could be conducted. These included the country's origins as a collection of widely-dispersed colonies of Britain and France, which led to a decentralized federal form of government that assigned to the provinces many of the powers important to planning, including municipal institutions and property and civil rights. They also included European concepts of the public and private interests in the ownership and use of land which, until recently, conveniently ignored the interests of the Indigenous peoples of these territories.

Showing the Way illustrates the pivotal role of World War II in the evolution of planning in Canada. The requirements of Canada's role in the conflict transformed the country's economy and established a clear role for the federal government in housing and community planning. As the book demonstrates, the spirit of postwar "reconstruction" that infused the country was as much about city building as anything else.

World War II not only brought Peter Oberlander to Canada, it also brought Walter Gropius to Harvard's Graduate School of Design along with many of Europe's leading architects and urbanists. As the first Canadian (or soon-to-be Canadian) to receive a master's (and later a doctorate) in planning from Harvard, Peter Oberlander soaked up from these intellectual refugees their concept of planning and architecture as social and democratic endeavours and brought this thinking back to Canada.

This book contains some fascinating vignettes about the impact of happenstance in the evolution of Canadian planning. They include the decision of John Bland, the Director of McGill's School of Architecture, to grant Oberlander, the stateless refugee, admission with advanced standing without a shred of paper evidence as to his qualifications. Then there is the way in which the President of UBC, Dr. Norman MacKenzie, a member of the Massey Commission, saw a chance to advance his vision for UBC as the catalyst for a new postwar society in the case for Canadian-trained planners that Oberlander and Humphrey Carver made to the Commission on behalf of CMHC. Perhaps the happiest of the happenstances was the professional then personal partnership that Peter and Cornelia Hahn began at Harvard, which brought to Canada an outstanding practitioner of one of planning's sister disciplines: landscape architecture.

Peter Oberlander believed that his most important legacy was the contributions made by hundreds of students who received an education in planning from the UBC School of Community and Regional Planning. This book documents only a few of the fascinating stories about the impact of these people in Canada and throughout the world.

Canada was (and still is) a small country in which individuals with the values and vision of citizenship can make a difference. Peter Oberlander's story illustrates the importance of citizenship and city-making to a secure and peaceful future, not only for Canadians but for all of humanity.

In that sense, *Showing the Way* helps us to realize that we are all global citizens.

Vancouver, British Columbia
March 2018

CHAPTER ONE:

PROPHETS HONOURED
IN THEIR OWN TOWN

The Vancouver City Council meeting of November 25, 2008 was the last for the mayor and council elected in 2005; it had been one of the most acrimonious terms in living memory. Early in the term, the city had watched with pride as Mayor Sam Sullivan took a turn with the Olympic flag in his wheelchair in Turin, Italy in anticipation of the 2010 Winter Olympic and Paralympic Games in Vancouver and Whistler.

The good feeling soon soured. Sullivan had sponsored a new concept known as "eco-density" which, while neatly encapsulating the environmental benefits of higher density, had become a subject of controversy with a divided council where deep suspicions lurked about the Mayor's motives and tactics. There had been a bitter 88-day strike by civic workers (dubbed "Sam's strike" by some) that had frayed tempers on all sides. By the fall of 2008, trust and co-operation among council members — even those of the same stripe — had almost completely broken down. Confidential documents had disappeared — possibly stolen — from *in camera* meetings, and the police were called in to help the political arm find out where they had gone. Some doubted the wisdom of this step, given that the chief of police had had to apologize for a prank: he had left a bullet-riddled human-silhouette shooting-range target on the city manager's desk. Earlier in 2008, Sullivan had lost his bid for renomination as mayor to fellow Non-Partisan Association Councillor Peter Ladner, who would later be defeated, setting the stage for a decade in power for the opposition Vision Vancouver party.

Both of the guests of honour had been in City Hall many times for many different reasons. On this occasion, they had been told to come to the Mayor's Office prior to attending the council meeting. They were told they could leave their belongings there for safekeeping, which led one of the guests to question facetiously whether this was wise in the light of recent allegations of theft from the offices of city politicians. After receiving reassurances on this point, they were ushered into the council chambers at 3:45 p.m.

On behalf of Council, Mayor Sullivan announced that the guests, Heinz Peter Oberlander and Cornelia Hahn Oberlander, were to be granted the Civic Merit Award in honour of all their achievements and contributions to the City of Vancouver. He stated that this was the first time in the city's history that the Civic Merit Award had been given to a couple. He also noted that such awards required the unanimous approval of City Council and wryly added that this proposition was the only one which had received such approval in Council's soon-to-be-expired and rancorous 2005-2008 term of office.

Sullivan began with the citation for Cornelia Oberlander. He noted that she had started her landscape architecture practice soon after her arrival in Vancouver to join her husband Peter in 1953. "She started bringing to Canada her vision for outdoor spaces that provide pockets of nature in urban environments." he said, noting her involvement in designing landscapes for non-market housing and play spaces for children. "Her talent and knowledge brought her together with some of our country's finest architects for major projects including the National Gallery of Canada and the Canadian Chancery in Washington, D.C. In Vancouver, we have her to thank for helping to make Robson Square and the Vancouver Public Library great public spaces...Mrs. Oberlander has always combined her technical expertise with a concern for the cultural, social and environmental context of each project."

The Mayor cited Cornelia Hahn Oberlander's many national and international recognitions, including five honorary degrees "so far," and, he said, "I am delighted to finally see Vancouver recognize her for all she has done for our cityscapes."

Accustomed by this stage in her life to playing second fiddle, Cornelia told the council she had expected her remarks to be "a P.S." to the remarks of her husband Peter, "my partner for life," but she provided a "pre-script" instead. She recalled what a small town Vancouver seemed to be on her arrival but noted the importance of a number of citizens groups such as the Community Arts Council, the Housing Association and the Community Planning Association of Canada who were trying to "bring this town into the new light of the latter part of the twentieth century" and "...we had one goal: to establish a Planning

Department which was concerned with all aspects of the growth of the city." A highlight in 1970 was her collaboration with Arthur Erickson for the design of the government complex at Robson Square which had attracted worldwide attention. She described her dream for "new ideas for a greener city with open spaces and public transportation so that we do not have to flee the city on weekends." Such a city would offer public support for the arts, be multicultural and take a modern approach to stormwater management, ecological design, and climate change. The future city should have more biomass through the planting of trees, urban agriculture, and green roofs. This dream could only be achieved through teamwork involving all professions and the city's political leadership.

Next, Mayor Sullivan summarized the contribution of Peter Oberlander, the first Canadian to receive a master's and a PhD degree in planning from Harvard, and who went on to establish the first graduate school in planning in Canada at UBC. In 1970, he became the first Secretary of the federal Ministry of State for Urban Affairs, working with a former fellow student at Harvard, Pierre Trudeau, and another Vancouverite by adoption, Ron Basford. Among the achievements of that Ministry were the first federal-provincial-municipal partnerships for urban development and the use of federal lands for the creation of such important urban spaces as Vancouver's beloved Granville Island. (Here, Sullivan recognized the presence in the public gallery of Madeleine Nelson, the widow of Ron Basford, former Minister of State for Urban Affairs.)

Peter Oberlander, the Mayor went on, was the first Canadian to serve as the President of the Association of Collegiate Schools of Planning, the American Society of Planning Officials and the Alumni Council of the Harvard Graduate School of Design. Sullivan referred to Oberlander's many-faceted involvement in the United Nations Human Settlements Program (HABITAT), which "promotes socially and environmentally sustainable towns and cities with the goal of providing shelter for all." The establishment by Peter Oberlander of the Centre for Human Settlements kept a focus at UBC on the issues raised at the first UN Habitat Conference in Vancouver in 1976. This conference had set the stage for the more modern iteration of this meeting, the World Urban Forum III, involving not only governments but representatives of the private sector and civil society, which had been attended by more than 10,000 people in Vancouver in June 2006. The Mayor noted that Oberlander had served the City of Vancouver in more formal roles, including as a Trustee and Chair of the Vancouver School Board and as a Member and Chair of the Town Planning Commission. In the latter capacity, Oberlander played a key role in Vancouver's decision to reject freeways within the city.

When Peter Oberlander came forward to receive the Civic Merit Award certificate from the Mayor, he exclaimed, "It's printed! It must be true!" He continued:

> To be honoured in your home town is a great honour. To be honoured with your lifetime partner is indeed a unique honour. And there's one more: unanimity from this Council is truly unique. I have appeared before this Council many times, never to unanimity about what I have had to say. In fact, it's the first time in my experience that there was no uproar as to what I proposed.

He recalled five events which changed his life and involved the City. First, when he arrived at UBC in 1950 he found that Dr. Norman MacKenzie, President of UBC had secured a seat *ex officio* for a representative of the University on the Town Planning Commission. Peter Oberlander assumed this seat in 1953, taking over from Frederic Lasserre. Second, he noted that he had used his influence to advocate for greater professionalism in planning and decision-making at City Hall, participating in the hiring (and later the firing) of the City's first Director of Planning, Gerald Sutton-Brown. Third, he was instrumental in the City's decision to reject freeways and to retain public access to "our birthright, the waterfront." Fourth, he cited his role in attempting to replicate in Ottawa the coordination among functions he had pursued at City Hall, in the high state of tension arising from the October Crisis (brought on by political kidnapping and murder by Quebec separatists) in 1970. A key achievement there had been the discovery that the federal government was the largest landowner in every Canadian city, which led the establishment of systems to ensure that this land was used and reused for the perpetual benefit of the people of Canada – and never sold. The fifth event was the augmentation of the United Nations' involvement in the human environment to encompass a concern with human settlements, through the conferences and other activities that had been previously referenced by the Mayor.

In his closing, Peter Oberlander referred to his work with Mayor Sullivan on the concept of "ecodensity," a term that encompasses both the economic and ecological dimensions of urban sustainability. Referring to the School of Community and Regional Planning, he stated:

My greatest joy when I look back on the past half-century is the graduates that we have launched into Canada, North America and the globe. We have launched not only the first but the best professional planning school in Canada…The idea that Dr. Larry MacKenzie seeded in 1950-51 has come to fruition. His university is the leading university in this field.

Slightly more than one month later, on December 27, 2008, Peter Oberlander passed away at the age of 86.

Peter Oberlander and Cornelia Hahn Oberlander[3]

In the introduction to her 1987 book *Cosmopolitan Culture: The Gilt-Edged Dream of a Tolerant City*, Bonnie Menes Kahn states, "The great city, the cosmopolitan city, the subject of this book, is one where diversity has created a temporary tolerance, a thriving exchange among strangers. And the project of the place, by force, by design, by chance or coercion, the project is an attempt to benefit from the presence of newcomers and outsiders. Big cities witness it on a grand scale."

Mozart was not from Vienna. Shakespeare was not from London. Peter Oberlander and Cornelia Hahn Oberlander were not from Vancouver. But all prospered in an atmosphere of tolerance and the celebration of creativity that is the essence of great cities. The lives of Peter and Cornelia demonstrate what citizenship means on national and international levels and gained wide recognition. But the roots of this citizenship were always local — in their adopted city.

CHAPTER TWO:

COMPASSION IN THE RUINS OF EMPIRE

Peter Oberlander was a member of an Austrian Jewish family who had lived in the countryside since the fifteenth century. The family name Oberlander, translated into English, means "over the land." Peter's great-great-great grandfather Arthur Oberlander began a modest wine-making and grape-growing business in the small town of Krems, approximately 70-kilometres upstream from Vienna on the River Danube. Krems was located in a steep valley, mid-way between the centre of power (Vienna) and Winzer, the heart of Austrian wine-making territory.

In Austrian rural society, wine-making was considered a tough enterprise due to its requirements of discipline, patience, and back-breaking efforts in response to the fickle weather along the northern fertile lands of the River Danube. The Oberlander clan persisted in the business for a century despite these challenges.

Paul Hofmann, in his seminal work *The Viennese: Splendor, Twilight and Exile*, deconstructs Vienna's rise and decline in Austrian society. He spells out how, in the spirit of the enlightenment in the eighteenth century, Emperor Franz Joseph propagated tolerance and inclusion of the Jewish communities. This created an opportunity for the Jews to participate to a certain extent in Austrian social, economic and political life. They quickly gained prominence in the commercial and financial sectors. The impact of this inclusion was felt by the Oberlanders.

By the mid-nineteenth century, industrialization was contributing to the growth of an urban middle-class in Vienna. Urbane Jewish groups used this opportunity to organize themselves as a religious and cultural community. This created further opportunities to participate in the political life of Austria. The Viennese Jewish middle-class quickly established itself within Vienna's intellectual and artistic life. This class not only contributed many of the creators of this *gutes Leben* (the good life) as musicians, scholars, literati, physicians and theatre personalities but also provided patrons and audiences for this robust talent and creativity. They participated in city beautification projects and municipal affairs having finally realized a sense of belonging to a place, security, and a feeling of being at home.

Meanwhile, in Krems the Oberlander family's grape crops were frozen in the unusually severe winters of northern Austria in the late 1800s, prompting Adolf Oberlander, the third-generation winemaker, to switch to the brandy-making business. This decision provided the family with greater economic security. On October 2, 1889, Adolf Oberlander had a third child, Fritz, Peter's father.

The Oberlanders emerged as a business family in Krems due to the efforts of Adolf Oberlander. They were no longer winemakers but had risen up the social ladder as an established, middle-class, Jewish, business household. Along with his siblings, an older brother and sister, Fritz had access to primary education and high school. But the periodic business trips to the bustling city of Vienna gave young Fritz a peek into the vitality and glamour of Viennese society. Major influences such as the rise of socialist politics and the potential for access to a larger socio-cultural and political life beckoned him. As a result, Fritz Oberlander would be the first in his family's five generations to leave the family business and Krems and to pursue an urban education. He enrolled at the University of Vienna.

It was not easy. Continuing waves of anti-Semitism made for an often-hostile political context for young Jewish adults like Fritz. He gradually reconciled himself to the harsh reality that even higher educational institutions in a sophisticated city were not immune from this influence. Nonetheless, Fritz undertook undergraduate, graduate and doctoral studies. With the completion of his studies in political science and law in 1912, he became the first Oberlander to earn a university degree. By that time, his fondness for Vienna, in spite of its challenges, outshone the appeal of the modest, conservative and austere world of Krems. Like so many migrants to cities in a process to which his son would devote his life's work, Fritz experienced the push of the limited opportunities in primary industry combined with the pull of the city's vitality, diversity, and opportunity. Fritz chose the urban setting of Vienna to settle down.

Membership in Austro-Hungarian society exacted from its citizens (including Jews) certain responsibilities and duties. Among these was the requirement was that all able-bodied Austrian men be enlisted in the Imperial Army. Fritz volunteered to serve in the Army for a year on the assumption that this would help him avoid being drafted at a later date. He was appointed as a cavalry officer and spent a year (1912-1913) in Hungary and Italy, where he learned to speak Italian. Fritz was also fluent in French, the *lingua franca* of prewar Europe, in addition to his native German. As he was nearing the end of his volunteering assignment, fate intervened to extend his military career and change his life forever.

The unexpected assassination of the heir to the Austro-Hungarian throne, Archduke Franz Ferdinand of Austria, by a young Bosnian Serb on June 28, 1914, resulted in a month of diplomatic tension that was called the "July Crisis." Austria handed over a "July Ultimatum" to the kingdom of Serbia, a set of unacceptable demands with the intention of provoking war, which it did. Known as the Great War, World War I ultimately commandeered the energy of the great economies and societies of the world in the twentieth century, namely the Allies (the United Kingdom, France, and the Russian Empire) and the Central Powers (Germany and the Austro-Hungarian Empire).

Fritz Oberlander would end up spending five long years in war service. He was terribly wounded twice, once on the Polish-Russian front and once again on the Italian front, by shrapnel and bullets in his stomach. His war service and injuries were a life-transforming experience for him. He was shifted to the War Ministry in Vienna, where he spent two years until 1918 behind an office desk. It was in this position that Fritz focused on humanitarian work that sought to advance social justice. On November 11, 1918, the Great War drew to a halt in an uncomfortable and ambiguous armistice.

At the Paris Peace conference in 1919, the Allies imposed a harsh peace on the Central Powers. They laid out peace treaties for new international relations between various countries. The Treaty of Saint-Germain in 1919 resulted in the reconfiguration of Central Europe. The German and Austro-Hungarian empires ceased to exist, although their responsibility for starting the war – at least in the minds of the victorious Allies - did not, and new states were created from the ruins of empire. One sign of hope for a more peaceful future was the creation of the League of Nations, an intergovernmental organization formulated by the victorious Allies.

No country was more transformed by World War I than Austria. Having entered the war as the dominant part of the dual-monarchy Austro-Hungarian Empire with hegemony over a vast territory, the Austria of the post-1918 era was a much smaller and weaker state struggling to meet the challenges of social and economic reconstruction. Margaret MacMillan described Austria in *Paris 1919* as follows:

> Its picturesque and impoverished mountains and valleys clustered around the former imperial capital of Vienna, whose magnificent palaces, vast offices, grand avenues, parade grounds and cathedrals were built for the rulers of 50 million subjects, not 3 million. "We have thousands more officials than we need," the prime minister complained to a sympathetic American, "and at least two hundred thousand workmen. It is a fearful question to know what to do with them."

The new Republic of Austria comprised the German-speaking Danubian and Alpine Northern provinces. The successor states of the Central Powers were deemed liable for causing the war and had to pay economic reparations to the Allies over a period of time. With the collapse of the Austro-Hungarian Empire and its economy, the support among the German-speaking non-Jews for Anschluss (union) with Germany increased.

In the early twentieth century, the concept of citizen rights was quite novel and not fully developed in Eastern Europe. The descendants of those who gave up their lives fighting wars were mostly forgotten. Fritz was deeply aware of this. With the end of the war in sight, he had transformed into a humanitarian soldier, one who sought social justice and civil rights for those marginalized by the catastrophic events of the Great War. He was particularly energetic in challenging the new state to secure proper treatment for two of the main affected groups: the widows and orphans of Austrian servicemen, and the non-Austrians left stateless by the redrawing of boundaries to create new countries, not only Austria but Hungary, Yugoslavia and Czechoslovakia.

As a result of its reduced status, postwar Austria struggled with famine, distress, and in-migration of German-speaking residents of the former Habsburg Empire and men who had enlisted in the army during the war and had returned to unemployment and hunger. Many of the people isolated as a result of the Great War had problems that were more than social or economic — they were stateless. Although they were residents of Austria, they were not accepted as citizens and, lacking citizenship documents, they were unable to travel outside of Austria to find a future in a more hospitable environment.

Fritz Oberlander established a private legal practice in postwar Vienna that was heavily influenced by a passion for social justice. He worked to assist individual refugees caught in the limbo following the end of the war, particularly to make available to them some form of internationally-recognized documentation. An improvised solution was the Nansen Passports, which were internationally recognized travel documents issued to stateless refugees by the League of Nations between 1922 and 1938. They were named for their promoter, the statesman and polar explorer Fridtjof Nansen who served as the League of Nations High Commissioner for Refugees. An enthusiastic internationalist, Fritz joined the League of Nations Association and created in his household the sense that citizenship entailed global as well as local and national rights and responsibilities.

On the personal front, Fritz Oberlander sought to renew contact with acquaintances and friends in Vienna he had had before the Great War broke out. As a university educated and trained cavalry officer in the Austrian Imperial Army, Fritz was an eligible bachelor in Viennese Jewish circles. At a party organized by a middle-class family one winter evening, Fritz was introduced to Margaret Josephine Braun. Amid the chatter, the clinking of wine glasses, the smells of traditional Viennese foods and desserts, the young couple danced the evening away.

The Oberlanders and Brauns were not really strangers. The families knew each other from being part of a tight circle of liberal, Jewish, business families. Like the Oberlanders, the Brauns were an affluent, urban middle-class business family; in their case, they were associated with the Austrian textile industry. Their business networks spread across Moravia to the eastern end of Hungary. They represented a long line of textile traders and manufacturers who settled in Vienna in the nineteenth century and established a shirt-manufacturing factory called Brother Brauns. Margaret had been born to Alexander Braun and Rosa Weihsberg on August 1, 1892. The Braun household was large, with four girls and four boys. Tragedy struck when Alexander Braun passed away at a young age. His widow and children were looked after by the extended Braun family, leading to tight-knit familial bonds among the Brauns. Raised in the liberal Jewish traditions of urban Vienna, Margaret had access to education. She studied in a Ladies College that combined commercial and finishing school.

Although the Great War was over, the conditions in Vienna were dismal. People were poverty-stricken, food was rationed, and the economy was non-existent. The time was definitely not right for thinking of marriage and establishing a household, not at least until one was able to have a regular source of income.

It took Fritz Oberlander and Margaret Braun two years to consolidate their position. In August of 1920, the couple had a Viennese wedding.

Margaret Oberlander immediately stepped into her new role as Mrs. Oberlander under the watchful eye of Fritz's mother. Fritz purchased a large, elegant apartment in a northwest neighbourhood called the Ninth District of Vienna or Alsergrund. It was connected to the *Ring Strasse,* a landscaped boulevard that followed the route of the fortifications of the walled city. Modelled on the nineteenth century Parisian boulevards of Baron Haussmann, the *Ring Strasse* enclosed the inner city of Vienna like a horseshoe with its two ends touching the Danube River embankments. It housed important government and administrative buildings, the residences of the elite and public parks. Location along the *Ring Strasse* denoted the high social standing of a family.

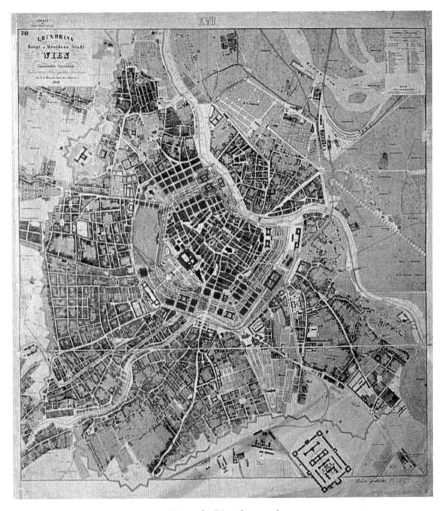

Vienna's *Ring Strasse*[4]

The dynamism of political life in postwar Vienna led to the creation of various uneasy coalitions whose members ranged from conservative ideologues to social democrats in the national government. This leadership, comprising middle-class intellectuals (both ethnic Germans and Jews), strove to create a citizenry that was community-minded, honest, and industrious while attempting a social experiment in redistributive justice. The central urban project undertaken by this government was to supply housing for the working classes, comprising super-blocks called *Höfe* (courts) with multiple communal facilities. The Oberlander family lived in one such *Höfe* on 41 *Währinger Strasse* in Alsergrund. Opposite the apartment building was the University of Vienna's Institute of Organic Chemistry. Next door was the *Währinger Strasse* elementary school, the School in the Park. Alsergrund comprised mixed-use areas dotted with three- and four-storey walk-up apartment blocks planned around a central courtyard. The neighbourhood did not have single-family houses. Such socially-conscious urban projects helped the Social Democrats win the electoral support of the Austro-Jewish community, particularly since the opposition parties were mostly anti-Semitic conservatives.

A year after the Oberlanders settled in their new home, their first-born arrived. Heinz Peter Oberlander was born on November 29, 1922. Fritz and Margaret doted on their little one. The apartment block had an attached garden that was communally managed by the residents of the building. The Oberlanders lived on the top floor; there were no elevators at the time. There was a winding staircase with smooth polished marble steps that rose from a small foyer at the main entrance. There were family residences on the second, third and fourth floors. At the ground level, there was a bookstore and other shops. Peter's baby carriage was tied up on the first-floor stairway landing. Margaret pulled it out when she took him for an evening stroll to the nearby garden. Fritz had his legal practice in an office which he shared with another lawyer on the second floor of the apartment building. Fritz's mother ran a laundry shop that was on the ground level adjacent to the courtyard. She had her apartment on the second floor.

As a toddler, Peter was a poor eater. Margaret suspected that he was a little sickly, so she spoon-fed him his meals every day. But Peter would not open his mouth until he saw the Number 38 trolley coming along the narrow *Wahlringer Strasse* in front of the apartment. Luckily the Number 38 ran regularly every day of the week. It still does. Peter was sent to the nearby school in the park to complete first and second grade. At the age of six, he was sent to the *Gymnasium Wasagasse,* a traditional Austrian secondary school that at the time was favoured by the Jewish bourgeoisie, whose sons represented half the school's population at that time. He travelled to school every morning by trolley or street car. The traditional school curriculum emphasized the sciences as well as classical and modern languages. Peter studied both Latin and Greek and participated with other students in various language competitions.

Gymnasium Wasagasse Secondary School, Vienna[5]

Like most inner city schools at the time, the *Gymnasium* was a very urban school. It had no playground or yards, as the building fronted right on the sidewalk. Students went to the Royal Parks of Vienna for their major recreational activities, including soccer once a week. Peter seemed not to have minded the atmosphere of the *Gymnasium,* but others did, including Harry Seidler, who was to become his lifelong friend and colleague and a highly-respected Australian architect. "This particular school was run like a military academy," Seidler later wrote. "It was the horror of my existence. It was tough, it was strict. You had to jump up when you were called to attention; you had to study Latin and Greek, and you had to memorize. Some of the people who ran it were ex-army officers." The routine and rigour were relaxed somewhat every year when the students would have a week off for a skiing trip as part of a school program. Sport was considered to be an important part of the learning process.

In 1929, Peter was blessed with a baby brother, George, who recalls:

> The earliest story I was told about Peter was the day I was born, and he went to school and told his teacher and class that he now was a "twin." The teacher was amazed and corrected him saying it must be a brother or sister. The word for "twin" in German is *Zwiling,* and he needed to be corrected since our mother did not have twins. Since that early time, Peter has been very careful in choosing his words since he did not like to be corrected — although he did love being an older brother, and I have always been proud to be his little brother.

Peter shared his room with his baby brother. With its view out into the *Währinger Strasse,* the apartment included five large rooms: the children's bedroom, parents' bedroom, living room, dining room and a private study, plus a maid's room, kitchen, and bathroom. As Peter grew up he was given his private study room next to the dining room. The house had a big kitchen where the boys spent most of their time while at home. They had a maid who took care of their daily routines under the keen and watchful eyes of their mother and grandmother. The children's meals were eaten with the maid, not with the grownups. The large living room had a grand piano. Peter would spend many hours at the French-styled windows in the living room where he could see the Vienna Woods and the hills in the distance.

Both the Oberlander and Braun families were practitioners of liberal Judaism, and Fritz and Margaret Oberlander raised their sons in this tradition, which was an important influence on them and their extended families. Fritz Oberlander was president of a group founded on *Haskalah* or the Jewish Enlightenment. He eventually went on to play a critical role in the Viennese Zionist movement in the 1930s, when anti-Semitic literature was being reintroduced by Nazi propagandists.

In 1933, Adolf Hitler's rise to power in the German Reich introduced a fresh wave of anti-Semitism in Europe. Deeply disturbed by these events and uncertain of the future that lay ahead for Jewish communities in Austria, Margaret's brother, Bernard Braun, and his family left Vienna for good to resettle in England. Very few Jewish families took such drastic steps, but this move would prove to be fortuitous for the Oberlanders.

In 1935, the Austrian government recognized Fritz Oberlander's commitments to civil and political rights by awarding him the Knight's Cross, one of Austria's highest honours, for his service in the cause of those deprived of rights and privileges as a result of the Great War. This further reassured the Oberlanders that the rising waves of anti-Semitism were just a momentary phenomenon.

The seeds of a strong spiritual life were sown in the boys as they were growing up. They visited Alsergrund's synagogue regularly for their prayers and festivals. Like most synagogues at the time in Europe, it was built behind other buildings so that it was not directly visible from the street. The community had to go through a corridor to get to the main door of the synagogue. One reason for keeping the synagogue tucked away from the main street was to protect and secure Jewish people and sacred places from anti-Semitic activity. (Three decades later, Peter would be instrumental in founding the liberal-tradition Temple Sholom in

Vancouver, Canada, with its vast and prominent frontage in its current building on Oak Street.)

Despite the fears in the backdrop, Peter's bar mitzvah was grandly celebrated in 1935 in the Alsergrund synagogue. George Oberlander reminisces about the big party that his mother had organized at home after the ceremony:

> I remember it so vividly. Peter was thirteen, and I was five and a half. My parents ensured that I was given lots of presents for his bar mitzvah. I was in my room with my friends, and he was in the main living room with his friends and adults celebrating the bar mitzvah. My parents wanted to make sure that I was not discriminated against.

Most of the Jewish families in 1930s Vienna continued to practice their religion and culture, but they avoided broadcasting it lest they had to face negative consequences. The Oberlanders were the same – they neither hid their Jewishness nor did they overtly advertise it. The traditional Jewish holidays of *Yom Kippur* were celebrated by the Oberlanders, and they broke fast with Fritz standing by his mother *Oma's* side because that was the tradition. *Oma* would prepare scrambled eggs and herring that would be served to break the fast. Sometimes the Oberlanders stayed at home and invited family and friends to come over. Occasionally, they would be invited out.

An important holiday from the very beginning for the Oberlander family was *Hanukkah*, the commemoration of the rededication of the Holy Temple (the Second Temple) in Jerusalem at the time of the Maccabean Revolt against the efforts of the Seleucid Empire to assimilate the Jews and ban their religion in the second century BC. Fritz had made a very incisive argument to a young and impressionable Peter. He had said, "That was the year in which the world changed because if we would not have fought and succeeded, Judaism would not have survived. Critically Christianity and Islam would never have been born. So, this was not a minor holiday." Fritz taught a young Peter that *Hanukka* was important because people seldom celebrated historical holidays as they did religious ones.

Visiting family and friends was an important aspect of social life for Peter while he was growing up in Vienna. They visited his mother's siblings and extended family and quite often their grandmother who lived next door. The Oberlander household, like any other middle-class family at the time, had a rich

Viennese diet of pot roast, potatoes, vegetables, soups, breads and pastries. Both Peter and George relished the rich Austrian-style pastries and desserts that Margaret baked herself. She prepared *matzah* ball soup on the Jewish holidays, a long-standing family tradition.

Fritz organized professional meetings and Zionist activities at his office. He was an excellent orator and deeply committed to the Jewish community. His other love and commitment was the Free Masons, in which he was the Master of the Viennese lodge. Margaret, on the other hand, was committed to the family: husband, sons, in-laws, siblings, nieces and nephews. She played a role in Masonic life because she occasionally chaired the ladies group. She had a little circle of friends through this. In all, Peter and George grew up in a professional, middle-class family that was very much committed to the economics and politics of the country.

As a teenager, Peter revealed a mischievous side to his personality. Every morning on their way to the *Gymnasium Wasagasse,* Peter and half a dozen of his friends would hop off the streetcar at *Berggasse Einundzwanzig* where Sigmund Freud lived. There the father of psychoanalysis would be lost in thought "contemplating the world from his wonderful alcove balcony, and he would always do this while stroking his silver beard. The moment he would spot us imitating him stroking our chins, he would be mad as hell," Peter chuckled. As an adolescent at the time, Peter knew nothing about Freud's intellectual prowess. He seemed like a "weird character" to the teenagers. But then in 1937, Freud published a book on Moses and Monotheism that created a major connection between the Jewish Community and Freud. After reading this treatise, Oberlander senior spent hours extolling the virtues of Freud's latest masterpiece.

An image that made a deep impression on Peter while he was growing up in *Alsergrund* was the *Votivekirche* or "Votive Church." It was a Catholic church constructed in the Neo-Gothic style of architecture in the late nineteenth century. Designed by Heinrich von Ferstel and built as a "votive offering" meant to gain favour from a supernatural power, the church was the brainchild of Emperor Franz Joseph's younger brother established after a failed assassination attempt on the Emperor. The white sandstone formed a contrast to the sea of green trees in which the building was set. Peter frequently talked about this building with his brother George or with his friends because of its imposing scale, design, and presence.

What fascinated him was how effortlessly the two slender towers of the *Votivekirche* rose magnificently, seeming almost to touch the sky above. The crucial elements of the building were the towers, the gabled portals and the gallery with a series of statues expressing their stories. By night the building was lit up, which gave the impression of its white sandstone presence floating in the still darkness. For Peter, the *Votivekirche* was more than a historic landmark located at the site of the failed assassination attempt and at the junction of the *Währinger Strasse* and the central *Ring Strasse*. It was a powerful aesthetic and personal experience that was deeply etched in his mind. The poetics of open and built space, the interplay of form and function and the mastery of the architect shaped in this adolescent a fierce desire to pursue architecture as a calling.

Votivekirche (Votive Church), Vienna, Austria Ca. 1900[6]

Before the coming adverse circumstances surfaced, Fritz Oberlander ensured both his sons enjoyed their urban childhood with a good exposure to nature through skiing, bicycling, and swimming. George recalls how Fritz Oberlander patiently and lovingly taught him to ski:

> I knew skiing because I was put on skis when I was five years old by my father. He would stand in front and my uncle behind me to shoot down a 1,200-foot hill. I can still vividly see the trees coming at me. I never went skiing directly with Peter because he was with the older boys on those events.

There was obviously a considerable degree of separation between older and younger siblings at that time. Peter interacted more closely with the older boys whereas George had friends his age as company. It was the summer vacations that brought the Oberlanders together — adults, and older and younger siblings. The emphasis on sporting activities instilled by Peter's father led him to become involved in *Maccabiah* (Jewish Olympic) games at the age of thirteen after his *bar mitzvah*. He was a member of the *Maccabiah* soccer club in Vienna.

Peter also enjoyed Viennese opera, a taste he acquired from Margaret who was a dedicated patron of the Viennese arts. Season passes for Saturday operas at the *Volksoper Wien, Burgtheatre* or the *Akademietheatre* were always a welcome treat for an urban adolescent stepping into the adult circle of life. Another interest was the movies, an integral cultural artifact of adolescent Jewish-Viennese life; Peter was a regular at the *Votiv Kino* and *Studio Moliere*. It was to be another lifelong passion.

But life was more than the artistic pleasures of cinema and theatre, and the rigours of the *Gymnasium*. Fritz Oberlander imparted a strong sense of Jewish identity, heritage, and philosophy in his sons. Heavily influenced by his father's work, an adolescent Peter read *Der Jundenstaat* (The Jewish State) written by Theodore Herzl, a young Jewish journalist, to analyse the notion of anti-Semitism. This document was sneered upon by established Jewish-Viennese scholars and the literati of the day. The sense of deep-rooted security, arising from centuries of peaceful co-existence with non-Jewish communities, led Viennese Jews to ridicule their fellow Jewish peoples in Eastern Europe as the gatekeepers of some archaic idea of Zionism. In *The Viennese: Splendor, Twilight and Exile,* Paul Hoffman suggests that although anti-Semitic literature was frowned upon in the early twentieth century, vivid novels such as *die Stadt ohne Juden* (The City without Jews, 1922) and *die Freudlose Gasse* (The Street without Joy, 1923) by Hugo Bettauer, a Jewish journalist, were early warning signs foretelling the onset of anti-Semitism in Austria in the next decade.

In early March 1938, Peter embarked with his schoolmates on the school's annual ski trip to the Tyrol. The Oberlanders' lives were about to change forever.

CHAPTER THREE:

THE DAY EVERYTHING CHANGED

Peter Oberlander's brother George remembers looking out the window of their apartment on the morning of Saturday, March 12, 1938 to see a unit of Germany's 8th Army marching down the *Währinger Strasse*. After years of agitation and ultimatums, Adolph Hitler had annexed Austria, an action that became known as Anschluss.

One surprising aspect of the Anschluss was the speed with which Austria was absorbed into the Third Reich. Literally overnight, everything from flags to senior government personnel was replaced to reflect the new order.

For Peter and his friends on their ski trip in the Tyrol, the impact was immediate. As he later recalled, "At that point, our high school teacher separated the Jewish from the non-Jewish students immediately. We were locked into a cabin when everyone else went skiing." To his friend Harry Seidler, he said, "This is the end. I think we'll have to get out of here."

The following day, the students returned by train to Vienna. The non-Jewish students were driven home from the station, and the Jewish students had to walk.

> By that time," Peter recalled, "Vienna had already been occupied and was in a beleaguered state where the German troops – and Austrians for God's sake – were already arresting Jews on a mass scale and making them scrub the walls and floors in a very denigrating fashion. I remember the day because my first reaction was "When are we leaving?" And my father said, "Well, what are you talking about? These are Nazis, and we belong here; we stay here, and this is where we have grown up; besides which, this will not last."

Adolph Hitler announces the *Anschluss* on the
Heldenplatz in Vienna, March 15, 1938.[7]

Peter's father did not realize he was a target. The Nazis' approach was to round up and replace all the leaders in order to prevent any resistance. As the head of the bar association, Fritz was one of the first to be arrested. On Tuesday, March 15, the Gestapo came to his office, arrested him, destroyed his records and smashed his furniture. He was taken to court. Peter Oberlander summed up the situation:

> The charges were typical. As a Free Mason, he had connections with England and France and was [thought to be] plotting against the state. In defending the innocent, he was not obeying the laws of the day because he was taking sides. Being a Jew was another valid reason for incarceration.

The judges were the men who had been clerks in the court when Oberlander had appeared as an attorney a few days earlier. To no one's surprise, he was sent to prison. There he experienced a foretaste of the horror that was to descend on Europe. As Peter described it:

The so-called concentration camps had yet to come. What the Gestapo in those days did was learn how to do it. This is where the Gestapo literally learned how to kick the hell out of people, get confessions, get admissions of guilt of one sort or another and bring humiliation on people who had already established themselves in some fashion and became icons of certain causes. My father spent four months in a jail that was built for the Roman Empire. The whole question of retaining and incarcerating people had not yet been perfected. Particularly in Vienna, the Germans had to teach the Austrians how to do it.

One of the first concentration camps the Germans established in Austria was at Mauthausen, near Linz. Its intended purpose was to provide slave labour for the Wiener Graven stone quarry. Mauthausen was classified as a "category three camp". This meant "*Rûckkehr unerwünscht*" (return not desired) and "*Vernichtung durch arbeit*" (extermination by work). Fritz Oberlander was among the several hundred prisoners transferred to Mauthausen when it opened on August 8, 1938.

Faced with single-handedly maintaining a household with two sons aged 8 and 15 who as Jews had been banned from their school, Margaret Oberlander struggled to cope with the devastating blow her family had suffered in the increasingly ominous atmosphere of post-Anschluss Vienna. She became ill and required surgery that left her in a weakened state.

Eventually, some of Fritz's non-Jewish former colleagues in the legal profession, at great risk to themselves, were able to secure his release, but only on the condition that he sign away all his assets and leave the country within 24 hours. As George Oberlander recalled, "There was a huge lift van that was a big box standing on the street into which we put our furniture; it was shipped off to Trieste in Italy and confiscated by the Italians at that point." They never saw any of their possessions again.

The family's supporters were able to arrange for plane tickets to allow them to flee Austria; this would have been a considerable feat in the circumstances at that time. Hostility and danger pursued them right to the door of the airplane. George Oberlander's memory is vivid:

> I had to carry a portable typewriter; it was my job. When we got to the airport, a storm trooper saw me carrying this little portable typewriter, and he wanted to take it away from me, and I would

not give it to him, and I outran him, and we got on to the plane. We flew from Vienna to Prague and then from Prague to London.

The Oberlander family's 400 years as part of Austrian society were over.

In summing up the family's experience later, Peter Oberlander took pains to acknowledge the help they had received:

> The local involvement was fundamental because the Viennese welcomed Hitler's Anschluss. But it also had a positive side, and I want to make this clear. My father ultimately came out alive because of the support of several important friends who intervened, including the Deputy Minister of Justice who schooled with him. There were compassionate gentiles who ultimately intervened. He escaped with life and limb because of the support that several very key legal and political friends exercised, particularly in those days when it was all improvisation. No one knew how to do it.

The outcome could have been worse, and for millions it undoubtedly was.

This "local involvement" by Austrians in planning and executing the Anschluss explained the incredible speed and thoroughness with which the deed was done. At about this time, the term "fifth column" came into use, having been invented during the Spanish Civil War by the Republican General Emillio Mola, who bragged that as his four columns of troops approached Madrid, a fifth column inside the city would support him and undermine the government from within. Fifth columns became a key element in Hitler's attempt to conquer Europe in the early days of World War II a year later, when Denmark, Norway, and the Low Countries fell in rapid succession. The decisive effectiveness of this technique did not go unnoticed in Britain, and this led to measures that would cause further grievous damage to the Oberlander family.

When the family arrived in London, they stayed with Margaret's brother Bernard Braun who had seen the writing on the wall with the rise of the Hitler movement in 1933 and had moved with his family to England. Within this welcoming environment, the family began to put their lives back together. Peter and George were enrolled in school in London, but their immediate challenge was learning English. Fortunately, Margaret spoke English, and she could type, so she was able to work at two part-time jobs.

The family's biggest concern was with Fritz, who emerged from his experience a broken man. Peter remembered it this way.

> My father was in very poor shape, so he needed both emotional and medical help. Obviously, there were some physical marks on his back. [George Oberlander said that he had also lost a couple of teeth.] It was not so much that as it was the terrible destruction of the individual person – the human being, the illegitimacy of the destruction. All his life he was on the other side, and suddenly he was the object of that emotional and physical attack. So, he had to come to grips with that injustice and his inability to do anything about it or about others that he defended before, including members of our family.

There were professional challenges as well. Fritz was a highly-respected practitioner of law in the Austrian legal system, which was derived from Roman law. His expertise was of virtually no use in the English system of common law which was standard not only in Britain but also in virtually any other country in which they could conceivably settle where they would be reasonably safe. He spoke little English, and for a time he and his sons took language classes together as part of their adjustment to the new setting. Listening to Judy Garland on the radio and attending movies in English were a combination of education and pleasure for Peter.

The family's status in that setting was tenuous too. At the time, the maximum period for which the British government would issue visas was six weeks, which could be extended once by a further two weeks, after which the family could presumably be deported back to Austria. The outbreak of war in September 1939 swept this factor away.

Ultimately, Peter's father found work that allowed him to channel his bitterness to a productive end while he healed and developed his English. He went to work at Bloomsbury House, a unit that tried to help Austrians get out of Vienna and anywhere in Austria. His work mainly involved filling in forms and other tasks to help refugees re-establish their identity and their lives. Peter described it this way:

> There was the whole process of trying to justify and obtain visas. This was a closed world, and unless you had a piece of paper you

could not move. It was again a question of identity, proving who you are and trying to develop a process that would ship people. England was not a permanent destination, that was for sure.

In this role, Fritz was also able to pursue his primary personal objective, which was to get his mother, his sister and other members of his family out of Austria and to England.

In Europe, the slide into war continued, propelled by Adolf Hitler's incessant provocations. Germany annexed much of Czechoslovakia in September 1938, and the nadir of Prime Minister Neville Chamberlain's policy of appeasement was reached in the Munich Pact at the end of that month. The experience served to galvanize the recognition by Britain and France that war was virtually inevitable, and their energies were refocused — none too soon — from avoidance to preparation. They set about establishing defensive alliances with Turkey, Greece, Romania, and Poland. Germany occupied the rest of Czechoslovakia in March 1939 and formed a full military alliance with Italy in May. A non-aggression pact between Germany and the Soviet Union in August 1939 forestalled the possibility of a two-front war for Germany and the stage was set for the invasion of Poland. This occurred without a declaration of war on September 1, 1939, and prompted declarations of war on Germany by Britain, most of the members of its Commonwealth, France, and others.

Observing these developments from London, the Oberlander family must have felt some relief that Hitler's aggression would be resisted and perhaps regret that, for various reasons, none of them could do much to help. Accompanying these thoughts would have been the recognition that the outcome of the conflict was far from certain and that they might be uprooted again or worse.

One of Britain's first steps in defence of its citizens reflected a long view: the nation's children were relocated from cities such as London to places less vulnerable to attack in the coming air war, either elsewhere in the country or overseas. So it was that Peter and George Oberlander were enrolled in a boarding school in Folkestone, a port town on the English Channel southeast of London in Kent. Their first night was difficult for George, who recalls:

> The school we were in, in London, was just day school, and we were together with our parents at night. At Folkestone, we were separated from our parents. Peter was with the older boys, and I was with the younger boys, and I remember the first night at Folkestone, I was

terribly annoyed and crying all the time with having to be with strangers. My English was not great either yet. They found Peter, and he came and consoled me; that is how we started my education in boarding school. Peter was always my bigger brother and always helped me out when I needed it.

In due course, Peter and George's parents and grandmother (whose extrication from Austria Fritz had accomplished) relocated to a boarding house in Folkestone so as to be able to provide help and support to the two young boys. The family was out of immediate danger, but the war was never far from their minds. "There we observed every night when the Nazis would fly over Folkestone to bomb London and so we could alert people in London," George remembered.

It seemed that an environment had been established in which George and Peter could resume their education and their parents could work on preparing themselves for the family's future, whatever it might entail.

The boys were able to come home from boarding school on the weekends. On Sunday, May 12, 1940, they were in the boarding house in Folkestone. Peter described what happened next.

> Someone knocked on our door and said, "May I speak to Master Oberlander?" I was fifteen at the time. "Would you come with me for a few questions?" By this time, my grandmother had arrived, fortunately, and she said, "Where are you taking him?" He kept saying, "Just a few hours, a few questions, and we will bring him right back." I was studying for my matric. So I said I wanted to take my matric materials. "Just a few, not too many." So I took a bag, a shirt, my books, and a toothbrush as a teen who was preparing for matric. That's the last time I saw my grandmother and my parents for a long time.

It would be years later and half a world away.

The security situation in Britain at that time was grave. After the fall of Denmark and Norway in April, on May 10, 1940, Hitler invaded France, Belgium, Luxembourg and the Netherlands. Winston Churchill became British Prime Minister.

The activities of fifth columns had figured prominently in the German sweep of Europe. Then, as now, there was conflict between security concerns and the maintenance of a free and open society. In World War 1, Britain had introduced the *Aliens Restriction Act* that required foreign nationals to register with the police and authorized their deportation in certain circumstances.

At the outbreak of World War II, there were about 80,000 people of German or Austrian nationality in Britain who could conceivably be German spies or operatives. Fifty-five thousand of these, mostly Jewish, were refugees. A set of tribunals was established to categorize these according to perceived risk: A (high security risk) B (doubtful) and C (no security risk). Initially, the British government interned 568 persons in Category A; those in Categories B (around 6,800 people) and C (around 65,000 people) included most of the refugees from Nazi oppression. Those in Category B were free, subject to certain restrictions, and those in Category C were entirely free. With the rapid advance of Germany in Europe, of course, this situation was made more complicated by bringing under German control large additional populations, including people whose loyalties might be uncertain and who might have an influence on nationals in Britain.

Churchill moved swiftly to respond to the threat perceived to exist from the presence of these "enemy aliens," particularly in the event of a German invasion, which seemed imminent. Peter Oberlander's arrest was a consequence of the government's first decree, under which were interned male Austrians and Germans between the ages of 16 and 60 living in "Protected Areas" on the threatened sectors of the coast. The family's relocation from London to Folkestone on the coast had exposed them to fresh danger.

It likely would not have mattered, ultimately, where he was, because Churchill, unable to make a clear distinction between any who posed a risk and the vast majority who were refugees from the Nazis, then issued the notorious order to "collar the lot." Male and female refugees in Category B were interned. The detention of male refugees in Category C, ordered in June, was under way when the policy of internment was halted in July. This ultimately caused the internment of some 27,000 foreign nationals, including about 4,000 women, most of whom were Jews who posed no security risk.

Churchill acknowledged the impact of these actions in a speech to the House of Commons on June 9, 1940 after the near-disaster at Dunkirk:

> We have found it necessary to take measures of increasing
> stringency, not only against enemy aliens and suspicious characters
> of other nationalities but also against British subjects who may

become a danger or a nuisance should the war be transported to the United Kingdom. I know there are a great many people affected by the orders which we have made who are the passionate enemies of Nazi Germany. I am very sorry for them, but we cannot, at the present time and under the present stress, draw all the distinctions which we should like to do.... There is, however, another class, for which I feel not the slightest sympathy. Parliament has given us the powers to put down Fifth Column activities with a strong hand, and we shall use those powers subject to the supervision and correction of the House, without the slightest hesitation until we are satisfied and more than satisfied, that this malignancy in our midst has been effectively stamped out.

The handling of the initial phase of Peter's internment bore the signs of a hastily-assembled approach that resulted from the sudden change in leadership and strategy at the top of the government. He recalled:

The place I was moved to was Canterbury Cathedral School, and I spent the first week on the gym floor of Canterbury Cathedral School. At that point, I had assembled half a dozen of my old friends because they came from other schools. That new cluster of people was like family. So we were lifelong friends as we assembled there and moved together through the camps. There was a type of camaraderie, but it was not like you could take your books and go home the next day. We moved from camp to camp and, ultimately, ended up at the Isle of Man. That was the longest period in any one camp in England. The next thing was, we were moved to Glasgow. Now there was always this uncertainty because no one was sure what would happen next or why you were there. We could not communicate with our parents. We could not write to our parents nor could they contact us because they didn't know where we were, and we were not allowed to send letters. So the break with the family was pretty crucial to our life.

In Glasgow on the River Clyde in the summer of 1940, there was considerable confusion, as hundreds of internees were mustered for a purpose that was to them unknown. Four ships were in the port (the S.S. *Duchess of York,* the M.V.

Ettrick, the S.S. *Arandora Star* and the M.S. *Sobieski*), and it became clear that the internees were to be departing on them. Peter's experience with internment had already taught him never to be first in line or to volunteer for anything, so he and his friends stalled while the first of the ships was loaded. They watched with anticipation: if a ship went up the Clyde, it meant another internment camp in Scotland; if it went down the Clyde, it was departing for parts unknown.

The first ship went down the Clyde. The *Arandora Star* sailed solo and was torpedoed and sunk by a U-boat off the west coast of Ireland with the loss of more than 800 people, many of them internees. Peter got on the last ship, the M.S. *Sobieski.* While she was being loaded, a cargo sling split open and Peter's suitcase, with the last of his belongings, was dropped overboard; it was later recovered. "Halfway down [the Clyde]," Peter recalled, "it was obvious that one of the ships had been torpedoed and lost." The *Sobieski* joined a convoy that assembled off Greenock, Scotland. They were going to cross the Atlantic.

M.S. *Sobieski*[8]

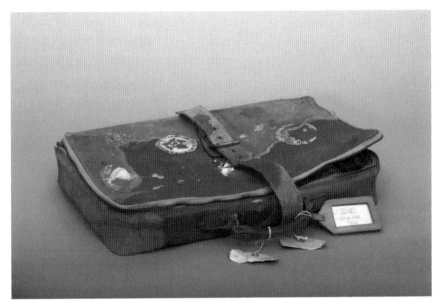

The suitcase that belonged to Peter Oberlander during his internment[9]

Peter's description of the experience years later is vivid:

> The ship was a leaky bucket. There were two things about the MS
> *Sobieski,* for the record: it was a miserable, overcrowded, underfed,
> over-disciplined misery. What was much worse was that this is the
> place we came to be identified as prisoners of war together, with
> those Germans who had been captured — members of the Luftwaffe
> and the Army that captured Holland, France, and Belgium. We
> travelled cheek to jowl with something like 500 officers of the
> Luftwaffe and the German Army. It was pretty obvious that about
> 800 of the passengers were not prisoners of war but Jewish refugees,
> many of them Yeshiva students, aged 16 to 17, with ear locks, black
> hats, and caftans. The Germans began taunting the refugees, and
> began to sing the most obnoxious songs possible, which all spoke
> to the same thing, which was how they were going to kill the Jews.

Some minor physical skirmishes broke out and eventually the two groups
had to be separated for everyone's safety.

Conditions got steadily worse, particularly after the ship ran out of fresh water
and the only recourse was to make tea using salt water. In an ironic turn of events,

the German prisoners of war began agitating for their rights to decent treatment, including adequate food and clean bedding, under the Geneva Convention. The ship's attempt to respond to this pressure led to some slight improvements for all the passengers.

Although the passengers did not know it, the *Sobieski* was bound for Canada. The British authorities had told the Government of Canada that all the passengers were prisoners of war, which meant that Canada had to admit them under the Geneva Convention.

The long-standing — if shameful from today's perspective — policy of Canada was not to accept refugees, particularly Jewish refugees; it was rigorously enforced by Frederick Blair, head of Canada's immigration branch from 1936 to 1943. In his 1941 Annual Report, Blair wrote, "Canada places a greater emphasis on race than on citizenship." In the most notorious incident, Canada had refused permission for the M.V. *St. Louis*, with more than 900 German Jewish refugees aboard, to dock in Halifax in 1939. The ship returned to Germany, where many of the refugees later perished in the Holocaust. One official, when asked how many Jews should be admitted to Canada, replied, "None is too many."

The British had blandly assured the Canadian authorities that all the passengers were prisoners of war because they knew Canada would never have agreed to accept them had it known that Jewish refugees were among them. British officials only admitted that there were refugees in the group after the ships containing them had sailed.

Peter recalled the gasps of shock from the Canadian authorities when the *Sobieski* docked in Quebec City and began to disembark hundreds of men who were clearly not German prisoners of war. One Canadian sought to make sense of it all by suggesting that those who appeared to be Jewish refugees were really disguised fifth columnists who had been cleverly swept up by the mother country, proving Churchill's suspicions to be well-founded. In fact, quite the opposite was true: the British government had begun to realize that its policy of rounding up and deporting detainees was a vast overkill (it had revealed not one spy), not to mention a waste of strategic resources; it was abandoned later that summer. Had Peter Oberlander and the others been able to remain in Britain, they would likely have been freed within a year.

The Canadian government was outraged that they had been hoodwinked by the British government and felt humiliated and betrayed. Underlying all those emotions was recognition of the huge political problem presented by this inadvertent departure from an anti-Jewish immigration policy that, it must be said, enjoyed wide support among Canada's nervous population at the time.

All of the passengers were transported to an arena in Trois-Rivières for "processing." This included being frisked and surrendering all their possessions "for safe keeping" to the members of the Home Guard who were responsible for them. Peter's request for a receipt was ignored, and he never saw his possessions again. The only thing of value he was able to keep was a ten shilling British note which he had sewn in his shoe. He was later able to exchange the note for $2.80 in Canadian funds, which he described as his "beginning stake in Canada." With considerable understatement he later described his experience as "a complex and ambivalent" welcome to Canada.

It was at the arena in Trois-Rivières where the internees were finally separated from the German prisoners of war. This brought the worst of the abuses to an end, but it did little to clarify the future of these reluctant and unwelcome new arrivals. Although there was no evidence that any of them offered a threat to Canada's security, their release was out of the question, largely because of the implacable determination of Frederick Blair to keep Jews out of Canada, but also because of the political problem their presence represented. Prime Minister William Lyon Mackenzie King had written about the prospect of helping Jewish refugees in his diary on March 29, 1938: "My own feeling is that nothing is to be gained by creating an internal problem in an effort to meet an international one."

The reality in the summer of 1940 was that hundreds of Jewish refugees were now on Canadian soil. They could not be returned to Britain because they had no status there, and the United States wasn't interested in helping. At one point, it was rumoured that the internees could be returned to Germany and Austria in exchange for Allied prisoners of war, which would have meant continued incarceration and almost certain death. For the Canadian authorities, the operative principle seems to have been "out of sight, out of mind," and the internees were transferred to a series of isolated camps in Quebec and New Brunswick. They were not permitted any illusions. One guard told Peter, "The only way you will be allowed to stay in Canada is six feet under."

Camp B70 was established in Ripples, New Brunswick, near the mining town of Minto. On August 12, 1940, a Jewish holiday, Peter arrived by train with 710 other men and boys who were led on foot to the 22-hectare site. B70 had been a camp for relief workers during the Depression, and it was considered suitable for this new purpose because of its isolation in rugged country, which would discourage thoughts of escape. And there was work to be done.

Peter recalled the experience as follows:

> At the beginning it was very tough. We worked very hard. I learned how to cut trees. I became an expert. We developed "pit props" — 16-inch diameter logs that are necessary to keep the mine shafts of the neighbouring area intact. So we harvested the pit props of New Brunswick for summer and winter.

They were paid 20 cents per day and worked six days per week. They were issued uniforms made of denim with a large red circle on the back of the jacket and a red stripe down the pant leg so that they could be easily identified. Peter never wore denims for the rest of his life.

And yet, as Peter later stated, there was an upside:

> The important thing was that, at that point, we began to build our lives again. Those who knew taught those who did not know. So that was really the beginning of my architectural education. So we had built into this whole process, first without permission and gradually with permission, this learning and teaching for people my age. The older ones were teachers. That was a very important part.

One of Peter's most important teachers in camp was Wolfgang Gerson, a fellow prisoner. Gerson's experience was described by his son, Martin, as follows:

> My father was born in 1916, so he was 6-7 years older than Peter. He was already a trained architect from the Architectural Association at London, England. He came from a family of architects from Hamburg. His father and uncle were prominent architects in Hamburg. My father graduated from architecture school in 1933 and did not get a school leaving certificate, due to the sudden changes in rules after Hitler's rise to power in Germany. His parents were sure that he was not going to get into an architecture school in Germany, so he was sent to London. Initially, the thought of his parents was that the Germans would come to their senses and all this would blow over. My father and his cousin could then come

back and work in the family business. But things did not work that way.

Wolfgang and Peter were later reunited in 1956 as faculty members at the School of Architecture at the University of British Columbia, where Wolfgang continued a distinguished design practice, including elegant buildings such as the Vancouver Unitarian Centre at 49ᵗʰ Avenue and Oak Street.

There were other manifestations of resilience in the camps, including communities of observant Jews who practiced their faith in the teeth of fairly strong anti-Semitic sentiment among the guards. Peter observed, "I think the most important thing that set that group apart was that they had a form of ritual which even the most miserable kind of internment circumstances couldn't prevent them from continuing."

A more objective but more damning account of the way men were treated in the camps came from Alex Paterson, the British Commissioner of Prisons, who was sent by the British government to assist the Canadian authorities. In a report elegantly titled *Report on Civilian Internees Sent from the United Kingdom to Canada During the Unusually Fine Summer of 1940,* he wrote:

> The uniform an internee is required to wear is both degrading and unworthy of a civilization that believes in encouraging the individual, rather than treading on his soul. It was disturbing to find distinguished university professors dressed as clowns. The red circle, which is commonly supposed to be a target for the machine guns, is a shabby insult to men who are ready to wear the red cross.

At first, discipline in the camps was very strict. "You didn't have any moments to yourself; you were observed for every moment of the day," Peter remembered. Gradually, things became more relaxed, and the internees' efforts at self-education came to be viewed as constructive rather than subversive. Arrangements were made for internees to travel to Camp M near Sherbrooke, Quebec for examinations to confirm their educational progress, and they spent time at other camps in New Brunswick and Quebec. But they were never beyond the watchful eyes of the guards during these outings.

Responsibility for the camps was shared between the Army and the Secretary of State for External Affairs, and as it became clearer that the internees posed no security threat the latter agency exerted more influence on the day-to-day administration of the camps. The internees were granted refugee status in July 1941, but they still had no documentation of their origins, education or any other aspect of their lives.

Meanwhile, Peter Oberlander's parents, distraught with the internment of their elder son in Canada, arranged to leave Folkestone to move to New York. In September 1940, they sailed in a convoy out of Southampton for Montréal so that they could attempt to reunite with Peter. They were devastated to learn from Canadian officials that their son would have to be returned to Britain before being released.

Fritz Oberlander had an acquaintance in Montréal, Ben Robinson, from their mutual association with the League of Nations in Geneva. Robinson was part of the small Montréal Jewish community and a prominent lawyer. Before the family moved on empty-handed to New York, Fritz sought out Ben and, according to Peter, said, "Look — do something about this boy." Through Ben's efforts the Canadian authorities were persuaded to accept Peter's innocence and his release was approved in November 1941.

It was a difficult and hostility-ridden process to the very end. Ben and his wife Tony drove to the internment camp to pick Peter up on the day he was to be released. They arrived at 3:45 p.m. on a Friday afternoon. Tony decided to wait in the car. The camp commandant told Ben the office was closing at 4 p.m. and there would not be time to process Peter's release. They would have to come back on Monday. As time dragged on, Tony became concerned about the delay and came into the commandant's office. When informed of the situation, she said, "Are you telling me that we are fighting a war for people's liberty, and you aren't able to release an innocent man, so he can sleep in a clean bed on Shabbat?" The commandant realized he had met his match. Peter was released immediately and was forever grateful to Tony and Ben for their courageous support on this and many other occasions.

The dominant impression Peter had about his life from March 1938 until November 1941 was of the utter lack of choice, of all the decisions being made by people and circumstances beyond his control rather than by his own free will. Although still constrained by legal, educational and financial factors, he relished the freedom to take control of his own destiny.

CHAPTER FOUR:

NEW BEGINNINGS

Across the border in New York City, the Oberlanders had already begun their second life far away from home in Vienna. George recollects the struggles his parents went through in creating new roots on foreign soil and enduring the pain of their elder son being trapped across the border in Canada. George describes his parents as belonging to "the Victorian age where children were protected from the harsh realities of life."

Fritz Oberlander faced a number of obstacles to becoming the sole bread-winner in their newly adopted country. His training at the University of Vienna and experience as a lawyer were of limited value in the completely different context of the American legal system. Perhaps as important was the physical and psychological damage caused by his experiences since the Anschluss. As a man with deep commitment to the cause of human rights, he never really got over what had happened to him and his family and, with Peter interned in Canada, it was still going on.

In New York, Fritz Oberlander worked at many different jobs, both day and night, to help make ends meet. From selling sausages packed in dry ice in a suit-case to immigrant and Jewish families in Washington Heights during the day to working in a factory that manufactured sequins for women's dresses at night, his erratic work schedules took a heavy toll on him. His wounded but indomitable spirit, however, kept him going. George describes his father as a professionally broken man but someone who had not given up on life. Fritz Oberlander eventually landed a more secure position, but one that would contribute to his early death in 1953. He became a clerk at the Modern Industrial Bank at 5th Avenue and 10th Street. He worked in the vault, looking after its maintenance and the safekeeping of records. The sides of the safety deposit boxes were made of steel, and they had to be oiled often. The fumes from the oil, combined with the dust, ultimately affected his lungs.

Margaret Oberlander had a rather tough second life. In Austria as a home-maker, in Peter's words, "she was a busy lady who ran a big house." Although it was uncommon for women to be employed in paid work at the time, Margaret went to work in New York out of sheer financial necessity.

Her first paid job was cleaning homes. This comedown in status was a terrible psychological blow to her. Her skills were more portable than those of her husband; she was fluent in French as well as German, and she could type. English was a second language for her, but she managed to get some work in a New York-based law firm. She prepared correspondence in relation to restitution and other matters relating to claims against the German and Austrian governments after the war. She primarily translated documents from German to English and vice-versa. She took the subway every day to work. As a legal secretary, she managed to supplement the family income. Ultimately, she would spend three decades in that occupation, retiring at the age of 94.

As the Oberlanders struggled to gain a toehold in Manhattan, Peter's repeated attempts to join his family in New York after his release were futile. The Canadian and American immigration policy towards foreign war internees at the time posed many challenges. Probational release from the internment camp did not permit unrestricted mobility even within Canada, let alone the ability to travel outside the country. Without any papers to prove his legal status in any country, Peter was technically and legally stateless and a non-person resident. George Oberlander recalls that after being released on probation from the internment camp in Quebec, Peter briefly enlisted in the Canadian Army. He hoped to reduce the implications of being Jewish in wartime Canada and to help establish himself as being worthy of Canadian citizenship.

Shortly after the family's arrival, in December 1940, George (then 10 years old) was sent by his parents by bus to meet Peter, but George did not have the necessary paperwork to cross the Canadian border. He was stopped at the port of entry at Rouses Point in northern New York State. Peter travelled to the border and was successful in persuading the Canadian immigration personnel that the brothers could be briefly reunited in the office at the port of entry. (Peter's impact on George was considerable and continued into their adult years. Years later, George noted that "Peter influenced me to get into the same business as he was in as a city planner." The younger Oberlander brother went on to earn a master's of science degree in urban planning at Columbia University and to a distinguished career in Washington, D.C. with the US National Capital Planning Commission, serving as Associate Executive Director.)

Meanwhile in Montréal, Ben and Tony Robinson continued their efforts to help the son of Ben's friend Fritz. Their sponsorship of his release from camp required them to post a bond in addition to their guarantee of Peter's benign status; in other words, that he was not a danger to the Canadian state, that he was living with them and that he was a non-political person.

Peter's "non-person" status, coupled with the Robinsons' moral, financial and emotional support, greatly shaped his new life in Canada. Peter remembered that time clearly in an interview with Irene Dodek for the Jewish Historical Society of British Columbia's oral history project focused on Jewish war internees:

> I arrived in Montréal on a Friday night. On Monday morning, Ben Robinson took me to McGill. He pointed me to the office of the Director of the School of Architecture, John Bland. I will never forget the day. Apart from what I knew, and my coat, I had nothing. I said, "I want to study architecture." The time was November and the term had begun in September. So I was obviously late. Secondly, students needed records. I had nothing. He accepted my word that I had done these subjects, and I had some advanced standing, and I was given admission into the second year of architecture, because he trusted me! He had restored my confidence that somebody would trust what you had to say not because you had a piece of paper.

Due to Peter's personal circumstances, including a prohibition on travel outside of Quebec, McGill's School of Architecture was effectively his *only* choice. Fortunately, it was an excellent school with compassionate, creative and socially-conscious mentors and peers. This was more than just an opportunity to study or earn a degree for Peter. For a non-Canadian, Jewish youth, direct admission to an undergraduate program in architecture at McGill with advanced standing in wartime Canada meant that, instead of questioning his legal status, someone accepted his word and said, as Peter phrased it, "Okay, we will give this a try."

The trust that John Bland placed in a "non-person" teenager, on that cold, windy, afternoon in the fall of 1941, injected a wave of self-confidence in Peter. He felt respected and trusted at face value for the first time since his arrest in

1940. He also learned a lesson that would guide him in his future as an educator, which was: always have faith in what students tell you regardless of what is on paper; it will almost always work out for the best. In Peter's words,

> I came out of the inferno of Europe, and I was in a very uncertain, ambivalent state. McGill restored my life. I'm very much in debt both to John Bland, personally, and those four years at McGill... it was a place that allowed me to in a sense regain my balance, my own strength, my own trust in myself and encouraged me to go on.

Professor John Bland, Director of the McGill School of Architecture 1941-1972. McGill News 1973.[10]

But education meant expenses, for tuition, books, accommodation, and meals. The Robinsons gave Peter the interest accrued on the bond they had posted for his release, which helped Peter manage his daily expenses and pay his tuition fees for the first term in architecture. In his second year, he was awarded a university bursary. This support formed the foundation for Peter's new beginning in Canada as an architect, planner, future citizen and citizenship court judge. Moreover, he was about to be immersed in the latest thinking sweeping his chosen profession.

In the mid-twentieth century, the rise of the Modernist architectural movement generated new thinking about land as a *tabula rasa* that would house the modern city. CIAM, *Congrès Internationaux d'Architecture Moderne* (International

Congresses of Modern Architecture) was series of conferences that unleashed new ideas about city building in Europe that began in Switzerland in 1928. In his book on CIAM, Eric Mumford states that "From the beginning, CIAM was conceived of as an instrument of propaganda to advance the cause of the architecture that was developing in Europe in the 1920s…the formation of CIAM appears to be a defining moment in the formation of a new approach to architecture." CIAM's Athens congress in 1933 suggested a new urban planning framework that viewed the physical city as the sum of four segregated central functions: dwelling, work, recreation, and transportation. This powerful set of ideas influenced both theory and practice in architectural circles in Europe. As Ala Damaz, Peter's classmate and friend, recounts, with the new wave of modernist thinking ushered by the Athens Charter, "everything was history."

At McGill, Peter was part of a small, tightly-knit group of students and teachers. Damaz recollects that most undergraduate students were foreigners from former British colonies in India, Afghanistan, Africa and South America, who had been re-routed to North America with Allied Nations Scholarships due to the outbreak of the Second World War. The class environment was truly global and diverse for its time. As most students were "war refugees", they were treated protectively at McGill; they had an opportunity to rebuild their lives in Canada.

Another of Peter's peers at McGill was Blanche Lemco (later known as Blanche Lemco van Ginkel). She particularly remembers Peter among her peers at McGill. Peter had always enjoyed being in the outdoors on adventures such as his annual skiing trips at the *Gymnasium*. Skiing trips ensured lively and interesting conversations, helping him to put away the internment experience briefly. The presence of the Laurentian Mountains created opportunities for skipping classes together and heading out for group skiing excursions. He particularly enjoyed skiing trips on the Maple Leaf Trail, or up to Saint Agathe and skiing down Hill 69 back to Saint Sauveur. There must have been some awkward moments; some ski hills at that time were closed to Jews. Exhausted from a long skiing day, the group would head back home by train. As a relatively small class, the students spent plenty of time together socializing, exploring and studying. The students ahead of them by a year were their "demi-gods". The juniors, in turn, looked up to Peter's batch for inspiration. This made students from all the years close colleagues. John Bland ensured that *his* students were kept together.

Peter's professors at McGill included John Bland, Arthur Lismer (one of Canada's iconic Group of Seven artists), Gordon Webber (a modernist painter and professor of design), Frederic Lasserre, (who would go on to head UBC's Architecture School), Freddy B. Taylor, Harry Mayerovitch, Percy Nobbs, and Harold Lee Fetherstonhaugh. Bland played the role of mentor and taught design and the history of modern architecture. Taylor taught drafting and architectural drawing. Peter recalled how Lismer introduced Webber to McGill. Webber came from Chicago and brought with him "the whole Bauhaus tradition red hot out of Mies [van der Rohe] and Chicago." Lismer and Webber got together to develop basic design and foundational drawing courses. Nobbs taught heraldry, and Mayerovitch, a local practitioner, would conduct weekend classes that provided rich insight into real-life architectural practice. In addition, many other local practitioners were invited to the school to showcase their work, take courses or spend time with students in the design studios.

But learning according to Peter was not only between students and teachers. Learning occurred in the everyday interactions among his peers within the classroom and across the years. One such peer was Alvaro Ortega. Ortega had undertaken a summer internship in France with Le Corbusier. This gave Ortega an important influence over his junior peers. In a conversation with Jim Donaldson, chronicler of the McGill school, Peter described his interactions with Ortega: "I'll never forget the fact that at one point I tried to borrow a pen from him, and he wouldn't let me have it. And I said, 'What's wrong?' and he said, 'Well, because the master had it in his hand, and I won't let anyone touch it!'"

Steeped in this new world view represented by Bauhaus and CIAM, Peter emerged as a modernist with a difference, one whose focus was on the social and political aspects of architecture. His concern was people, community and the social impacts. Building on this ethos, Peter chose to design a housing project for his architectural thesis in his final year at McGill. Harold Lee Fetherstonhaugh, Peter's thesis supervisor, opposed this project because he did not feel that it qualified as architecture. Peter had made the ultimate mistake. He had not chosen to work on a single, institutional building of significance such as a hospital, school or church. Instead he had opted to design socially relevant student housing modules between McGill College Avenue and Bleury Street. Despite stiff opposition from his supervisor, Peter persisted. Fetherstonhaugh was very upset by Peter's stubbornness and chose to ignore his candidacy for a prestigious award at McGill. However, despite this setback, Peter stayed his course, re-conceptualizing student housing through a socio-cultural lens. It was only through the intervention of John Bland, his mentor and the school director, that Peter was able to graduate.

By 1944, Ortega was a graduate student at Harvard's Graduate School of Design (GSD). He maintained a line of communication with Peter across the borders. He wrote enthusiastically to Peter that Walter Gropius, Marcel Breuer, G. Holmes Perkins and Martin Wagner were teaching at the GSD. These well-known architects were surely a valuable resource for any enthusiastic, novice modernist, and Peter was keen on pursuing his advanced architectural education.

Modernist ideals propagated by CIAM were mainstreamed in eastern parts of wartime America through the prominent faculty involved in architecture schools. These ideals were set out in *Can our Cities Survive? An ABC of Urban Problems, Their Analyses, Their Solutions: Based on The Proposals Formulated by CIAM,* written by José Luis Sert and CIAM and published in 1942. It was intended to generate popular support for CIAM's vision within pragmatic American urban development circles. One proponent of this approach was Walter Gropius. It was Gropius who had helped Sert's book project see the light of day. However, in postwar America, the New York CIAM Chapter for Relief and Postwar Planning shifted its agenda towards postwar reconstruction in Europe. Although Peter could identify emotionally with the cause of European reconstruction, his focus was firmly set on the future of planning and cities in North America.

Peter graduated from McGill in the summer of 1945. With the end of the war, he once again made attempts to reunite with his family across the border, but his efforts were futile. Just before the war had ended, Peter had worked with the National Research Council (NRC) as a staff architect. Although he was unaware of it at the time, he was part of a team that designed a nuclear research facility at Chalk River, located northwest of Ottawa. His superiors in the team were happy with his work and encouraged him to pursue graduate studies. He was recommended for and won a prestigious NRC Mechanical Engineering Fellowship to support graduate studies in planning. Peter seized this opportunity as a route to Harvard's Graduate School of Design to pursue a master's degree in city planning.

Peter was clear early on that he chose Harvard not to get a paper degree but for the spectacular lineup of internationally renowned faculty at the GSD to which Alvaro Ortega had alerted him. Peter joined the City Planning Program at the GSD in the fall of 1945. Two subsequent Wheelwright fellowships in the second year at Harvard made completion of the two-year graduate program possible. But the support that was most critical was the NRC scholarship which gave Peter a one-way entry into the US with a guaranteed return to Canada, *all without a passport*. This scholarship not only provided Peter with the mobility he badly needed, first to reunite with his family and second to access graduate education at Harvard, but it altered his non-person resident status in Canada. It opened a new horizon and new possibilities in terms of education, professional possibilities, and reunification with his family.

In Boston, Peter had elected to live in a student residence, and he was apprehensive about who his roommate might be and whether they would get along, given Peter's unique background and unfamiliarity with American society. On arriving at his room, he was delighted to find that his roommate was none other than Harry Seidler, his childhood friend from primary school days in Vienna and a fellow internee in the Canadian camps. Seidler had taken an undergraduate degree in architecture at the University of Manitoba and had, like Peter, been attracted to the GSD by the glowing array of talent on the faculty. He would later become one of Australia's foremost architects and planners.

In addition to living with Seidler in Boston, Peter discovered a new set of friends who he called "ex-patriots at Harvard." There were six of them. The common thread that imbued a sense of cohesion among them was that they were novices who had chosen Harvard for its teachers and were seized with the burning question of what they were going to do with their young lives. John Creswell Parkin, Jean Sutherland Boggs, Jean Barnes, Charles Edward Trudeau (brother of Pierre Trudeau who studied Public Administration) Seidler and Peter comprised the team of six. This was a close-knit group (in fact, Jean Barnes soon married John Parkin) who often had lively discussions and went skiing together. Weekend skiing trips up to Stowe and the Harvard skiing cabin would be planned to begin on Friday at 4 p.m. For Peter, graduate school was not only about studies and young minds questioning their uncertain futures; it produced new friendships that would transform into lifelong partnerships.

The Graduate School of Design at Harvard was a large entity with three departments — city planning, architecture and landscape architecture. Besides the "ex-patriots", Peter befriended students from the landscape school. This led to the beginnings of a personal friendship with a young graduate student from the landscape architecture department, Cornelia Hahn. In the fall of 1946, a group of students, including Cornelia Hahn and Peter Oberlander, attended a picnic. The site was Walden Pond, in Concord, Massachusetts, made famous by Henry David Thoreau's reflection on simple living in natural surroundings, *Walden: Life in the Woods*. It was a popular summer swimming destination among students, locals, and tourists.

Peter cherished such moments of bonding with friends, especially as he worked towards integration into North American society and tried to put his internment experience behind him; he rarely revealed the traumas he had experienced to others. His memories of Europe were refreshed when he discovered a *gugelhupf* on the picnic table. The Jewish communities of Vienna considered the *gugelhupf,* a traditional European fruit cake, to be a *Viennoiserie* i.e., a "thing of Vienna." Growing up in Vienna, Peter had enjoyed *gugelhupf* baked by his grandmother, and so he had a weakness for it. He delightedly approached the picnic table and helped himself to another slice of the largish ring-shaped cake set upon a cake stand. He inquired about who had made it and was introduced to Cornelia Hahn.

As the classmates sat around chatting or swam in the Pond, Peter enjoyed the raisin, almond, and cherry brandy flavours of the *gugelhupf,* which suddenly transported him back to Vienna. Cornelia's memory of the moment is vivid:

> When I met him at Walden Pond he skipped stones with me. He jumped over tree trunks, and he never talked about the past. I had no idea what he had gone through since 1938. We were always going forward. We never dwelt on the past. I was lucky to be from the family I was from. He was able to distance himself from his pain and struggle of the war years because his head was always full of ideas: build things, make town plans.

As they gathered their mats and repacked the picnic basket, Cornelia hoped that she would see Peter again.

Who was this young lady who had managed to refresh memories of Vienna in Peter's mind on that outing?

Cornelia Hahn was the daughter of fully-assimilated German Jews, Lotte Beate Jastrow Hahn, a horticulturalist, and Franz Hahn, an engineer. She was born in Mulheim, located in Rhineland, Germany. The socio-economic consolidation of the Hahn family began with the European Industrial Revolution. Cornelia's paternal great-grandfather was Albert Hahn, a man of vision who moved to Grosenbaum in 1890 to start a steel mill, the *Hahn'schke Werke.* After three decades, it employed thousands. Grosenbaum gradually emerged as a coal and leather town.

Cornelia's grandfather taught economics and history at the University of Berlin and was later an elected city councillor. Their son Franz Hahn was raised as a liberal-minded, socially-conscious individual who eventually studied engineering. Like his parents, he did not observe the Jewish way of life and consciously chose to assimilate himself into the cosmopolitan ways of Berlin between the wars. The family devoted themselves to the cause of public housing and welfare-related projects.

Cornelia's maternal ancestry had similar secular, liberal roots. The Jastrow family's origins can be traced to the small town of Rogasen in present day Poland. When her maternal grandfather was sixteen years old, he aspired towards an urban life and left home to register for high school in Breslau. Cornelia's mother, Lotte Beate Jastrow was born into an assimilated Jewish, academic family, to Ignaz Jastrow and Anna Seligmann Jastrow in Berlin. Ignaz was an economist, historian, and professor of political science at the University of Berlin. Jastrow's position in society offered his daughters a cosmopolitan upbringing among the socially-conscious intellectual and artistic elite of Berlin.

When Lotte and Franz were married they moved to the small coal town of Grosenbaum, the site of the Hahn steel mill. They had two daughters, Cornelia and Charlotte. To create a safer space for the growing family, Lotte Beate Hahn chose to move away from the coal town to a village near Düsseldorf. The new home gave Lotte and Franz access to professional, cultural and literary circles which boasted the likes of the Bauhaus master, Walter Gropius. Cornelia's parents were influenced by the Bauhaus school of thought and, gradually, Gropius became an influential colleague and a friend of the Hahns.

The new home also had a garden, and Cornelia and Charlotte spent hours enjoying the beautiful landscape around them. The memories of growing up in an environment not shrouded in coal dust but in the serenity of nature left a deep mark on the impressionable Cornelia. However, this new life, new friends and a new way of being were to abruptly change when tragedy struck the Hahns.

In 1933, Franz Hahn suddenly died in an avalanche accident. On January 30 of that year, Adolf Hitler became Chancellor of Germany and the transformation of the country by the National Socialist Party began. The situation for Lotte, Cornelia, and Charlotte was brought to a head by *Kristallnacht*, infamously referred to as the "night of the broken glass," a German pogrom against Jews in

Austria and Germany on November 9-10, 1938. Assisted by travel documents arranged by her brother, Kurt Hahn, Lotte Beate and her two daughters boarded a train out of Düsseldorf. They were travelling third class to avoid attracting attention. An SS officer was going through the train checking papers. An American, sensing what would happen if the officer discovered the mother and her daughters were fleeing the country, engaged the officer in conversation, stalling his progress until the train began pulling out of the station, and he had to get off.

With help from an American lawyer, a friend of the Hahns, they sailed aboard the *Queen Mary*, arriving in New York in February 1939. When Cornelia reached the United States, she decided to follow in the footsteps of her mother and maternal aunt, Elizabeth Jastrow, a well-known academician, and pursue higher studies.

From the age of eleven, Cornelia had never wanted to be anything but a landscape architect. She enrolled in Smith College, one of the Seven Sisters colleges, in Northampton, Massachusetts where she earned a liberal arts B.A. After graduating from Smith, she chose to study at Harvard University, which had admitted only male students until 1941, the year when the US entered World War II. A steady decline in the enrollment rate of male students had been produced by the competing demands of military service. This compelled the authorities at Harvard to admit women "temporarily." That is how Cornelia along with other women students began graduate studies in the landscape department at Harvard's Graduate School of Design.

Peter was extremely busy; the GSD program demanded an all-out commitment, and he worked at various jobs during the vacations. It was, therefore, two terms after the picnic at Walden Pond before Peter asked her out to a movie. The screening of *You Can't Take It with You* at a local cinema seemed the perfect opportunity, although the ironic relevance of the movie's title to their young lives to that date may have been lost on them.

That evening, Peter arrived at Cornelia's apartment only to inform her that he had to turn in an assignment for Martin Wagner's city-planning studio on new town design. Peter was keen on making a good impression on Wagner in the studio, so he made a deal with Cornelia. If she helped him for two hours with the landscaping details for the new town study, they could catch the late-night show. Although disappointed, Cornelia was no spoiled sport. She showed Peter into the common living area that she shared with a roommate. As Peter set up his T-square, drawing board and papers on her study table, she hurried to get out her landscape reference works.

All the work had to be done manually. Peter and Cornelia never made it to the movie. They worked forty-eight hours straight on the drawings of the new town project through many cups of coffee and excited conversation breaks. Cornelia's roommate was furious with them for "burning the midnight oil." At the end of their work session, Cornelia and Peter ran with their boards and the drawings to Hunt Hall at the GSD where the drawings were mounted with 10 minutes to spare before the deadline. "It was most stimulating," she recalled, "and Peter got an A."

That evening etched an important impression in the minds of both the young students. In Cornelia's words, she "fell in love with Peter because of his intellect, his energy, and scintillating ideas." The coy friendship at Walden Pond was transforming eventually into something more profound. It would, however, be seven years before it became a lifelong partnership, of loyalty, creative ideas, and mutual support.

It is now recognized that Harvard's Graduate School of Design was a place where some of the most progressive thinkers, many of them refugees like Peter from oppression in Europe, brought together the values that would drive the postwar reconstruction of the destroyed cities of Europe and the expansion and suburbanization of the cities of North America. The leadership was provided by Walter Gropius, Chairman of the GSD, whose Bauhaus thinking had transformed European architecture before he had had to flee Nazi Germany. A condition of Gropius' acceptance of the post was that he be joined by Marcel Breuer, a Hungarian-born modernist, architect and furniture designer. Another Gropius associate on the faculty at the GSD was Martin Wagner, the former Chief Planner of Berlin who was a demanding but rewarding taskmaster for the young Oberlander in a relationship that was enhanced by the latter's ability to converse with Wagner in German.

Gropius stressed that there was "no finality in architecture, only continuous change." He perceived architecture as a transformative tool that adapted to the ever-changing and dynamic needs and forces in society. To him, modernism was an idealist philosophy in which everyone had a duty to build a better world. And it was timeless. Years later, in 1964, in a letter to students, Gropius wrote:

> For whatever your profession, your inner devotion to the tasks you
> have set for yourself must be so deep that you can never be deflected
> from your aim. However often the thread may be torn out of your

hands, you must develop enough patience to wind it up again and again. Act as if you were going to live forever and cast your plans way ahead. By this, I mean that you must feel responsible without time limitation, and the consideration whether you may or may not be around to see the results should never enter your thoughts. If your contribution has been vital, there will always be somebody to pick up where you left off, and that will be your claim to immortality.

Peter and Harry Seidler spent the rest of their lives exercising that belief.

Walter Gropius and Harry Seidler in Sydney, 1954[11]

Another influence on Peter Oberlander at Harvard was Catherine Bauer, the self-taught expert whose seminar on housing transformed his thinking. In a comprehensive biography of Bauer that he wrote later with Eva Neubrun, he said, "Following her model, I devoted myself to figuring out how to change the world, not how to accept it."

The late Alan Armstrong related a story from Peter Oberlander's days at Harvard. Jean Sutherland Boggs was PhD student at Harvard's sister university for women, Radcliffe. She would later have a distinguished career in fine arts scholarship and development, including being the first female director of the National Gallery of Canada. While at Radcliffe, Boggs periodically held salons in her home, at which students and guests would debate the issues of the day. One evening the subject was the role that national governments in federated countries should play in the affairs of cities. Peter attended, and strenuously put forward his view that healthy cities were vital to a nation's economic and social well-being and should, therefore, be an important theme in national government policies, particularly housing and planning. His opponent, a young Quebecker, argued equally vigorously that, in Canada at least, cities were part and parcel with "municipal institutions," which were the exclusive domain of provincial governments into which any intrusion by the federal government should be steadfastly resisted. His name was Pierre Elliott Trudeau, and he must have been convinced by Oberlander's argument at some point in time because as Prime Minister he tapped Oberlander to head up a new federal Ministry of State for Urban Affairs in 1970.

As Peter progressed through graduate school, he and Harry Seidler worked through their vacations to support themselves at school and gain relevant professional experience. In the winter of 1945 during Harvard's Christmas recess, they were at the office of celebrated Finnish architect Alvar Aalto in Boston. They were assigned the task of drawing the plans for the Baker Dormitory at the Massachusetts Institute of Technology (MIT) in Cambridge. Penelope Seidler, Harry's wife, fondly remembered a little anecdote Peter shared with her when she visited him in Vancouver in the summer of 1988. Aalto used to drink *aquavit,* a caraway--flavoured Scandinavian distilled beverage often consumed during festive seasons such as Christmas. Aquavit purists often sipped it slowly from a small shot glass. Aalto seemed to be one such purist. He would make his daily rounds around the architects' drafting boards in the office, with a small paper cup filled with aquavit. Peter and Harry always froze when he approached their drafting boards with their drawings meticulously detailed in Rotring ink pens. They feared that "Aalto's paper cup would disintegrate, splashing the dark beverage all over their drawings, thus ruining their hard work and compelling them to start all over again."

At Harvard, Peter had the opportunity to reflect on the philosophical ideas of the modernist urban agenda propagated by CIAM and synergize them with the social beliefs he had forged from his liberal upbringing in Vienna and his personal experience with the impact of World War II. The uncertainty of the postwar times reinforced Peter's belief that the architectural profession could no longer neglect the importance of the social, political and cultural life of cities where the well-being of people should be the core concern. This required architecture to break free from its disciplinary preoccupations with individual buildings, aesthetics and built form. The need of the hour was for architects to address housing issues affecting whole communities and the emergent urban form shaped by large projects and facilities needed for reconstructing cities. It was a belief that had nearly scuppered Peter's career at McGill, but it was gaining more currency at Harvard.

Finally, graduation day arrived on June 5, 1947. It was a sunny afternoon, and the selection of the guest speaker at convocation could not have been more appropriate to this moment in Peter's life. General George Marshall had played a leadership role in the Allied campaign in Europe; Winston Churchill had called him "the organizer of Victory." In the postwar world, Marshall had become US Secretary of State, with the delicate task of ensuring that all of the former combatants could participate in peace and prosperity. In words that seem incredibly quaint from the perspective of 2018, he shared the philosophy of the US government as it approached the postwar era:

> It is logical that the United States should do whatever it is able to do to assist in the return of normal economic health in the world, without which there can be no political stability and no assured peace. Our policy is directed not against any country or doctrine but against hunger, poverty, desperation, and chaos. Its purpose should be the revival of a working economy in the world so as to permit the emergence of political and social conditions in which free institutions can exist. Such assistance, I am convinced, must not be on a piecemeal basis as various crises develop. Any assistance that

this Government may render in the future should provide a cure rather than a mere palliative.

The United States — and the world — had learned a lesson from the hard, punitive and transitory peace that had followed World War I.

This speech foreshadowed the creation of the European Recovery Program popularly known as the Marshall Plan. Marshall's focus on the role of national governments and peacekeeping in Europe's economic recovery and a stabilized global condition greatly impacted Peter's thoughts. This speech was one of the factors that helped Peter to look beyond the unforeseen circumstances that had brought him to America and dream of a new life far from Europe. It further reinforced his ideals for modernist planning approaches in architecture and the planning of cities that were rooted in Bauhaus thought and Viennese socialism. Mike Harcourt, former premier of British Columbia, suggested 60 years later that, "Peter started working on issues of cities and sustainability in the 1950s and he, therefore, is one of the early pioneers of the urban century in which we now find ourselves."

After Peter graduated from Harvard, he did not immediately apply for the doctoral program. He was conscious of the moral and legal obligations he had in Canada, especially due to the faith and trust placed in him by the Robinsons, John Bland and his seniors at the National Research Council. He returned to Canada in the summer of 1947 with the hope of contributing to Canadian society as a trained planning professional. He quickly accepted a contractual position with the National Research Council.

On his return to Canada, he must have been struck by the contrast with his "complex and ambivalent" first arrival in Canada just seven years earlier as a stateless internee, an innocent casualty of a conflict whose outcome was anything but certain at the time. His experiences in the camps had hardened his survival instincts but had also forged deep friendships based on trust and common interest. His education in design and planning, starting first in the camps and then at McGill and Harvard, had equipped him to make a contribution to a new society and had convinced him that Canada was the place where he could pursue that goal.

CHAPTER FIVE:

A NEW SCHOOL FOR A NEW PROFESSION

The federal government's approach to Canada's prewar Depression housing needs had been firmly rooted in a philosophy that housing was a private good to be provided to families by private industry. The role of government was to facilitate the operation of that industry by providing security for the financing of home ownership and the construction of rental housing. This comfortable stance was quickly swept aside by the urgent needs of the wartime mobilization effort.

World War II was a crucible for Canada: it is often said that the country entered the war as a colony and emerged as a nation. One of Canada's key roles in the war effort, in addition to providing men and women of courage and determination, was the production of the materials, supplies, and equipment needed in the struggle for survival against the evils emanating from Germany and Japan. Niceties such as the constitution were set aside under war measures legislation to enable the country to fulfill its responsibilities to the Allies. Canada witnessed a steady rise in industrial employment from metal and energy industries pressed into the war effort.

Most industries were established around the suburban fringes of cities and small towns. Munitions and explosives plants were built in Ontario and Quebec, aircraft manufacturing developed in Ontario, Quebec, British Columbia and Manitoba, shipbuilding facilities were expanded in British Columbia, Quebec and Nova Scotia, and the military transport plants in Ontario and Quebec were the foundations of the future automobile industry.

The housing needs of hundreds of workers who had migrated to these areas remained unaddressed due to housing and material supply shortages, resulting in double occupancy in single homes and overcrowded conditions. Resolution of Canada's housing problems quickly became critical to the nation's economic and military requirements because of the need to provide housing for wartime factory workers and their families.

The federal government's response to this challenge was the creation of Wartime Housing Ltd. in 1941 to build rental housing for war workers and (later) veterans. Wartime Housing Limited was one of nearly 30 crown companies reporting directly to C.D. Howe, the Minister of Munitions and Supply (fondly and appropriately remembered as "the Minister of Everything,") who is properly credited for mobilizing the Canadian economy to be a powerful force in the conduct of the war. Wartime Housing Ltd. built an enormous amount of rental housing primarily for low- and medium-income workers and their families.

In 1943, the federal government began to look at the housing and community planning needs that would prevail in postwar Canadian cities through an Advisory Committee on Postwar Reconstruction. This Committee's report foretold the need for a comprehensive national-level housing policy that would aid postwar national economic development. It also revealed that both the Depression and war years had resulted in a drop in homeownership and increased demands for rental housing associated with the war economy. The need for a postwar housing policy for low-income families and the provision of low-rental housing for an important segment of the population was becoming increasingly evident.

The government's response to these needs was the *National Housing Act,* enacted in 1944. It resulted in the creation of the Central (now Canada) Mortgage and Housing Corporation on January 1, 1946 to house returning war veterans and to lead Canada's housing programs.

Following his brief employment at the National Research Council after his return to Canada from the United States, Peter was hired by CMHC as its first planning professional. His first assignment was to prepare comprehensive data on the existing 36,000 wartime housing units spread across the country that had been developed during the war years. With the creation of new planning frameworks to regulate and reconfigure housing policy in Canada, officials at CMHC were contemplating the future of wartime rental housing stock, specifically whether to remodel, rehabilitate or sell the units to the existing occupants.

CMHC finally sold the housing stock to the occupants in a move that some observers see as a lost opportunity for the public sector to take a necessary role in the provision of housing for those left out of the private market. The idea was at cross-purposes with the private-enterprise principles of the government of the day, which recoiled from the prospect of becoming a landlord for thousands of Canadian households. Instead, the government embraced an approach that focused on home ownership through the involvement of private developers and builders in the housing sector.

As part of his work assignment at CMHC, Peter was also sent to England. As he later put it, the directive he had been given by his Canadian bosses was to "learn something from those guys (the British) and tell us (Canadians) how to do it." (Cornelia was not impressed: "Why would you go back there?" she asked. "They threw you out!") He spent a year in England. His exposure to the reconstruction of London by the London County Council and the ambitious new town projects provided Peter with deep insights into planning and implementation of city-building processes.

He soon learned that the urgent task in Europe was to address the socio-economic turbulence, loss of life, statelessness and physical damage to European cities and the countryside caused by the war. In September 1947, Peter attended CIAM 6, popularly known as the Bridgwater CIAM convention (1947), which was the first postwar meeting of architects and urbanists that specifically focused on the question of the reconstruction of devastated European cities. Policymakers and architect-planners in Europe struggled to generate solutions through intervention in the economy, in society, and in planning of cities through the reconstruction process. As was soon to become clear to Peter, the postwar situation in Canadian cities was more nuanced; "reconstruction" would mean making up for time lost to Depression and war by repairing and expanding an urban fabric that was mostly intact.

In London, he also reunited with Pierre Trudeau who was then at the London School of Economics and Political Science (LSE). Trudeau had chosen to continue his master's dissertation at the LSE through an exchange program. However, he stayed on and registered in a doctoral program that exposed him to the principles of socialist economics. Trudeau and Oberlander socialized often, taking a Christmas skiing trip to Europe in the winter of 1947-48.

During his sojourn overseas, Peter travelled through the Scandinavian countries in Europe to get a first-hand understanding of postwar housing developments, planning regulations, and infrastructure projects. He learned a good deal from these experiences that would be relevant to his future work in community planning research at CMHC in Canada.

Peter Oberlander returned to Canada in July 1948 to become the CMHC's first professional planning employee at a time when all levels of government in Canada were seized with the urgent task of reconstruction.

CMHC was the government's chosen instrument for facilitating the provision of housing primarily through the private sector under the *National Housing Act of 1944*. This legislation reflected a broad approach, authorizing CMHC to provide:

- Mortgage loans offered through financial institutions to prospective home-owners, co-operatives, builders and limited dividend housing corporations;
- Guarantees to life insurance companies undertaking the construction of low and moderate-income rental housing;
- Grants to municipalities wishing to undertake slum clearing for the construction of low-income housing; and
- Support for housing research and community planning (Part V of the Act).

At CMHC, Peter Oberlander engaged in developing programs under Part V to support research and education in the housing field. From the beginning, the corporation's research and education mandate was interpreted broadly to include what would now be called "capacity building" within the country's private sector, educational institutions, and civil society organizations.

On the civil society front, CMHC sponsored the creation of the Community Planning Association of Canada "as a means of organizing public education and of encouraging citizen participation in community planning." These are remarkable words in the context of the late 1940s, when "citizen participation" had until recently simply meant supporting the war effort and "community planning" was scarcely being done in most communities in the country.

CMHC also supported a number of university research projects at that time, including a study of provincial legislation conducted by McGill University, a study of social and economic aspects of housing in metropolitan Toronto carried out by the University of Toronto School of Social Work, and a study of urban development and housing survey techniques done by the University of British Columbia School of Architecture with the co-operation of the Vancouver Housing Association.

One of the grants was of particular note: a grant to McGill University to support five fellowships to post-graduate students taking a special seminar course organized by the McGill Physical Planning Committee (precursor to the

McGill's School of Urban Planning). Candidates for the fellowships, which were also supported by the Province of Quebec and the City of Montréal, could be drawn from any of the social or physical sciences and could proceed to a master's degree in their own faculty. It was the beginning of interdisciplinary planning education in Canada and the fellowships were the forerunner of CMHC's scholarship program.

Some understanding of the ultimate impact of the fellowship program can be gained from the observations of Moshe Safdie who was one of the early recipients of a CMHC scholarship in 1960. Renowned architect, designer of Habitat at Expo 67 and Member of the Order of Canada, Safdie recalled in 1997 how the CMHC scholarship changed his perspective on architecture and its relationship with planning:

> I had started my thesis. I should say that an important event for me and to give credit to CMHC where credit is deserved, they had formed that new scholarship, at the time it was new, of studying housing, picking one student from one school of architecture in Canada and sending them off in the summer to study housing on the continent. That was the first year that they formed the scholarship. And I was picked. I remember Michel Barcelo, École des Beaux-Arts, Université de Montréal, and discovering separatism on the trip. And, you know, we travelled and then we went to Ottawa and worked at CMHC. And I came back saying, "I'm going to do housing for my thesis called A Case of City Living." And that work became sort of the program for the thesis, and I was going to do housing.

An opportunity for CMHC to present itself on the national stage came with the appointment of the Royal Commission on National Development in the Arts, Letters and Sciences, which was established by Privy Council Order on April 8, 1949. Often referred to as the "Massey Commission," this inquiry was chaired by the Honourable Vincent Massey, Chancellor of the University of Toronto, who later became the first Canadian-born Governor General of Canada. Its agenda was essentially the cultural and scientific reconstruction of postwar Canada.

During the course of its two-year inquiry, the Commission held 114 public hearings throughout Canada, at which some twelve hundred witnesses appeared.

The Commission received 462 formal submissions and many hundreds of letters from Canadian citizens.

Norman Archibauld Macrae (Larry) Mackenzie, President of the University of British Columbia, was a member of this commission. In the early 1940s, amid the anxiety and sacrifice of wartime Canada, the University of British Columbia had seen a change in its administrative command. A new board of governors, a new president, and a new chancellor were appointed. The new president, Norman Mackenzie, was a Nova Scotian. Mackenzie was a farmer, a former serviceman and then a trained lawyer with a distinguished career in international law. He headed the University of New Brunswick for four years before moving west to UBC in 1944; indeed, for a number of months prior to Peter Oberlander's release from camp, they would have been within a few miles of each other.

In addition to his role as UNB president, Dr. Mackenzie had served as the Chairman of the Reconstruction, Rehabilitation and Postwar Development Committee of New Brunswick. He identified peace, security, freedom, prosperity, plenty and the good life for all Canadian citizens as the key features that would be desirable for a better Canadian future. On a global scale, he believed that in the postwar geopolitical climate a new international organization similar to the League of Nations would be needed to achieve these ideals both within Canada and internationally. He recognized that the adversity of war had yielded full employment rates and boosted industrialization and urbanization processes.

In Mackenzie's analysis, five factors lay behind this growth. First, the war had generated a unity of purpose from coast to coast across Canada. Second, there had been a demonstration of the benefits of the federal government acting in the larger public interest despite tensions with provincial governments. Third, the country's fiscal strength gained by high taxation and successful large-scale government borrowing from citizens through Victory Bonds had been demonstrated. Fourth, the political will to regulate, intervene and act had been developed. Fifth, and finally, there was the creation of a strong wartime economy and markets. He was cognizant, however, that the postwar period would transform these "conditions and attitudes" drastically, so the transition of the economy from war to peace would need to be managed carefully to avoid a lapse into recession or depression.

By the winter of 1944-45, it was clear that the war would soon be over. British Columbia, like other provinces, was preparing for the sudden increase in war veterans and returning servicemen. Mackenzie eagerly prepared for them to return and be offered admission to UBC, as Canadian universities across the country were now legally obliged to do, thanks in no small measure to his efforts. His vision of UBC's role as the war ended was to train a new generation of professionals — doctors, lawyers, teachers, engineers, and architects — to create a new, civilized, tolerant, educated society in British Columbia that would contribute to the social, economic and cultural life of postwar Canada.

To achieve his vision, Mackenzie launched the expansion of UBC — its physical space, student enrolment, diversity of course offerings, faculties, programs and essential resource facilities for student and faculty use — to suit a variety of professional, research and academic needs. This was in keeping with a promise that Mackenzie made at his formal installation ceremony at the Autumn Congregation in the Women's Gymnasium on November 1944.

> The University is a society of scholars…It must, too, be ever alert to the importance of freedom…free Universities are possible only in a free country and in a free world. For myself, I will do what I can for British Columbia, for the University of British Columbia and for Canada, and with the co-operation and support which I know I will get from the rest of you, I believe we can, together, accomplish a great deal.

In 1949, CMHC was invited to appear before the Massey Commission. CMHC management was reluctant because they had no clue about what they might contribute. Peter remembered the Corporation's conundrum:

> The one thing the Feds wanted to avoid was being deeply involved. Constitutionally, it was not federal territory. Municipal affairs were under the provincial governments. I had just started to work at CMHC. David Mansur was our President who brought to the Corporation his enviable record of having marshalled enormous wartime production resources through the promotion of popular investment in Victory Bonds. His deputy was John Young, the youngest Brigadier General in the Canadian Army and its former Quartermaster General. In search of some meaningful task, he commandeered me to prepare a submission to the Massey Commission on behalf of the Corporation, inventing whatever tenuous link I chose between the Corporation's and the

Commission's mandates. Humphrey Carver, a long-term friend and genial spirit, was drafted to work with me.

British-born Carver had been an active advocate for public housing since his arrival in Canada in 1930. At the time, he was Chair of CMHC's Research Committee, and he would later chronicle his experiences and observations in a memoir titled *Compassionate Landscape*. He was particularly impressed with Peter Oberlander's energy and enthusiasm, noting how Peter would spontaneously click his heels together when crossing the street. Carver also recounts that Peter grew a moustache at this time in an apparently unsuccessful attempt to present a greater *gravitas*.

Oberlander and Carver worked all night on the brief on what could be done in relation to city planning within the larger mandate of the Commission and its focus on areas of federal jurisdiction.

Oberlander and Carver's submission reflected their own experience and perspectives. It was clear to them that, after the war, city planning was an urgent matter in the economic and social reconstruction of Canadian cities. Canadian provincial and local governments had more often than not relied on American, British or French expertise in designing and planning their cities. Trained, qualified Canadian planners were scarce at the time, and all had had to leave the country to acquire a professional education. Urban renewal or city design at the time was primarily the domain of architects who doubled as architect-planners. In essence, the submission stressed that the country needed Canadian planners trained in Canada. To the utter surprise of Oberlander and Carver, the Brigadier approved the submission and instructed them to present it to the Commission the next day during its public hearings in the Supreme Court building on Wellington Street.

The need for a home-grown Canadian approach to planning was more than a nice idea. Years later, Eli Comay, Commissioner of Planning for Metropolitan Toronto and, ironically, an American with left-wing views who had fled the McCarthy era in the United States, found sites for "tips" in early maps of Toronto prepared by British planners; he had to find out from colleagues that "tips" were garbage dumps! Bob Williams, one of the first Canadian-trained planners, recalls that even in the 1960s "The planning department in Vancouver was all Englishmen in those days. No Canadians need apply…there was no way that I would ever have been employed in the Vancouver City Planning Department."

Later, after having been elected as a city alderman, Williams was blunter with the planning staff: "You know and I know the process; you do a windshield survey of the neighbourhood. One of you bloody Englishmen drives down in your car and says yes, no, bad, good, da da da, and then you make some decisions about moving the bulldozer in."

Although Oberlander and Carver could not have known it at the time, their appearance before the Massey Commission was one the first and most important steps in creating a Canadian culture of planning and urbanism.

As the Commission members settled down in their chairs for the day's hearings, Peter was summoned into the chamber to make his presentation. Peter quickly glanced through his brief, composed himself and began his presentation. If Canada aspired to bring about a cultural renaissance in the postwar years, it would need well-planned and beautiful cities. His argument was simple but powerful:

> If we are serious about rebuilding, designing or expanding Canadian cities, it has to be done by Canadians. We can no longer sustain importing European and American ideas for municipal problems in Canada. The role of the CMHC should be to support education, not hire planners from abroad to design new subdivisions in Canada.

If the Massey Commission's vision of a cultural and scientific renaissance were to be achieved, it would be achieved in cities which were planned, designed and managed with this purpose in mind. Such cities would have to be built by Canadians for Canadian people according to Canadian values, goals, and objectives. The bottom line was that "better cities would create the opportunities for the arts in Canada, but they required Canadians to be city planners who were trained at Canadian universities."

Decades later as an Emeritus Professor at UBC, Peter recalled the basic premise of his argument to the Massey Commission:

> After the war, it was clear that Canada would go through enormous transformation. What was less clear was the quality of that transformation and whether a cultural focus would be there or whether it would be entirely economic and political. We...said, "look, if you are serious about the cultural future of this country, there is only one place you have to start and that's the city

because that's where music, drama, literature — all the arts — are encouraged, practiced and flourish." In addition, the city itself is our greatest artifact because Athens, Jerusalem, Paris, Vienna, and London are places where civilization which has something to do with civitas or city happens. We made the case for the city. And if you say it's about the city, then you must start there. And this is the important thing mainly — training Canadians to build better (Canadian) cities. Up until now, there was no education in the (Canadian) university dealing with the city, city improvement and city building.

To some, it might seem to be an odd statement coming from a European-born, U.S.-trained planner who had only lived in Canada for a few years, but it underscored Oberlander's comprehension of Canada's needs and his commitment to its future, notwithstanding his accidental and unpleasant introduction to the country.

In their submission to the Commission, Oberlander and Carver cited the role of Paris-based Jacques Gréber who had recently been invited to prepare a plan for the National Capital Region and would suggest a grandiose Champs-Élysées for that city. In British Columbia in the 1920s, the provincial government and the City of Vancouver had called upon Harland Bartholomew from St Louis, USA to advise on plans for Vancouver and its region. So, cities in Canada were being planned — where they were being planned at all — by American, English or French planners.

The perspective presented by CMHC on the interdependence between cities as the cradles of a national culture, planning education and the role of the university struck a chord with the keenly observant Norman Mackenzie.

The day after the submission to the Commission, Peter received a phone call at his CMHC office from Mackenzie who had left a message for him asking, "Would you have breakfast with me at the Château Laurier?" Peter had never met Mackenzie and had only a vague idea of what Vancouver and UBC were. They met at the Canadian Grill at the Château, then as now the social epicentre of political Ottawa. Mackenzie introduced himself to Peter and then introduced Peter to his colleague Dr. Fred Soward of the UBC faculty. After Peter had shared the gist of his presentation with Soward, Mackenzie with characteristic directness said, "How would you like to come to UBC and experiment with your idea of an academic educational program in urban planning?" It was an opportunity for Peter to embark on a new journey that involved not just talking about the need for and role of planning education in postwar Canada but actually applying his ideas in real life — to move from ideas to action.

At the time, Peter was in a contractual position with CMHC. Having invested in Peter's training in Britain, CMHC did not want to release him from his duties, but Norman Mackenzie was keen to get Peter quickly on board to UBC. The astute politician that he was, he managed to persuade CMHC to provide Peter with a paid leave of absence for two years.

Peter arrived in Vancouver in the cold and wet winter of 1950. The winter edition of *The Ubyssey*, the university student newspaper, announced, "University appoints Town Planning expert," saying, "the University of British Columbia to keep pace with the rapid development of its province and communities has appointed Professor H. Peter Oberlander to the staff of the School of Architecture."

When the Massey Commission's final report was published in 1951, its recommendations mainly focused on the creation of new national institutions that became the Canada Council and the Social Sciences Research Council and on improvements to the mandate of the Canadian Broadcasting Corporation. In its commentary, it acknowledged the importance of architecture and planning in Canada's cultural life. Its broad endorsement for more federal support for the arts and social sciences in the form of grants to universities and fellowships for students was implicit, if not explicit, recognition of the importance of research and education in housing and community planning as set out by Oberlander and Carver in the CMHC submission. The Commission does, however, appear to have been careful to confine the focus in its more specific comments to areas of clear federal jurisdiction, as evidenced by the following excerpt from the report:

> ...it was urged that the Federal Government recognize the importance of community planning and aid it, insofar as this lies within its power. Regional directors, now used by the Central Mortgage and Housing Corporation, should be employed, we were told, for all federal projects and should work closely with provincial and municipal governments.

In the autumn of 1950, with the support of CMHC, a two-year post-graduate diploma course in Community and Regional Planning was created at UBC to respond to the growing need for qualified planners with professional status. In the light of the postwar expansion of villages, towns, and cities, due to rapid population growth, the university was considered to be the logical centre for studying the problems arising from such conditions and for instruction in the methods of dealing with them. Peter Oberlander was nominated to supervise UBC's first planning school and was appointed as the Secretary of the Directing Committee chaired by Professor Henry Angus.

What did Peter Oberlander bring to this role? Although he was not yet 30, Peter had life experience and education that equipped him with a strong conceptual framework for the development of a graduate planning education to suit Canada's circumstances in the 1950s. As an undergraduate architecture student, Peter had been influenced by his experiences as an observant middle-class citizen in Vienna and his exposure during his internment to others interested in architecture such as Wolfgang Gerson and Harry Seidler. His obvious enthusiasm for architecture may have contributed to John Bland's humane decision to admit him into McGill. In his graduate years at Harvard, his thought process had been profoundly shaped by a number of influences, including Martin Wagner's new town studios, Gropius' Bauhaus tradition, CIAM's European modernist ideals of contemporary city planning, the student debates both formal and informal with his friends at Harvard and the attractive possibility of becoming a citizen of Canada on his return. As a planning practitioner, his training in England and subsequent work with CMHC led to his contribution to the concept of a greater role of senior governments in responding to the urbanization process in Canadian cities. These experiences also helped Peter to comprehend the need for a sense of social responsibility and citizenship in planning professionals which would focus on solving inequalities and addressing the needs of postwar Canadian society, something Gropius had promoted at the Harvard Graduate School of Design.

At McGill and Harvard, Peter had expanded his concept of the role of the architect and planner from a focus on single buildings as works of art to an understanding of the relationship of buildings with people, economic activity, environmental resources and the urban landscape. His training at Harvard led him to understand planning as a modernizing tool but also as a humane one; he recognized the need for it to be responsive to people, cultures, and societies located in a specific regional setting. The radical new thinking about cities and postwar reconstruction prompted by CIAM, the sense of social responsibility instilled by Gropius and the new reconciliatory path forged by the Marshall Plan all combined to create the ingredients for Peter to envisage a particular form of planning and pedagogy that could be pressed into creating innovative solutions for communities and their regions in Canada and globally.

In Peter's vision, the planning profession offered new opportunities to engage a breadth of areas of study and skill-building to address postwar needs. He was acutely aware of the inter-relationships between the process of postwar urban reconstruction and the design of new cities and communities in a way that combined the roles of architecture, economics, environmental science, and sociology. Judy Oberlander, Peter's daughter, recalls how he was "able to transcend his own personal experience of the internment and then think about the changes in a larger context. He always had an incredible ability to look forward. He was always thinking about the next project."

Peter Oberlander's appointment was a part of a much bigger picture of change in Canadian universities and particularly the role of the University of British Columbia under the outstanding leadership of Norman Mackenzie. The driving force was the spirit of postwar reconstruction, which was fuelling a reorientation of educational priorities towards a larger role for universities in postwar Canadian economy and society, especially in British Columbia. By the 1950s the federal government was funding universities across Canada, traditionally recognized as provincial jurisdiction.

Being politically astute, Mackenzie had an ear to the ground when he recognized that increasingly people in Canada were demanding equitable access to employment, social services, social security and material wealth. In short, after the economic depression and the war people were interested in the pursuit of a good life. They looked towards governments to be leaders in meeting these needs beyond the role of private enterprise.

MacKenzie imagined three distinct phases in reconstructing postwar Canada. The first would be the emergency period immediately after the war which would involve rehabilitating and employing returning war veterans. Next would come the redirection of industrialization beyond a war economy and, finally, a stronger Canadian peacetime economy would emerge.

P.B. Waite's biography of Mackenzie, *Lord of Point Grey*, describes him as a "six-foot-tall bear of a man, ruddy-faced, an articulate orator to diverse audiences, unorthodox in thought with an excellent memory for people and a complete politician." He liked to learn what was going on with students, faculty, the administration and the ground staff as he walked around UBC with his pet collie. Waite describes him as a "tough, able squire" who took to UBC quickly on his arrival in 1944, for a term that would last 18 years. President MacKenzie was extremely popular, especially with the students.

Mackenzie believed strongly in universal access to education. Being a democrat at heart, he dismissed the idea that education was for the privileged few. According to him, it was the taxpayers' money in British Columbia that was subsidizing the costs of faculties and facilities at UBC. So, UBC's responsibility was towards the people of the province and was not confined to the ivory towers of academia. In his view, "the more education for more people the better." With this in mind, he travelled all over the province telling British Columbians about *their* university.

Norman Mackenzie was a doer, a man of ideas but also a man of action who spread a new understanding about the relationship of "gown" and "town" among British Columbians in general. Drawing on his personal struggles to obtain an education after returning from service in World War I, Mackenzie was instrumental in developing policies that supported university admission and federal financial support for returning war veterans. He also championed the idea that universities should be deeply embedded in the societies within which they existed i.e., they had to serve the community that sustained them, or they would never survive.

UBC's specific mission at the end of the war, in Mackenzie's view, was to train the professionals — doctors, lawyers, engineers, architects and teachers, many of them veterans — who would be needed to build a new, modern society in British Columbia, to tap the potential resulting from 10 years of economic stagnation, the feverish industrial mobilization for the war and the pent-up demands for family formations that would lead to what would later be known as the "baby boom."

Education (known then as Teacher Training) was already a key professional program at UBC. It was headed by Dr. Maxwell Cameron, a UBC graduate whose first teaching job was at Powell River, a company town on British Columbia's mid-coast (It would later be the subject of one of the UBC School of Community and Regional Planning's first planning studios). After the abrupt departure of the high school principal there, the school board offered him the position of interim principal, which he accepted on the condition that it be a permanent appointment. Cameron, thus, became at 20 years old, the youngest high school principal in British Columbia's history. The arrival of the new Home Economics teacher, Hazel Robertson, also turned out to be a significant event. In 1933, after a top-secret romance, they resigned their positions in Powell River to get married and pursue further education. Cameron earned the first PhD in education from the University of Toronto and taught there for a time before accepting UBC's offer to return to the west coast in 1939. Unfit for active military service because of his fragile health, Cameron served as a civilian air raid warden during the nightly blackouts implemented in Vancouver as defence from threats of air attack on the city by Japanese forces. As the end of the war approached, he threw himself into preparation for the influx of veterans and the postwar demand for teachers and teaching positions.

With Mackenzie's active support, Cameron was appointed as a one-man royal commission to study school administration and finances across the province. The Cameron report on Educational Finance was completed in 1945 and its recommendations were accepted in their entirety by the government. The report recommended a new formula for school finance and an administrative reorganization of school districts in British Columbia. Much of that administrative architecture remains in place today.

The week the Royal Commission's report was completed, Hazel Cameron gave birth to their youngest son, Kenneth, who would receive a master's degree in Community and Regional Planning from UBC twenty-five years later and is the author of this book. Although Max Cameron's untimely death in 1951 when Kenneth was six prevented any great direct exposure to his father's career, Hazel Cameron made sure her sons knew what a remarkable time it was in UBC's history. Ken Cameron remembers hearing from her about Mackenzie's mission for UBC and how returning servicemen responded to it. "Many of Dad's students were war veterans who were raring to go; they wanted to get their education and get out there."

To fulfill Mackenzie's mission, UBC needed new facilities and fast. Army huts moved from various camps in the province were temporarily installed at UBC to accommodate classes and offices. These huts made way for modernist buildings that Damer and Rosengarten suggest "gave tangible expression to the mood of reconstruction," although the pace was often agonizingly slow, with huts and other temporary structures persisting on the campus into the twenty-first century.

Historians identify Norman Mackenzie as a leader who was driven by a spirit of social reform rooted in the belief that societal progress was possible through social leadership. On reading his elaborately detailed speech notes, one also realizes that Mackenzie strove to inculcate a sense of responsibility and citizenship in students through their education at the University. He argued that a sense of responsibility should emerge from consideration of what an individual "ought to do rather than what one should do." For Mackenzie, a sense of responsibility should emanate from parenthood, citizenship, and morality and go beyond mere law observance to create a conscientious modern citizenry. It was thinking that that resonated strongly with Peter Oberlander in relation to his own experience with many less noble ideas of citizenship.

Until the 1940s, the concept of a planning profession did not exist in British Columbia. Moreover, planning was seen as a technocratic process, managed by public administrators and politicians mostly detached from the public view and opinion. The idea of planning was centered on the application of professional values and expertise to essentially local problems of urbanization such as housing, sanitation, transport etc.

Peter Oberlander recalled that the implications of the Fraser River flood (1948) in the Lower Mainland had helped municipal administrators recognize that the river was actually a natural force that imposed risks that transcended municipal boundaries. Therefore, any effort to provide protection against flooding had to be undertaken on a broader scale; there was no point in one municipality spending money to dyke the river if neighbouring municipalities did nothing. In British Columbia's rugged terrain with its areas subject to flooding, geotechnical and seismic risk, the importance of understanding natural resources and human settlement in this light caused environmental and resource planning thought to extend across jurisdictional boundaries and focus on a larger regional setting. As he became accustomed to his new setting in a functioning democratic society, Peter realized the significance of understanding institutional dynamics, engaging communities and developing a regional perspective for the success of planning initiatives.

Here again, Central Mortgage and Housing played a key role, this time in promoting a positive political context for planning in British Columbia. In 1947, a British Columbia Division of the Community Planning Association of Canada was formed with CMHC support. The provincial government of the day was a Liberal-Conservative coalition, which was in its death throes and rife with infighting and corruption. Tom McDonald, who had served as both President of the British Columbia Conservative Party and Secretary to the provincial division of the Community Planning Association of Canada, used his considerable influence to press for legislative amendments to allow the creation of regional planning areas and for the creation of a regional planning board for the Lower Mainland, which took place in 1949. One of Peter's first extra-curricular assignments after his arrival in Vancouver in January 1950 was to help set up the Lower Mainland Planning Board in a consulting capacity.

All this was backdrop to Peter's primary role at the University of British Columbia, which was to establish Canada's first professional, graduate planning program. His first responsibilities included surveying the existing courses related to planning already available at UBC to understand what gaps existed. As a result of his experiences in academia and practice in Canada, the United States, and England, he saw that planning was increasingly an interdisciplinary realm linked to a diversity of fields ranging from architecture, sociology, economics, and engineering to the physical sciences and public administration. It was, therefore, essential for a graduate program in professional planning to introduce students to the breadth of such sub-fields in addition to some depth in a particular area of their choice. This meant that not only was the curriculum to be of an interdisciplinary nature, it also had to guide students through a process of study that could empower them to develop decision-making processes and policies that would generate and strengthen a Canadian culture of planning.

Peter enjoyed teaching two courses at the UBC School of Architecture — the history of architecture and a planning course for architects — as he developed a more specific planning curriculum for future planning students. The Director of the School was Frederic Lasserre who had been Peter's studio master at McGill, and so he felt very welcome. As a professor, Peter was very interested in bringing the academy to the community, what he called "town and gown," an approach that echoed President Mackenzie's effort to forge strong bonds with all communities in the province.

Peter Oberlander's vision for the planning school was staunchly supported by Frederic Lasserre and by Leonard Marsh, Director of the School of Social Work, Dean G.E. Robinson of the Faculty of Arts and Sciences and Dean Henry Angus of the newly formed Faculty of Graduate Studies. Prior to Oberlander's arrival at UBC, both Lasserre and Marsh had already been active in planning-related circles in Vancouver and British Columbia.

Peter and Dean Angus knew exactly what they wanted in terms of a program. In Peter's words, it would be "a graduate program that would allow a melding of subjects of multi-disciplinary education in an interdisciplinary fashion." Angus championed the cause of the planning school with the UBC administration and negotiated for a two-year graduate diploma program in Community and Regional Planning. SCARP was the very first unit of the Faculty of Graduate Studies. Angus even suggested how Peter should position SCARP vis-à-vis other faculties and departments: "Relate and link to everyone, be subservient to none." This lesson resonated with lessons Peter had learned in the camps and remained with him during his time at SCARP.

Henry Angus, UBC's first Dean of Graduate Studies.[12]

Personally, Peter had a distinct European style — being private, yet extroverted. He loved politics and believed in jumping in, rather than sitting back and watching things happen. Having had exposure to some of the best talent in architectural and planning thinkers in America and Britain, he had learned to be creative and entrepreneurial early on, finding ways to conceptualize, mainstream and shape institutions that could work at the local level in relationship with higher levels of government. He had a charisma that helped him support and enhance relationships with people. This nature made him an enormous stimulus to other people and a great collaborator. In all, these qualities helped Oberlander develop friendships and institutional positions not only in UBC's administrative echelons but also within the local Vancouver planning department, the provincial division of the Community Planning Association of Canada in British Columbia and local architectural firms. Being tenacious and committed to his ideas and work (and still single), he lived in an attic on Allison Road and walked to work at the School of Architecture each day.

The name chosen for the planning program reflected not only Oberlander's carefully thought out concept of human settlement but also the need to avoid the pigeon-holes created by certain terms in the Canadian constitution. First, it was to be an independent, professional school, which would not be subsumed by dominant disciplines such as architecture or the social sciences. Second, the program would focus on a community of people, not on more artificial ideas of a city, municipality or other entities defined by jurisdictions and law. Third, the communities of people would be identified through their relationships within a given environmental resource base as a regional setting. Therefore, the name of the School, when it was formally established as a separate entity in the Faculty of Graduate Studies in 1958, incorporated these concepts, reflecting its acknowledgement of and commitment to both communities and the region as two important and interdependent scales of planning.

Thus, in 1951, the Community and Regional Planning program was formally established within the School of Architecture. The program comprised coursework and a thesis to be completed in a period of two years. However, as Peter recalls,

> We needed students. I was able to persuade few students to take a chance. The first cohort of four students registered in a program that did not exist, under an academic who had never taught before, subjects that were alien to them and with a vague future for jobs. So they were the pioneers.... Those four students....because they took a chance in every sense of the word. I made only one promise to them: that in the two years that they took to learn these subjects

I would guarantee them a master's degree. Their commitment and my guarantee got SCARP started.

The four pioneers were: Bill Paterson from UBC with undergraduate degrees in social work and sociology; Gerard Farry from geography and economics at UBC; Clive Justice with a University of California Berkeley degree in landscape architecture, and Gordon Arnott with a University of Manitoba architecture degree. A grant from CMHC provided seed funding for SCARP to get the program started. In addition, the CMHC fellowships for study and research in planning supported students in this new field in postwar British Columbia.

In March 1952, Peter wrote an engaging piece in *The Ubyssey* to promote the new program. He carefully outlined why the School focused on community planning as opposed to town and country planning. Peter explained how nothing was new about planning or city building as an activity and how it had evolved since antiquity. What was new in the twentieth century, however, was the *purpose* of planning cities and the *methods* being drawn on for city building. No longer was city planning meant to glorify God or any specific ruler, nor was it meant to control rebellious citizens. The planning program at UBC was seen as a way to "guide the development of our cities and towns for the good of man and the benefit of the community as a whole." For this reason, the program was open to students from the natural and social sciences to understand how to "relate their academic background to the professional practice of community planning." The core course was a workshop or studio in community planning in which students formed teams and attempted to solve real-life planning issues through the application of the skills and tools they acquired in various courses.

In 1952, Dean Angus convinced the UBC Senate to convert the diploma program to a degree program. As Oberlander recalled the discussion,

> The Senate had two questions: "What the hell is planning?" to which we replied, "Keeping bad things from happening," and "Where will these people work?" to which we replied, "They will create their own jobs," which turned out to be true. Many of the School's graduates went on to do new things or to define existing roles in a new way.

During the Christmas break in 1952, Peter Oberlander put in place the last — and in many ways the most important — component of his life. He and Cornelia were married in New York in a small ceremony on January 2, 1953.

Peter welcomed his bride to Vancouver and settled her in their rental apartment before heading off to New Westminster by streetcar for a meeting with the Lower Mainland Regional Planning Board.

In the spring of 1953, the first cohort of planning graduates attended their convocation ceremony at the UBC Point Grey campus. The four pioneers went on to have successful and noteworthy careers. Bill Paterson was the first director of planning for West Vancouver, later joining the United Nations to work in the field of international development planning for more than three decades. Clive Justice worked at the scale of local communities and regions as a landscape architect/ urban planner. Gordon Arnott evolved an architectural/planning practice that concentrated on building modern communities in Regina, Saskatchewan. The fourth candidate, Gerard Farry, contributed to the strategic management of urban growth and transportation planning in the Vancouver metropolitan region through the Greater Vancouver Regional District (GVRD, now Metro Vancouver). Thus, the four pioneers were involved in four scales of planning and urban development, from the local to the global.

In dozens of conversations recalling SCARP's history, Peter always stressed that the most significant achievement of the School was the contribution made by its graduates, which started with attracting the right students. The criteria for selecting students for the program were not conservative but eclectic. The emphasis was not only on marks and academic records but on ensuring that collectively the students had a range of backgrounds relevant to the program. Peter recalled:

> We chose students with some sense about learning multi-disciplinary aspects in an interdisciplinary way. We insisted that students had to have a background in one of the three disciplines, i.e., design, natural sciences and/or social sciences. They had to have literacy in their respective areas. Their entry into the planning school would then permit them to explore the other two disciplinary areas through the coursework made available to them. In admitting students, we were concerned about how well the students had done as undergraduates rather than what they had done. We could teach them how to plan, but we could not teach them how to read, write or think.

Diversity of background at the undergraduate level eventually became a norm for students who chose to pursue a master's degree in planning and professional practice throughout North America.

1962 was a year of financial crisis for the University. With an increase in enrolment as the Baby Boom generation reached university age, the facilities available for students were already overtaxed. The funding sources available until then were the federal and provincial governments, private industry, student fees and the National Research Council. UBC required new funding sources for capital expenditures for new classrooms, residences, administration, facilities and food services. The development and funding of post-secondary education — including the infant Simon Fraser University — became a provincial political issue.

In SCARP's initial years, the planning program was housed within the School of Architecture, where it shared space and certain funding packages that were available for students. The program negotiated with UBC departments — including geography, economics, and engineering — for faculty members to teach courses part-time to planning students. With the increase in program enrolment, however, Peter realized that SCARP would need its own faculty members if it was to expand as a program. He was constantly on the lookout for funding opportunities that could enable the expansion of the planning program through new faculty positions, an independent space for the planning school and financial assistance for students.

At this time, the Richard King Mellon Charitable Trust of Pittsburgh was developing an interest in university programs in urban planning across the United States. Having allocated in excess of $3 million to 10 US universities in the past, they had funded the Department of Urban Planning at the University of Washington in Seattle, Washington. Prof Myer Wolfe, the chairman of that planning department, had exchanged notes with Oberlander in this regard. In the fall of 1965, he helped Peter contact Joseph Hughes, the administrative trustee at the foundation in Pittsburgh to make a pitch requesting funds for SCARP's activities for the upcoming academic year. He also wrote a letter to the Mellon Trust outlining the program, activities, and curricula at SCARP, suggesting that the Trust might be interested in supporting SCARP financially. With this support from Prof Wolfe, Peter received a request from Hughes to submit a proposal outlining the relevant ongoing teaching and research activities at SCARP.

At about the same time, President Mackenzie's visionary support for SCARP and formidable connections came to the fore once again. The President returned from a salmon fishing trip on the British Columbia coast with Paul Mellon and told Peter that the foundation would be receptive to a proposal for significant funding for SCARP. He urged Peter to visit the foundation in Pittsburgh as soon as possible.

Peter was slated to attend the meeting organized by the five Canadian schools of planning to be held at Ottawa a few weeks away. He wrote to the Dean of Graduate Studies, Ian McTaggart Cowan, requesting permission to visit Pittsburgh after the Ottawa meeting to meet informally with the Mellon trustees to gauge their willingness to support SCARP's activities and to answer personally any questions they might have had about the school. McTaggart Cowan agreed.

"You'll need a new suit," Cornelia said. On his arrival in Pittsburgh, Peter went to Brooks Brothers to buy one of their suits, which by then had become part of his standard attire (the other components being bow ties and striped shirts). After accomplishing the near-impossible by getting Brooks Brothers to provide a new suit on hours' notice, Peter went on to the Mellon Foundation's offices. Cornelia later recounted what happened next.

> In the dining room at the Mellon Foundation, he heard a familiar voice and lo and behold, Uncle Kurt was sitting at the table behind him. [Hahn, then 83, was seeking funding for Outward Bound USA] My husband introduced his host to Uncle Kurt, and they chatted a bit. Later that evening Peter and Uncle Kurt met again at the airport. No planes were taking off because of a blackout in New York which was caused by overloaded use of electricity [It was the Great Blackout of November 9, 1965, which affected parts of Ontario in Canada and Connecticut, Massachusetts, New Hampshire, New Jersey, New York, Rhode Island, Pennsylvania, and Vermont in the United States.] This made Uncle Kurt apprehensive and reminiscent of the Blitz in London. However, Peter, being on the same flight, assured Uncle Kurt that everything would be okay and the airline confirmed that the plane would go the next day. Thus, they had to spend another night in Pittsburgh. The next morning, they met again on the plane, which luckily took them to New York. Peter had to go to the UN for a meeting and asked Uncle Kurt "May I give you a lift? I'm renting a car. Where are you staying?" "Oh, I'm staying at the Drake Hotel." "That is very near, I'll take you there." "Do you

know how to drive in New York, Peter?" asked Uncle Kurt and Peter said, "Yes. I'm a city planner." Thus, miraculously, Uncle Kurt was safely delivered to the Drake Hotel in New York.

By the fall of 1966, it was official. The Richard Mellon Trust had agreed to a $500,000 funding package for SCARP's teaching and research activities (more money than Uncle Kurt had received, Peter noted). The grant was the single, largest award to a Canadian planning school to that point and the first given to a Canadian university for the purpose of training graduate students. The letter and cheque were received by the UBC President's Office and the announcement was made in January 1967.

Disbursed over a period of three years, the grant provided funding for Mellon student Fellowships in City Planning and Urban Renewal, funding for faculty salaries and an amount to be used at the discretion of the School Director for faculty salaries or student fellowships. The letter from the Mellon Trust stated,

> This unusual and large grant was made to the UBC planning division in recognition of its leadership in professional education for city planning in Canada, and its success in training qualified practitioners for more than a dozen years. The purpose of this grant is to strengthen and expand the teaching, education, and research in urban and regional planning with special emphasis on regional resource development and conservation problems caused by rapid urbanization. Lastly, it will enable the division to enlarge substantially its teaching staff and range of students, and thereby contribute to a greater scope and depth for urban and regional planning in Canada.

The University recognized the timely nature of the grant, given the monumental task of producing a new generation of qualified planners to address the ever-growing problems of urbanization and change. By this time, SCARP had trained almost a hundred planners who were practicing in various parts of the world at federal, provincial/state and municipal levels of government and in international organizations.

The infusion of funds enabled Oberlander to recruit both practitioners and academics such as Brahm Wiesman (B. Arch McGill, 1948, just three years after Oberlander); Nirmala Devi Cherukupalle (PhD Harvard, social scientist);

William Rees (PhD Toronto, ecologist); Craig Davis (PhD Berkeley, economics); and V. Setty Pendakur, (a SCARP master's graduate and PhD Washington, transportation planning).

In recruiting these and other faculty with diverse disciplinary backgrounds, Peter laid the foundations for the interdisciplinary perspective that led twenty-five years later to SCARP becoming the first planning school to focus on sustainability. Some of the other stalwarts at the time were William Lane, a lawyer experienced in municipal and planning law, and Robert Collier, a specialist on demographic studies. SCARP students also had access to faculty in the Faculty of Commerce and Business Administration's newly established real estate program, including real estate studies pioneer Michael Goldberg and housing expert Richard Radcliffe.

Within the school, a core team emerged, comprising Peter Oberlander, Brahm Wiesman, and Bill Lane, all of whom were very close friends as well as colleagues. With an expansion of the faculty and the availability of funding packages for students, SCARP was able to offer a doctoral program.

By the mid-1960s, as the school absorbed more faculty and students, the everyday working of the Lasserre Building had to absorb new users and uses. The physical layout of the building with respect to faculty offices, an administration office, classrooms and studio space was refurbished to incorporate the planning program. Over a period of time, the planning classes and studios spread out to the nearby West Mall Annex, a structure built in an unfortunate effort at economy that resembled one of the army huts that had been salvaged after the war rather than a proper, purpose-built university building. Municipal planning law classes taught by Bill Lane were convened at the Law Faculty building on weekends.

Gradually, SCARP made provision for academic mentors for students. As mentors, faculty members were supposed to instill professionalism and collaboration among the students. A single mentor was assigned a group of students in a symbiotic relationship, a practice followed until this day at SCARP. At this time the school offered a Master of Arts or a Master of Science, depending on the student's academic strength and interests.

The new faculty members brought their own strengths of professional practice and teaching approaches to SCARP. The faculty appointments ensured a ferment of new ideas to complement the approaches established by the core team to enable students to form a rounded understanding of planning. They also resulted in deeper linkages to other departments within the University.

Practical application of planning ideas in the real world — turning ideas into action — was an important theme in SCARP's planning education, drawing on the experiences of faculty. For example, Wiesman had worked successfully as a city planner in Edmonton, as the Director of a new metropolitan planning agency for Victoria developing the regional plan for the capital region and finally as assistant director of planning in the city of Vancouver. His work in the trenches taught him how critical interdepartmental relationships were and how inseparable politics was from planning. As a representative of the planning department in council meetings in Vancouver, he had learned to make public presentations that lucidly explained planning intricacies to politicians. Observing Wiesman's expertise as a member of the Vancouver City Planning Commission led Oberlander to believe that Wiesman could make a valuable contribution as a teacher at SCARP. Wiesman guided the school for more than a decade in various capacities as professor, acting director, director and mentor to many master's and doctoral students. Wiesman's interest in the history of planning enabled him to supervise the first few doctoral students at SCARP working on this subject.

Although Oberlander and his colleagues felt that they were evolving an all rounded curriculum for planning students at SCARP through a combination of theory and practice, students, as is their occasional wont, sometimes disagreed with him. The year 1968 was a case in point. It was a rough year, with a sudden upsurge in student protests across North America against a background of social tumult generated by resistance to the Vietnam War and the assassinations of Martin Luther King and Robert F. Kennedy in the spring of that year. Students at UBC were affected by this ferment as members of the first generation born after World War II to reach young adulthood. The Ubyssey tirelessly reported on the happenings in the United States and its ripples into Canada.

On October 24, 1968, there was an appearance at UBC by American activist Jerry Rubin, a member of the Youth Independent Party. The Yippies, as they were called, had run "Pigasus the Pig" for President of the United States and had sponsored a demonstration against the Vietnam War at the Democratic National Convention in Chicago that led to a violent confrontation with police. After his speech, he led a protest march to "liberate" the Faculty Club (now the Leo and Thea Koerner University Centre), then the exclusive domain of faculty members.

As a first-year student at SCARP, Ken Cameron witnessed these events. He laughingly recalls, "My mother was proud to have been able to continue as a member of the Faculty Club after my father's death. I remember coming home and telling her that Jerry Rubin had gone wading in the Faculty Club reflecting pond, and she was utterly shocked and horrified." It was outrageous behaviour to the university establishment, but for the students, it was considered an incredibly gutsy thing to do. The feeling among the faculty was that the world had gone completely out of control for this kind of behaviour to occur.

Jerry Rubin at UBC[13]

The occupation continued through the night. In a retrospective in *UBC Reports* in 2007, Basil Waugh recounted that "Students drank the faculty's liquor, smoked their cigarettes, burned flags, and swam nude in the patio pool. Rock bands cranked out psychedelic jams until the small hours. Revolution, among other substances, was in the air."

Things threatened to get ugly the next morning when a group of UBC's engineering students, notorious at the time for their hostility to hippies and lefties, began gathering outside the facility and planning to clear out the remaining occupiers by force. Author and activist Stan Persky worked with philosophy professor Bob Rowen to convince those still in the club to depart peacefully. The incident sparked a process of self-examination at UBC that later led to students being given an increased role in the University governance. A key player in that process was the president of the Alma Mater (student) Society, David Zirnhelt, who would later serve as Peter Oberlander's executive assistant at the Ministry of State for Urban Affairs in Ottawa and go on to a career in British Columbia politics.

With this rebellious fervour on campus, the planning students would not be left behind. They decided to stage their own protests and voice their demands to Peter Oberlander. *The Ubyssey* reported in a tiny column called, "Planners revolt," that planning students were disappointed with the curriculum at SCARP. Having a high student-faculty ratio of fifty students to only four professors meant that there were challenges in communication between students and professors. Some of the other concerns students had were strict lecture attendance requirements, a rigorous exam system, and perceived callousness of adjunct faculty in two courses. The first-year students proposed that the school shift to a pass-fail system and re-evaluate core courses that were mandatory for students. The students accused some faculty of being too involved in consulting projects as opposed to mentoring students academically.

Ken Cameron recalled,

> One Friday afternoon, the students piled up all the furniture in one corner of the classroom. As soon as Peter Oberlander entered the classroom to deliver his lecture, the students presented their "non-negotiable" demands regarding their criticisms of the curriculum. They felt that the courses should be structured in a way that they have theory classes in the morning and practice-based classes in the afternoon. Steely-spined Oberlander tactfully informed the students that he would consider all their demands in evolving the curriculum.

After this, the students decided that the class should adjourn for a cooling-off period (at the Fraser Arms in Marpole, the closest pub to UBC at the time).

Over the course of the subsequent weeks, Oberlander helped the students to realize that the curriculum was the result of years of sustained effort and consultation in its conceptualization and implementation. Besides, the School's program was interlinked with diverse factors outside the department at the level of the Faculty of Graduate Studies and the University. He acknowledged that evaluating the curriculum to make adjustments was a useful process but overhauling the whole curriculum in a matter of days or weeks without discussions, time, identification of needs and funds was problematic. Peter neither capitulated to the students nor confronted them; instead, he stood his ground and allowed time and reason (plus the demands of ongoing coursework) to have their effect. For Cameron, it was an early lesson in Peter's skills in maneuvering through conflict by more subtle means than confrontation. In the end, Cameron discovered, the curriculum at SCARP continued to be pretty much the same as Peter and the other faculty had planned it.

Oberlander approached various organizations and individuals to secure funding for teaching and research activities at SCARP. A study by the American-based think tank, the Rand Corporation, had shown how the modernization of everyday life and technological advances would translate into reduced working hours, early retirement and longer life expectancy for societies in developed nations. This, in turn, would increase time available for leisure and recreational activity. Recreation would no longer be the privilege of the few but would be available to a larger section of the growing middle-class in rapidly urbanizing regions. There were discussions among planners in the United States and Canada at the time on how to go about developing leisure-based activities, and how to manage conflicts in the allocation of outdoor space between leisure facilities and other uses such as industrialization and resource development.

Once again, Cornelia's uncle Kurt Hahn came into the picture to influence Peter's thinking. As she recalled the occasion,

> Peter fitted so well into Kurt Hahn's ideas of global education. Uncle Kurt lived at Brown's Hotel in London. We flew into London from Vancouver. We were to have breakfast with Uncle Kurt at Brown's the next morning, so we stayed there the night before. Uncle Kurt always had three tables of guests for breakfast. He cruised between these tables discussing various things. He stopped by our table and asked Peter and me, "what are you doing about leisure?" At the time the Rand Corporation had predicted that we would have much more time for leisure. We would have to engage ourselves with activities. Based on this study by the Rand Corporation, Peter organized a fantastic workshop at UBC and in downtown Vancouver with the Parks Board on leisure activities. Conrad Wirth, a landscape architect, who was the head of the US National Parks Service, gave the keynote address. So, we could answer Uncle Kurt's question. We were so proud, you won't believe it. This became the basis for the Kona report on the community for leisure [see Chapter 6].

Oberlander was interested in exploring what criteria governed the usage of the natural outdoors as recreational space and the means of protecting natural resources from having their recreational potential compromised by human activity. For this purpose, he approached the Toronto-based Donner Foundation with a detailed project proposal to study and examine these criteria. The foundation responded with an $85,000 grant.

With this financial assistance, SCARP put together a research team to explore the specific quantity and quality of recreation space that should be reserved for use by future generations for activities such as camping, biking, hiking, skiing, summer cabins etc. Building on the relationship established earlier with

Myer Wolfe, the director of the urban planning department at the University of Washington, in securing the Mellon Foundation grant, SCARP proposed a partnership between the two planning schools on this project.

The result was a long-term, collaborative project to support teaching and research on the unique coastal region spreading from Seattle-Tacoma in Washington to Sechelt on the Sunshine Coast in British Columbia, now known as the northern half of "Cascadia". With $15,000 each from the Mellon Trust Fund for a period of two years, the two planning schools sought to test their "observations and criteria for space standards" from an earlier project in the San Juan and Gulf Islands in the broader region.

This collaborative effort was a small part of the larger multi-disciplinary, resource sciences research program that was created at UBC, in the fall of 1968, thanks to a Ford Foundation grant of $500,000. Involving the departments of forestry, zoology, ecology, agriculture, economics and planning, this research group headed by Dr. Crawford Holling studied the impact of human activity on the physical environment. It was in this context that both Oberlander and Holling decided to create a joint teaching position between the Institute of Animal Resource Ecology and the School of Community and Regional Planning, for a person with expertise in science and ecology who would teach and supervise students in planning.

The person selected was William Rees, an ecological economist now known for his contribution to the field of sustainability studies through the "ecological footprint" concept, a means of measuring the demands humans make on nature. Rees later recalled how this came to be. A biologist by training, he was interested in the human dimension of ecology. In the 1960s, particularly after the publication of Rachel Carson's *Silent Spring* in 1962, the consciousness about environmental issues was growing and Rees was involved in founding organizations that focused on his human ecological interests. Crawford Holling became acquainted with Rees through this work.

Oberlander had the foresight to imagine a role for a scientist trained in ecology within a planning school, Rees recalls. "Some planning schools at the time in North America were sending existing or about-to-be-retired professors to get a course in ecology or environmental studies to bring that thinking into the planning school."

When Rees met Peter in Vancouver, he was very excited at the prospect of being able to apply his ecological knowledge to human beings, planning and policy-making. When Peter described SCARP to Rees, he recalls,

> This really stuck in my mind, because I think it is a mark of the man. He said, "if you look around North America, you will see many schools with 'city and urban planning,' or 'city and regional planning.' But I chose the word 'community' because that term embraces a great deal more than the physical plan, the built environment which was so much the focus of American schools." He was conscious of the need to have a broad, transdisciplinary approach to what planning was all about. It wasn't just about land use planning but the integration of community, people, and places, diversity, and immigrants, and all of that into the urban landscape. And, of course, in a way that was ecologically sound and sustainable…There's no question that the man had a vision that was quite extraordinary at the time and that was reflected in the way the school was constructed.

The idea of introducing humans into the ecological realm was a very foreign concept at the time, and Rees was criticized by other ecologists who tended to see humanity as the enemy of nature rather than as part of it. Oberlander helped Rees counter this criticism by providing the opportunity for Rees to put forward the ecological perspective at SCARP with a course on the human ecology of planning, development and land use. Rees would later become the Director of the School, and he credits Oberlander and Holling with setting the pace in North American planning schools in recognizing that human beings and their activities had become a major ecological force affecting sustainability. Peter started the chain of events that led to SCARP being the first planning school in North America focusing on sustainability studies.

From the beginning, a community planning studio course was an integral and mandatory component of the SCARP program. This concept drew upon Peter's background in architecture and his experience at McGill and the Harvard Graduate School of Design. It had many advantages, including bringing the various disciplines represented among the students into focus on a comprehensive planning project approached in an interdisciplinary way. It helped students learn teamwork, and it provided practical experience in real-life planning situations. As with much that Oberlander did, there were other motives at work: the studios allowed municipalities to be introduced to planning without having to hire staff and consultants, and it created a potential employment market for SCARP graduates.

The studio for the first cohort at SCARP comprising four students and faculty was tasked with surveying and proposing a development plan for the Municipality of Maple Ridge in the Fraser Valley. Their project involved advising the residents of the town of Haney on its growth and expansion. Studios in subsequent years prepared planning reports for the Dunbar area in Vancouver, Banff, and the Fraser River region from Hope to Richmond.

A larger example of SCARP's efforts to become more involved in bringing planning concepts to British Columbia was announced in *The Ubyssey*, in the winter of 1965, "UBC group opening way for $40 million project." Oberlander had organized a student-faculty trip to northern Vancouver Island to study settlement and urbanization patterns in the towns of Port McNeill, Port Alice, Port Hardy, Coal Harbour, Alert Bay and Beaver Cove. This project was different from the usual studios because for the first time the provincial government was co-operating with UBC and other outside agencies in addressing of problems of settlements in rapidly urbanizing towns in the province's resource development regions.

The Minister of Municipal Affairs informed the Legislature that the provincial government would draw on the planning students' insights on the areas to gain new perspectives. Accompanied by Don South, the provincial planning director, and Tony Roberts, the director of planning for the provincial capital, the group travelled in "special radio-equipped buses, fishing boats, private cars, seine boat and logging company crummies" to meet with local businessmen, workers and residents to understand "how the community wished to see their towns develop and where they thought planning should come from." The students surveyed the various towns to get a sense of "social, economic and physical features" to understand the linkages between exploitation of natural resources and urban development.

This study trip led to the provincial government announcement of a plan to spend $40 million in "opening communication links in these areas." This project highlighted the need for planning at a different scale — the resource region — to resolve conflicts between urban and rural interests and between resource extraction and resource conservation and recreation. It set the stage for significant provincial initiatives in the 1990s such as the Commission on Resources and Environment.

From the time that he got established at the University of British Columbia, Peter Oberlander built his connections in planning and decision-making circles involving both pedagogy and practice, in keeping with Dean Angus' advice to "relate and link to everyone; be subservient to none." He became involved with the university's attempts to expand its facilities and improve the academic environment for students. In 1967, Peter was appointed to UBC's special committee for Campus Community Planning. He could see the need for planning graduates to be recognized by planning employers across the United States and Canada so that they could practice in either country. An institutional accreditation in both Canada and America ensured that a graduate degree obtained by a student in either country was recognized in both host countries. SCARP applied for accreditation to the US Planning Accreditation Board and received its accreditation in 1970. Peter was elected as the President of the American Society of Planning Officials in 1975.

Towards the end of his life, Peter Oberlander was asked to identify his most important achievement. As the remainder of this book will attest, there were a lot of achievements to choose from, but he unhesitatingly singled out the School of Community and Regional Planning. Asked about the most important aspect of the School, he equally unhesitatingly stated, "The students: without students you have nothing."

The clarity of his thinking conjures up planning education as almost a manufacturing process. You started with carefully selected raw materials, which would be students with demonstrated ability in one of the three areas of basic education (the design professions, the natural sciences, and the social sciences). In many cases, the students had had some experience after completion of their undergraduate degrees, not necessarily in a related field. "Where do you think Ken Cameron came from?" he asked an interviewer. "He was an IBM salesman when he came to see me about the School, and he explained to me the intricacies of my assistant's IBM typewriter. I picked him up!" Once admitted, the students experienced a carefully crafted multi-disciplinary program to build their competence to a minimum level in the three areas of basic education in an interdisciplinary process which drew upon real planning situations and issues, including studio and field work. As Oberlander and Henry Angus had promised the Senate, this process enabled the students to create their own employment.

The School's interest in its students didn't end with graduation. Ken Cameron says that "A degree from SCARP comes with a lifetime warranty on parts and labour," noting that at several challenging decision points in his career his thesis advisor, Brahm Wiesman, had contacted him with encouragement and suggestions. When Cameron wrote to Wiesman from Toronto about an opening with the Greater Vancouver Regional District (now Metro Vancouver) in 1978, Wiesman replied, "I'm on the Selection Committee [in fact, Cameron realized later that Wiesman WAS the Selection Committee] and you're already on the short list."

When Wiesman died in 2003, Ken Cameron and his colleague Hugh Kellas were asked by Peter Oberlander to be pallbearers at his funeral in Schara Tzedeck cemetery in New Westminster. "Until then, I had only the vaguest idea that Brahm and Peter were Jewish. I don't know what that says about them or me, but I think it meant that our commitment to better communities for humanity was more important than any personal attribute." Ever the teacher, Oberlander took Cameron and Kellas aside and said, "In our culture, we think a man should be buried by his friends rather than by strangers, so your role is to throw the first shovelfuls of earth onto the coffin in the grave. Then the others will follow." It was an approach Cameron would borrow six years later for his wife's interment.

Oberlander and his colleagues were extremely proud of the achievements of the students to whom they provided a planning education (and Oberlander was gracious in his praise of the achievements of students "processed" by the School after his term as Director ended).

An analysis of the fate of the students who graduated from the School between 1953 and 1972 is impressive: there were 43 people in senior positions, including 9 national bureau heads, 5 provincial bureau heads, 11 regional government planning directors, 6 city government planning directors, 8 principals of consulting firms and 2 university department chairs. When one considers that many of these positions would not have existed at the beginning of this period, it can truly be said that the graduates of SCARP created their own employment and/ or transformed existing roles.

As the current Director of the School, Dr. Penny Gurstein, observed in one of her last conversations with Peter, all the graduates were planners but a very impressive proportion of these became leaders. They embodied the principle established by Oberlander, drawing on his exposure to Gropius' ideas, that professionals had a social responsibility to act for a better world, not only as professionals but as citizens.

A review of the graduation statistics also demonstrates the dramatic impact of the funding Oberlander secured in the mid-1960s from the Mellon Foundation, the Donner Foundation and others. Fifty-six students graduated in the 15 years between 1953 and 1967, while the same number graduated in the five years between 1967 and 1972.

Looking back, one could take the view that the development of a home-grown tradition of planning, and a planning education system to go with it, in Canada were inevitable after World War II, and the growth and maturity of the profession today lend credence to that view. There is, however, no question that the UBC School of Community and Regional Planning played a key role in that process. It is a story of leadership and serendipity, from the early support for community planning and planning education by CMHC, to the vision of Norman Mackenzie for Canada and its universities projected through his role on the Massey Commission and as the "Lord of Point Grey," to the meeting of minds on interdisciplinary education with Henry Angus. The result was the creation of a program that has produced hundreds of professionals and leaders contributing to better places in Canada and around the world. Through the story runs Peter Oberlander's grasp of the importance of communities to humanity, his extraordinary conceptual ability as an educator, his energy, and his determination to convert ideas into actions for a better world.

There is a bust of Norman Mackenzie in a plaza at UBC, with a plaque that identifies the area as the "Norman Mackenzie Precinct," devoted to the fine and performing arts, architecture, and planning. The Precinct includes the Frederic Lasserre Building, which is still the home of the School of Community and Regional Planning. Nearby is "Oberlander Lane," so designated by the Board of Governors in 2013 "in tribute for the academic accomplishments of the late, Prof Peter Oberlander (1922-2008) and his wife Cornelia Hahn Oberlander. The Oberlanders were conferred Honourary Degrees from UBC (1998 and 1991)." Not far away is the Henry Angus Building, built in 1965 and originally housing the Faculty of Commerce and Business Administration and all of the social sciences, a reflection of the span of Angus' intellect and his support for breaking down disciplinary barriers in higher education. In a university known for its "edifice complex," and granting that the President's official residence is Norman Mackenzie House, the fact that this great leader is commemorated not in a building but in a "precinct" that brings various areas of learning together is an apt reflection of his approach and his achievements.

Dr. Norman MacKenzie and his bust[14]

CHAPTER SIX:

FROM IDEAS TO ACTIONS

Peter Oberlander brought more than a first-class graduate planning education to British Columbia and its University in January of 1950. After his powerless, stateless years of internment, he had responded enthusiastically to the views of Walter Gropius and others at Harvard that architecture and planning should serve the needs of the people rather than private interests. The best ideas in the world were worthless if there was not the capacity and the will to implement them. These concepts, accentuated by the spirit of postwar reconstruction, instilled in Peter a commitment to activism that would last for the rest of his life.

From the beginning, Oberlander conceived of the planning school as a place of professional training for a new breed of practitioners. This meant that there should be many opportunities for interaction between the academy and the practical world, both during and after completion of the students' programs. Such a concept faced a number of challenges. For aspiring schoolteachers, there were schools in which to pursue practicums and permanent positions; for aspiring lawyers, there were law firms and courts; for aspiring doctors, there were hospitals and medical practices. There was, however, not one professional planning position within the province of British Columbia, and even local governments were relatively scarce; 95 per cent of the province's land base was unincorporated territory — no counties, no rural municipalities or townships — there were local governments only in areas where the residents had voted to establish them. He needed to learn as quickly as possible about the local governments that did exist and to devise ways of convincing them of the benefits of planning and planners.

Oberlander was also convinced that a planning educator should have lots of engagement in the world of practice, and he consciously and successfully pursued opportunities for such engagement, notwithstanding the limitations set by university policy. For him, activism was a central part of the rights and responsibilities of a professional and a citizen.

The Lower Mainland Regional Planning Board

His first opportunity came shortly after his arrival in Vancouver when was asked to assist the newly formed Lower Mainland Regional Planning Board.

A decade of activism by professional and citizen advocates resulted in the establishment of the British Columbia Division of the Community Planning Association of Canada (CPAC) in the 1940s, under the chairmanship of J.A. Walker, executive engineer of the Vancouver Town Planning Commission. The BC division of CPAC launched its news bulletin titled *Layout for Living* to promote awareness, knowledge and participation among various resident groups in community planning at the municipal level.

At the first meeting of the BC CPAC in 1947, two resolutions were unanimously approved. The first supported the amendment of BC's *Town Planning Act* as an essential step to initiate the creation of provincial-level regional planning areas and regional planning boards, beginning with the establishment of a Regional Planning Authority in the Lower Fraser Valley. The second resolution called for a Planning Department for the City of Vancouver. A year later, the *Town Planning Act* was amended to enable the provincial government to set up regional planning areas defined by spatial boundaries and to establish regional-level planning boards.

Just as the institutional momentum for regional planning took root in British Columbia, disaster struck. It was a sudden crisis generated by the Fraser River floods in the spring of 1948 that eventually made regional planning in the Lower Mainland a reality. The devastation of this single event created the political will to implement a regional planning approach within the Lower Mainland.

The flood was the result of unusually hot weather that led to high snowmelt in the British Columbia interior and an unusually large "freshet," as the consequent swelling of the Fraser is known. As a result, the Agassiz dike gave way on May 26. As recounted by Harcourt et al., in a short time, large areas of the Lower Mainland were inundated, and the provincial government had to respond to the most destructive natural disaster in Canadian history. On May 31, 1948, BC Premier Byron Johnson declared a state of emergency. Peter later recalled how the Fraser flood "destroyed farmlands, houses, buildings, communities, and literally washed millions of acres of farmlands down the river."

This natural catastrophe created two planning-related opportunities. First, it compelled local governments to recognize the need to get serious about "a regional approach to planning" that would, among other things, discourage settlement in areas vulnerable to flooding and other natural hazards. Second, the flood established the need to build dikes to regulate the river and control its flooding.

To take stock of the conditions and possible actions to prevent recurrence of such a situation, in the summer of 1949 the Minister of Municipal Affairs, Mr. R.C. McDonald, invited members of the BC division of CPAC to meet with him.

In a memorandum submitted by the BC division of CPAC to McDonald, it was suggested that a master plan for the Lower Mainland Region could forestall premature or wasteful land subdivision and the expensive provision of municipal services to ad hoc growth. The issue of industry moving out of the central core into the fringe areas and its resultant pressures on land and resources could be addressed by looking at the relations between industry, transportation, housing and public utilities, thus giving suitable and meaningful direction that benefited the community and industry as well. In addition, the ad hoc conversion of fertile agricultural lands into subdivisions for expanding urbanization could be addressed through zoning controls. This would ensure an integrated land management system that protected natural recreational assets and agrarian lands to feed the population of the region. In addition, smaller municipalities and unincorporated areas who could not afford to maintain planning staff could be gradually drawn into systems of government to ensure the cohesiveness of the region to the benefit of its inhabitants.

Sensing the opportunity that the floods had created, the members petitioned the Minister to declare the Lower Mainland Region as a regional planning area under the new legislation and to authorize a regional planning board for it. On June 21, 1949, the Lower Mainland Regional Planning Board (LMRPB) was established and its planning area was gazetted by the Minister of Municipal Affairs. The Lower Mainland regional planning area's boundaries were based on a map prepared by the provincial Postwar Reconstruction Council in 1945 as reflected in a map prepared for the province by Harland Bartholomew and Associates. It extended from the Gulf of Georgia to the Village of Hope and from the US Border to the mountains north of the Fraser River. It comprised twenty-six municipalities and some unorganized territories. This Lower Mainland planning region of 1,600 square miles was to be planned as a single regional entity — the first time in Canadian history that such a project had been undertaken.

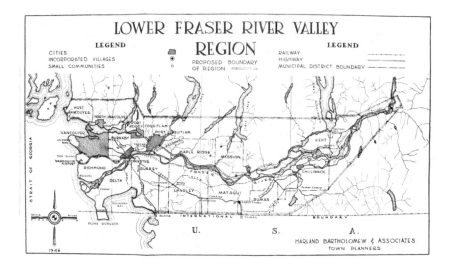

Lower Mainland Map[15]

The institutional structure of the LMRPB gradually took shape. The first meeting of the Board was organized in the fall of 1949 in New Westminster, the oldest incorporated municipality in Western Canada and a former provincial capital. The chairman of the Board was New Westminster Councillor and Chief Engineer of the Fraser Valley Diking Board, D.J. McDugan. Tom McDonald, having served as the regional Supervisor of the BC division of CPAC, was appointed secretary to the Board in addition to his institutional position of Chairman of the Vancouver City Zoning Board of Appeal.

Peter Oberlander, who was by then an assistant professor in UBC's School of Architecture, was hired by the LMRPB as a town-planning consultant to help the tiny staff of the Board to, in Peter's words, "invent the regional planning process." At the first Board meeting, Oberlander jumped right into the discussion with a recommendation that the Board's first task should be "to document the twenty-six municipalities and establish a character for the region." To initiate this work a budget of $20,000 was adopted with funding from various federal, provincial and municipal agencies such as the CMHC, the City of Vancouver and the provincial government as well as voluntary contributions from the other twenty-five municipalities.

Under a headline titled "Master Plan Starts Coordination of All Valley," the *Province* reported on the selection of a technical staff that would survey and coordinate the development of the twenty-six municipalities in the Georgia Straight Region. The staff comprised John Eassie, an engineer, A.D. Crerar, trained in urban geography and land utilization, and finally D.M. Churchill, trained in public administration and economics.

Peter's role as the Board's consultant was to guide the activities of the staff. The first step was data collection concerning development and growth in the Lower Mainland. The initial demographic studies conducted by the Board revealed a projected 50 per cent increase in population growth within a decade, leading to the need to designate the specific areas where such growth was to take place. Further, to support these populations the planners would recommend areas for work, residence, recreation, and industry in a way that preserved agricultural lands while providing for new needs and aspirations. Having completed a broad survey of the entire region and its various municipalities, the researchers created a character profile of each area revealing the population densities, economic activities, social facilities and zoning problems. Through graphs and drawings, the studies provided a visual imagery to enable residents and civic officials alike to understand the present situation while showcasing the possibilities and challenges involved in a long-term planning process.

The primary task identified through the first survey of settlement patterns by the Regional Planning Board staff was to advise municipalities on their powers to control *ad hoc* subdivisions of land that could be measured against certain desired standards for land holdings, acreage and plot frontage. The next task for the team was developing a detailed study of agricultural lands within the Lower Mainland Region to understand their potential in terms of land for urbanization and lands to be protected for the purpose of feeding the region's population. A regional strategy for transportation was also considered to address issues of increased automobile traffic and bottlenecks resulting from it. The planners developed the logic for street and house numbering system for the entire valley by taking suggestions from post office officials, map makers and the planning team. With its system of numbers for streets beginning at the Pacific Ocean and avenues beginning with 0 Avenue at the US border, this grid continues in use to this day.

As valuable as all this work was for the planning task at hand, for Peter it provided an equally important benefit: a comprehensive introduction to the issues, personalities and challenges of the School of Community and Regional Planning's home region.

As a consultant to the Board, Peter also had responsibility for shortlisting candidates for the position of Executive Director. Peter reported to the Board Executive that he had interviewed a number of potential candidates. He especially recommended James W. Wilson, an Engineer trained in Glasgow and at the Massachusetts Institute of Technology who had a graduate degree in planning from the University of North Carolina. His first position had been an internship with the Tennessee Valley Authority (TVA), one of the pioneering regional planning and development agencies in the United States. He had also worked with the BC Electric Company, forerunner to BC Hydro. The Board accepted this recommendation, and with the Executive Director in place, the LMRPB's office was located in New Westminster with a basic staff of a geographer, political scientist, two draftsmen and one stenographer with Jim Wilson doubling up as the Treasurer.

With the recruitment of the Executive Director, Peter's mandate as consultant to develop a general direction for the Board's program was complete. The LMRPB achieved high levels of success early on due to Wilson's pragmatic leadership. He was clear from the outset that the LMRPB had to "tailor its program according to its limited means on the basis of two cents per person living in the region per year and with no unallocated cash in the budget." Narissa Chadwick discovered the entrepreneurial nature Jim and Peter had needed when the latter spoke to her about the informal discussions of Board financing that involved the Minister of Municipal Affairs. The financing of regional planning, Oberlander recalled, happened at the Minister of Municipal Affairs' shoe store in New Westminster on Saturday mornings.

> Jim and I would go on the trolley to New Westminster and confront the Minister behind the cash register. That is where we would settle the budget for the first year and, ultimately, Jim and I convinced the Minister to allow the LMRPB to receive from the municipalities two cents a head as a contribution to the budget of the LMRPB.

In the coming years, the LMRPB produced ideas, reports and studies on all aspects of life in the region, culminating in an Official Regional Plan in 1966, which was formally adopted by the LMRPB, the municipalities and the province of British Columbia. Its central theme, *cities in a sea of green* — well-planned communities in a working landscape of farm and forest — has dominated regional planning thought and development to this day.

Years later, Peter evaluated the work of the LMRPB as a process and institution that achieved three things. First, it compelled municipalities to talk to each other and realize that they either had a future together or none at all. Second, for the first time a regional-level land use map was developed which provided knowledge of what existed within the region. Third, the plan became an instrument to introduce the specific geographic and environmental context of the region and bring municipal leaders into a continuing dialogue. According to Harcourt et al., the legacy of Canada's first regional plan is "the region of Greater Vancouver that we know today: a firm line between city and countryside, an outstanding system of regional parks, limited settlements in areas subject to flooding and a street numbering system that made logical sense."

The First Planning Studios: Maple Ridge and Powell River

At both McGill and Harvard, Peter Oberlander had been exposed to the studio component of education, in which a group of students work together intensively with faculty on a specific project guided by a design brief to produce one or more tangible outcomes which can include drawings, plans, models and written programs. Such studios bring into the modern world the ancient knowledge that as much can be learned by doing as by teaching and reading, and that there is no substitute for a hands-on experience as part of the design process.

Having a studio component of the new planning program offered another advantage: it allowed Peter to introduce planning as a process and planners as useful experts to the local governments in British Columbia as they prepared for the rapid population growth brought on by the baby boom that followed World War II. The contacts and knowledge Peter had developed through his work at the Lower Mainland Regional Planning Board provided a sound foundation for a process that would demonstrate how to turn ideas into action.

The first opportunity came when Reeve Solomon Mussallem, of the (then) 78-year-old Municipality of Maple Ridge, extended an invitation to Peter Oberlander to advise them about the possibilities of avoiding suburban sprawl in his municipality. This was the first municipality in British Columbia that had undertaken such an ambitious idea. Peter was determined to capitalize on this opportunity to kick start a process that would enable the municipality to translate planning ideas into specific outcomes. He made Maple Ridge the focus of the first community planning studio at SCARP.

The studio engaged SCARP's first cohort of graduate students, the "four pioneers": Bill Paterson, Gordon Arnott, Clive Justice and Gerard Farry. These students along with Peter Oberlander and Frederic Lasserre as faculty advisors took up the challenge of providing planning proposals to help guide development in Maple Ridge. Their specific task involved advising the residents of the town of Haney on its growth and expansion. In addition, in a time frame of three months they surveyed and proposed a development plan for the entire Municipality of Maple Ridge.

The students and faculty organized a four-day field trip to get a first-hand understanding of the area. Relying on data and reports from the Lower Mainland Regional Planning Board, Peter introduced the students to the suburban communities within the larger physical region comprising land, natural resources, people, human settlements, industries, culture and economy. It was a learning laboratory for the planning students that introduced them to the methods involved in preparing a community plan.

The time frame for the project was tight, given the constraints of the academic term and other courses the students were taking. Peter decided to focus on the stretch comprising the two communities of Haney and Hammond. This area was developing as a suburbanizing sprawl that would soon be neither town nor country. Through local discussions, LMRPB reports and the student's site visits, the team recognized that given the proximity of Maple Ridge to the emergent economic centre of Vancouver and the availability of land for building, population growth in the Haney-Hammond corridor was inevitable.

The studio provided students with an intensive experience in planning that developed an understanding of zoning conflicts, increased densities and the need for better public utilities. Physical site visits and immersion in the physical setting of the community provided insights that proved helpful to the students when engaging with civic leaders, local residents and administrative agencies. In addition, the challenge of translating broader planning goals into pragmatic objectives for a particular community in a timely manner ensured that students were not only trained in technical skills but also in collaboration, teamwork, project management and other practical skills of lifelong value.

At the core of the study was the now-familiar concept of the development plan, which could provide the basis for the amendment of existing regulations such as building bylaws and new instruments, particularly zoning regulations, going forward. If the work had stopped there, it would have been a reasonably defensible land use plan by the standards of the day, more or less "architecture writ large." It went far beyond that realm in two ways.

First, the proposals were positioned within the broader regional context provided by the Lower Mainland Regional Planning Board and related to the planning context of the Municipality of Maple Ridge as a whole. The study showed an eye for innovation and quality of life. Drawing on concepts from the reports of the Lower Mainland Regional Planning Board, such as *Land for Living*, the report identified the need for "creating a new type of subdivision with homes built on a "central path" such that no home opened out onto a major thoroughfare and pedestrian and motor traffics could be separated in doing so." In addition, it recommended physical connections between residential zones, educational institutions and play areas to ensure safety and efficiency.

Second, the study went well beyond the traditional scope of the development plan to explore issues that would need to be addressed if its concepts were to be implemented, if the ideas were to be converted to action. Two important issues were economic development and municipal administration.

The study team stressed the need for diversification of economic activities given the transitions then occurring within the larger provincial economy. In order to supplement continued reliance on the agriculture and resource industries, the study proposed the introduction of small scale, labour-intensive manufacturing. Such diversification could act as a safety net for household incomes that were otherwise vulnerable to fluctuations in the forest products and other resource-based industries. Potential industrial investors could build on the existing physical infrastructure, availability of developable land and existing community resources such as residential areas, schools, commercial and municipal services. However, the students identified the need for what they called, "high level urban services" such as sewers, roads, sidewalks and fire protection. These could in many instances be financed through the creation of local improvement districts for specific zoned residential areas so that costs could be allocated to the benefitting areas rather than becoming an additional burden on the general municipal tax base.

With respect to municipal administration, the students argued that to change the haphazard process of urbanization and its unplanned, sprawling outcomes, it was essential to initiate regulatory planning frameworks. They suggested a greater advisory role for the Town Planning Commission, the appointment of a technical committee for the area and a differential taxation system that would be based on access to, and delivery of, specialized urban services.

The study argued for the need to institutionalize the presence of trained planning experts within the municipal administration to ensure orderly growth. It suggested that the municipal council create a technical committee comprising the municipal clerk, a planner-engineer and the secretaries of the school and parks boards. The primary goal of such a body would be to move towards ongoing implementation of a comprehensive land use policy that would ensure compact residential neighbourhood growth through the efficient use of public utilities, transportation and community services.

In introducing the study report to the residents and the municipal council, Peter Oberlander stressed that the document was only an outline of the central concerns to be addressed in the process of producing a community development plan for Maple Ridge. The outline report was the first stage of a future series of detailed and comprehensive studies that would have to be carried out by trained planning professionals. He identified roles for both student work and jobs for trained planning graduates in these comprehensive studies.

Peter suggested that the students' work, constrained by the limits on time and resources, could be seen as the opportunity for municipal administrations to rethink and shape the future socio-economic growth of their communities based on valuable insights in terms of what to focus on, what issues and concerns emerged from a particular community, and what possible directions could be pursued to ensure balanced development.

So, the students' report created a basic road map. To make that roadmap comprehensive and tangible required in-depth surveys, studies and reports with respect to the various dimensions that community planning as an instrument had to offer. This work would require trained planning professionals who would not only undertake these tasks but also advise council members on the procedural and regulatory aspects involved.

The study had been undertaken in collaboration with the municipal council, the Town Planning Commission, the Maple Ridge Board of Trade and other civic organizations. In the fall of 1952, a public meeting was organized in Haney's

Agricultural Hall so that the residents could participate as a community in receiving the study report. Chaired by Jim Hadgkiss, chairman of Town Planning Commission and Reeve Mussallem, the meeting was packed with enthusiastic residents awaiting the ideas of the planning students from SCARP. While addressing the gathering, Mussallem congratulated the students for sharing a "wonderful plan," a first in British Columbia at the time. The council accepted the students' report for Haney, thanking the university for not charging any fee for the services provided to the Council. Eventually, the municipal council purchased 200 extra copies of the report from UBC to ensure its wide circulation.

The council thought it had scored a bargain by getting so much work done at no charge, and they had. But Peter had made a further step in introducing the benefits of planning to this local government and in creating career prospects for SCARP's graduates. Ideas would lead to action for the benefit of all concerned.

Powell River was the setting for SCARP's second studio in 1953. The community is in the resource hinterland of British Columbia's mid-coast where the Powell River Company, established by the Foley family from the United States, needed advice on how to preserve the quality of their company town called Townsite. This town was preplanned in accordance with the "Garden City" movement led by Patrick Geddes and had developed during the period between 1911 and 1930. Reflecting an attitude that was rare among industrialists at the time, officials of the Company had considered the development of a livable and healthy community for their workers as part and parcel of the development of the pulp and paper mill itself.

Aerial view of Powell River *ca.* 1956[16]

In another manifestation of this benign attitude, the Company was an annual benefactor to the University of British Columbia, in the sponsorship of Awards in Wood Chemistry. It is possible that UBC President Norman MacKenzie introduced Peter Oberlander to senior company officials seeking advice on preserving the character of their company town.

Four decades after its establishment, the pulp and paper mill and service businesses that had grown up around it were still the central locus of livelihood for the residents of the Powell River area. The ramping up of production rates during World War II resulted in the rapid growth of the labour force involved directly or indirectly in the mill. The consequence was increased population densities, overcrowding and degradation of existing structures within Townsite, which remained unincorporated. It also involved the spread of rental or ownership-based housing for workers and others in the neighbouring Villages of Westview and Cranberry Lake and unincorporated communities such as Wildwood.

However, company policy at the time confined its attention to the originally planned townsite. After the war, a few local social organizations, besides the company representatives, had become active in the larger region and were planning cultural and recreational facilities for these physically dispersed communities of workers in an ad hoc fashion.

In an attempt to influence new building activities and to address blighted worker housing conditions in and around Townsite, the company officials approached Norman Mackenzie to request UBC's in-house planning expertise. MacKenzie summoned Peter Oberlander to see how UBC could assist them. When this sudden meeting with Company officials presented itself, Peter immediately conceptualized the task as a physical planning studio for Powell River. With help from Frederic Lasserre, Dave Harper, a company agent who helped with the logistics for the studio and the financial grant to SCARP by the company President, Mr. Foley, for the expenses incurred in the planning studio, Peter created yet another opportunity for his students and the school of planning.

Since Powell River was far from Vancouver, the studio was convened in the summer break. Thus, in the summer of 1953, Oberlander and Lasserre travelled northwest by road and ferry with three planning students, J.B. Chaster, Robert Opie, and J.B. Macdonald, to meet officials at the Powell River Company office. Mr. Cooper, the onsite company manager, assigned his deputy the tasks of providing the planners with a tour of Townsite and ensuring they were supplied accommodation and meals for a period of six weeks to carry out their detailed surveys. Peter and Cornelia Oberlander had been married January 1953 and had taken an apartment in Vancouver's West End. If being alone for the summer in a new city and a new country was a challenge for Cornelia she didn't complain about it.

From the outset, Peter did not limit the project to the brief of planning Townsite's future alone. His focus was on the community within a broader region, as reflected in the name and entire program of the School and augmented by his experience with the Lower Mainland Regional Planning Board. Even in the context of a company town and some small satellite communities in the virtual wilderness, he was aware of relationship between land, settlement and natural resources that transcended artificial administrative boundaries.

In his initial meetings with company officials, Peter would have shared this "big-picture" thinking with them. He, therefore, conceptualized the studio in three components. In the first stage, students would study the on-the-ground realities of Powell River and its surroundings through a six-week reconnaissance survey. This would provide time to traverse the region and articulate a regional imagination. In the next stage, students would work in Vancouver for four to six weeks to collate their observations and, working closely with their faculty advisors, develop a set of recommendations and planning proposals to be undertaken in pursuit of short and long-term goals. Lastly, the students would present their findings to the client, the Powell River Company representatives, and outline an action plan for phased implementation.

The students recorded observations of vital problems confronting Powell River by immersing themselves in the everyday life of Townsite's residents. It was quickly evident that they needed to engage the three other residential communities of Cranberry, Westview and Wildwood which they discovered were integrally linked with Townsite through socio-economic activities and flows of people for work, residence and recreation. As they travelled through the far-flung areas on available public transportation, they spoke to mill workers, youth, residents, local commissioners, government clerks and agents, welfare officers, forest rangers and health officers and spent time in local clubs, the church, the dairy and the community centre. The planning students were able to develop a new regional perspective on the area's people, its natural resource base, economy and socio-cultural fabric.

This fresh viewpoint helped them identify the problems and challenges in the future expansion of these four communities, something the company had been unable to recognize as it had previously focused only on Townsite. The planning students and faculty identified the primary problem as the "lack of physical integration" of the far-flung communities, separated by jurisdictional boundaries but integrally connected through everyday activities, land and a natural resource base. Although the area had service industries, the pulp and paper mill and social facilities that supported the needs of the residents, administrative challenges resulted from the physical distance between the different settlement areas due to the natural terrain, poor transportation networks and "absence of social and physical planning."

Oberlander's primary intention for organizing planning studios was to entrench the consciousness and need for planning as a profession that not only engaged the problems and challenges British Columbians faced in the postwar era but created specific solutions for them as well. The Powell River Area study was the first of its kind in the northwest coastal area of British Columbia. It explored local conditions, problems, needs and challenges, to inform future policy directions for growth and expansion in housing, transportation, economic development and recreation. Building on this analysis, the study identified the need for a comprehensive regional planning program, regional-level planning institutions and a tangible goal-oriented community plan that would ensure a "systematic and orderly improvement and development of the region towards a common public interest."

The project's primary goal was to deploy "planning as a means of creating better communities" by orchestrating coordination of various community development projects with the aim of creating "meaning, purpose and unity in community undertakings." Through the mechanism of a comprehensive development plan, the aim was to create a set of common goals to respond to present and future needs. The geographic area for the development plan was not restricted to Townsite but was expanded to accommodate a larger regional imagination among the leaders of the four residential communities. Further, the plan was not to be viewed as a static model on paper but rather as a set of ideas that would be influenced by a variety of external and internal forces over time. Keeping abreast with these forces with help from trained technical staff, the leadership and their communities could evaluate the previously outlined goals and projects to refine and restructure the development plan as implementation proceeded.

The first critical action was, therefore, the delineation of the planning region called the Powell River Area comprising the four residential communities of Townsite, Westview, Cranberry Lake, and Wildwood. This would form the basis for the establishment of a Powell River Regional Planning Board comprising individual community representatives and technical staff such as planners. Such a board could generate the sustained commitment by communities and their leadership towards evolving locally- and regionally-specific planning programs and projects to strengthen the idea of a regional community as a legacy for the future.

The planning studio made the case for the creation of new planning institutions at the regional level and the ongoing requirement of technical staff as advisors to the board members. By suggesting the need for such institutions, recommending the role of planners within them and suggesting collaborations between senior government and regional organizations, the study created the basis for linkages between regional planning boards, municipalities, village councils and the graduate school of planning. This strategy ensured the continuous creation of planning jobs and internship opportunities for planning graduates from SCARP, a legacy that continues until this day.

Another outcome of the Powell River studio, as with the Maple Ridge studio, was creating the awareness of the benefits of having trained planners as technical staff. Such staff could conduct planning studies with respect to population growth, demographic composition and density patterns and containing smoke, odour and noise pollution from the pulp and paper mill. They could also play an important role as advisors to the regional planning board and oversee the ongoing maintenance and periodic updating of the regional plan. Regional institutions were not funded by government back then, so Oberlander suggested that local businesses and social organizations be approached to donate resources.

SCARP's collaboration with the Powell River Company resulted in graduation scholarships for academic excellence to the students involved in the studio. J.B. Chaster and Robert Opie from the second cohort at SCARP won the Powell River Company Ltd. Service Awards in Architecture for Special Project Study at Powell River. A further major outcome of the study was the consolidation of the Powell River District Municipality by the provincial government in 1955, incorporating Townsite, Cranberry Lake, Westview and Wildwood.

The Powell River Area studio had a transformative impact in multiple ways. It made the process of development decision-making tangible and concrete for leadership in four communities through the creation of shared goals in a comprehensive plan. It benefitted four physically isolated communities by creating shared visions for a better future. It highlighted the potential for harnessing the natural resource base in diversifying the economy, centered until then on the paper mill. It made visible the role of the planner as a resource that combined technical expertise with the ability to interpret people's needs. It generated the idea of regional-level institutions that could make democratic decisions for the larger area. The studio increased buy-in for the benefits of planning when the profession was in its infancy in British Columbia.

Perhaps most important from Peter Oberlander's point of view, the Powell River study proved that a studio component could contribute to a planning education by demonstrating the unique role planners can play in converting good ideas to useful action, as well as providing a "light at the end of the tunnel" to assure students that society would have useful work for them to do as professionals and would be willing to pay appropriately for such work.

Living and Working in West Vancouver

In the early 1950s, the Reeve (equivalent to today's Mayor) of West Vancouver, A. Hugo Ray, and the municipal council faced some significant challenges resulting from postwar population growth in the Greater Vancouver region.

Located northwest of Vancouver's downtown area on the north side of Burrard Inlet, West Vancouver was originally part of the municipality of North Vancouver. In 1912, it was separated from North Vancouver and incorporated as the Municipality of West Vancouver. During the Great Depression the municipality faced bankruptcy because its residents were unable to pay their taxes.

West Vancouver sold 4,700 acres of prime municipal lands to British Pacific Properties (BPP), owned by the Guinness family of Great Britain, for residential development that, in addition to bringing in new taxpayers, would create much needed local jobs. A plan for the initial stage of development was prepared for BPP by the Olmsted Brothers, a Boston-based landscape architecture firm famous for its designs for Central Park in New York City. The company agreed to construct the Lions Gate Bridge, a road connection from West Vancouver to Vancouver through Stanley Park, another job creation project which was completed in 1938.

The exigencies of the Depression and World War II delayed the realization of the immense development potential represented by a large supply of attractive residential land with a new road connection to downtown Vancouver. In the early 1950s, West Vancouver was a "dormitory town" with a majority of its residents either retired or commuting to jobs in Vancouver or North Vancouver. West Vancouver residents also relied primarily on Vancouver for social, cultural and some recreational services, although its beaches and mountains were important recreational resources for residents and visitors alike.

Faced with rapid residential growth, the municipality had no land that was appropriate for industry and, it was thought, limited commercial development potential, but it did have a stunning mountain and coastal landscape that residents wished to protect. Given the limitations of its residential tax base, and with near bankruptcy a fairly recent memory, the municipality clearly needed a game plan for the present, let alone the future.

The resolution approved by Council in authorizing the study in the spring of 1952 describes its intent very well:

RESOLVED:

THAT whereas the prospects of an Upper Level Highway, expanding use of Horseshoe Bay as a port, re-entry of the PGE [railway] and a new bridge over the Lions Gate pose development and service problems;

AND WHEREAS the practicable extent of physical planning will be limited to the capacity of the Municipality to meet the costs;

AND WHEREAS the Council recognizes the need for an Economic Study of the Municipality and a Physical Survey and development of Layout Standards;

a study be undertaken of living and working conditions in West Vancouver in anticipation of likely future requirements.

This was to be an economic analysis of the municipality as the basis for future planning.

Underlying the resolution were three core areas of concern: low-density residential development, coping with new infrastructure, and expanding public works projects to, among other things, provide jobs for residents. First, West Vancouver had to address the preponderance of single-family detached housing which did not generate sufficient tax revenue to support the public expenditures for these private properties in the form of roads, schools and recreational facilities. Second, the municipality had to address the issues arising from new public and transportation infrastructure projects such as the expansion of the Black Ball Ferry operation at Horseshoe Bay, an upper level highway and a second bridge connection to Vancouver. Third, the municipality had to figure out to maintain its urban standards of service in the face of growth, creating systems of sanitation, piped water supply, expanded bus services, improved recreational facilities, the provision of public safety services and redevelopment of the waterfront to cater to both residential users and visitors. All these challenges required capital expenditures which the municipality under the existing taxation system could not undertake.

It will come as no surprise to the reader that Peter approached his study of economic conditions in West Vancouver by viewing the municipality within the larger regional context of Greater Vancouver. From this perspective, West Vancouver was compared to a "trading nation," exporting what it could produce (mostly labour) and importing what it could not produce, including many types of goods and services.

Many years later, Ken Cameron was engaged in a discussion of economic development in the Greater Vancouver region when a participant said, "West Vancouver has no economic function because it has no industrial land." The Municipal Manager at the time objected strongly, saying emphatically, "West Vancouver most definitely has an economic function and an important one. It is the executive suburb close to downtown that every economically successful region needs." That role, so obvious today, was anything but clear when Peter Oberlander began his work in 1952.

His job was to generate an image of economic reality in West Vancouver based on the best available data (and what he assembled was impressive), and to suggest proposals for future directions and implementation measures. At the time, he did not have a private planning practice, so he worked on this project with the help of Cornelia. Dr. Ira Robinson, a new instructor and researcher at SCARP recently arrived from the U.S., assisted with the study, as did Bill Paterson, a student and one of the four SCARP "pioneers" who is acknowledged in the study report for his role "before and after his appointment as Municipal Planner." Another job for a SCARP graduate had been created!

To create an image of West Vancouver in 1952, Peter drew on a diversity of expertise from public administration agencies, academia, and local business and community groups. Since he did not have a team that could conduct extensive field surveys beyond the business survey conducted by Paterson, he relied on the embedded knowledge within the municipal administrative circles to understand the emerging concerns and challenges of urbanization and the aspirations of the civic staff and leaders for the future of the municipality. He drew on studies conducted by federal government agencies and statistical data sets on municipal-level details of population, business and income. Further, he drew on the networks of the West Vancouver Board of Trade to create awareness among its membership of the ongoing study and to get their feedback on specific recommendations regarding their prospective role. Finally, he drew on the strength of academia in developing the tools, methods and approaches to generate research data which was essential in generating a comprehensive picture of West Vancouver as a community and as a municipality.

The study revealed new relationships between income, occupations, economic activities and municipal finance. In addition to the economic functions of West

Vancouver, it also documented the recreation functions which, although smaller than the residential function, fostered the idea that diversification of residential, commercial and recreational sectors would yield to social cohesion as well as financial resilience.

In approaching the thorny question of a stronger municipal tax base, Oberlander carefully crafted the possibilities on the basis of the municipality's existing strengths and opportunities: "...the key to West Vancouver's wider tax base and, therefore, more secure municipal income, lies in diversification rather than any basic change in who lives in West Vancouver and what kind of buildings are built to house them."

He offered three possibilities, described rather quaintly as "a greater variety of residences at a high standard, a greater variety of shops and greater variety in recreation and tourist services."

The study recognized that the primary function of the municipality would be residential and that there was a need to provide more concentrated development and avoid the pressures for low-density residential development that could not pay for needed services. It proposed consolidated residential areas with a wider variety of housing types as well as consolidated development areas where housing, shops and services could be provided within easy reach of each other. The Upper Levels Highway could be used as an urban containment device by not allowing urban development above the Highway.

Peter suggested that West Vancouver exploit its conversion from a dormitory suburb to a corridor community by capitalizing on the flows of people to and through the municipality on their way to and from the Horseshoe Bay ferry terminal linking the Lower Mainland to Vancouver Island and what is now known as the Sunshine Coast. Therefore, the study recommended the identification of land to be zoned as commercial areas. To ensure diversification, it identified three types of shopping facilities *i.e.,* shopping centres near through traffic corridors, a local area for resident shoppers located at the intersection of neighbourhoods and individual "mom and pop" shops i.e., general stores within residential clusters.

By encouraging new commercial facilities and diversifying their types, West Vancouver could emerge as a commercial destination regionally. The best example was the Park Royal Shopping Centre, which opened in 1950 and was touted as the first enclosed shopping mall in Canada. The immediate benefits of such a policy were twofold. First, it would provide a new and stable source of municipal revenues through taxation. Commercial properties generally required fewer municipal services but yielded higher tax revenue compared to residential uses where the opposite was true. Second, it would provide employment for residents.

Recreation and tourism were the combined third function that West Vancouver could serve regionally. Oberlander suggested that the natural resource base of West Vancouver, comprising mountains, beaches, coves and floral landscapes, should be recognized as an asset for taxation by the municipality.

Although West Vancouver served as a recreational hub for summer and winter periods, it lacked a systematic mechanism to tap into the flows of people from within the metropolitan region. The study suggested that recreational centres could become a stable source of municipal income once facilities and services were provided for tourists and recreation seekers. Further, it proposed that the municipal council create a policy for preservation, protection and creation of unique recreational sites such as parks, playgrounds, beaches, hiking trails and marinas. A planning framework would be essential in order to develop these sites with supporting facilities such as hotels, motels, restaurants and ancillary services. Finally, but importantly, the study identified the need to keep the entire waterfront publicly accessible.

In the light of the increasing population densities and new functions identified in the study, the need for public open space was factored in as a possibility in the distant future. To address that concern, the study suggested the integration of both water-based and land-based recreational assets to create a "Blue-Green belt as a singular recreational development principle." These various facilities would require licences and in return provide tax income. Hence, not only would recreation lead to economic diversification it would also contribute to the well-being of the resident population who would also have access to these facilities.

The study showed how provincial grants and diversification of land use could yield revenues for the municipality. Taxation on new developments — residential, commercial and recreational — and fees charged for commercial and recreational licences would become new sources of municipal income.

A hallmark of Peter Oberlander's consulting work was the attention paid to recommendations for implementation, and "Living and Working in West Vancouver" was no exception. There were only two main recommendations, but both were weighty.

The first recommendation was a "land use policy for the Municipality's development" that could guide the preparation of a community plan to give effect to the diversification strategy outlined in the study. The second was that the Municipality create "a planning staff as an integral part of municipal government." This second recommendation offered an opportunity for Peter to flesh out his concept of a municipal planning function in a metropolitan setting.

It was not as if the municipality had not engaged in community planning. In fact, the Reeve and Council followed the requirements laid out by the *Town Planning Act*, drawing on advice from the Town Planning Commission or individual professional planning consultants periodically to address planning-related challenges and problems. Although these two sources of advice greatly shaped and enhanced the quality of life in West Vancouver, private planning consultants especially did not perceive planning as a continuous process.

Drawing on an incisive comment of a former Reeve in 1949, four years after a professional planning consultant had drawn up a comprehensive plan for West Vancouver, Peter Oberlander reflected that the Reeve's remarks on this experience reflected three insights. First, there was a growing awareness of the need for planning to be integrated within the work of municipal administration. Second, planning should be founded on adequate technical knowledge and local processes. Last but not least, planning had to be thought of as a continuous process, because it created certain outcomes that would be transformed in times to come, calling for further planning strategies. Taken together, these insights called for the recruitment of a full-time, in-house, professional planning officer within the municipal staff.

What would be the benefits? For Peter it was clear that, with a planner as a staff member, Council would be better informed, as it would have in-house access to research and technical advice on an ongoing basis. The Town Planning Commission's role would not cease; it would continue to advise the council on larger policy issues and their implementation based on the provisions and requirements of the *Town Planning Act*.

What would be the role and value of a municipal planning staff? It was the same question the UBC Senate had asked, and a clear and convincing answer was required for Peter be successful in his educational career as well as in meeting the needs of local governments to whom he provided advice in his various capacities. He had to justify the additional cost, in West Vancouver in this case, where money was tight. Peter however was committed to his belief that ideas were of limited value if not followed by implementation.

The role for the municipal planner, Peter wrote, could be three-fold.

First, it would entail advising the Reeve, Council and Municipal Manager on planning-related policy and programs. This could help the municipal administration stay updated and informed on provincial and federal government policy orientations. Using the framework provided by "Living and Working in West Vancouver," the municipal planner could undertake the preparation of a master plan. When the plan was complete, the planner could provide oversight of the day-to-day implementation of new improvement or expansion programs and could call for necessary revisions to the master plan. In response to the needs of a growing community especially in the light of the requirements laid out by the *Town Planning Act*, the municipal planner could initiate surveys for specific planning projects within the municipality. In addition, the planner had to periodically evaluate and update development and construction standards, keeping in mind the overall requirements of space, which would be possible only if the planner ensured a constant updating of municipal-level planning-related data.

The second function for the municipal planner would be to serve as a coordinator with respect to the physical development in the municipality. This could be achieved through a staff coordinating committee involving senior administrative officials who could provide an integrated approach to various planning and development projects. Such a committee would include the municipal manager, clerk, engineer, assessor and planner. For concerns involving schools or recreation the Secretary of the School Board and Superintendent of the Parks Board could be invited for advice.

As the third function, the municipal planner could be the institutional link between the municipality and planning-related agencies outside West Vancouver. Here the responsibilities would include liaison with the Lower Mainland Regional Planning Board, Metropolitan Health Committee, Metropolitan Parks Planning Committee, Greater Vancouver Water District and Technical Subcommittee of the Burrard Inlet Crossing Study. Contacts from this function would not only ensure that West Vancouver became an active participant in regional and metropolitan planning programs but also that its developmental goals were known and respected at the regional, municipal and community levels.

"Living and Working in West Vancouver" provided a clear strategic direction that not only enabled the municipality to navigate past the financial and economic hazards of the postwar era but crystallized thinking about the community's role and potential within the region that is reflected in the highly livable and successful place that exists today.

Tooling up: Community Planning Consultants and the PhD

By 1955, with the second SCARP cohort graduating, the curriculum and systems for the graduate program in planning were firmly in place. The benefit of the studios in providing opportunities for students to learn and demonstrate the value of planning in practical settings was well established. "Living and Working in West Vancouver" had provided a smooth transition for one of the "pioneers" from SCARP to a well-defined and recognized professional planning position.

Peter could see that, for his own academic and professional development, he would need two things. The first was a PhD, and as a master's graduate from Harvard he was admissible there, but the rule was that one had to start a doctoral program within seven years of graduation from the master's program, so time was of the essence. He started work on it in 1954.

The second thing he needed was a mechanism to allow him to pursue a private practice in community planning within the rules set by the university. At the time, the university was seen as a space for the "pure" pursuit of academic inquiries and did not permit faculty to engage in private practice. If a faculty member was in such an in-between position i.e., of one foot in academia and one foot in private practice, it was frowned upon as "double-dipping."

Various Canadian universities had developed such strictures on faculty members in the interest of students' needs so that faculty could focus on their commitments and responsibilities for teaching, research, and publication. Cornelia recalls, "The University made a stupid law that you are only allowed to work one day a month outside the university, and you were not allowed to make money from a private practice. It was pretty grim." When Ken Cameron asked Cornelia how Peter got around the university rule, she replied, "How did Peter get around anything? He was something. He would know exactly whom to go to and talk to and what to do."

Thompson, Berwick, Pratt & Partners (TBP) was a leading private architectural and engineering firm in Vancouver that was established at the turn of the twentieth century. The architectural fraternity in Vancouver at the time was a small group of professionals who had mostly worked and trained at TBP for practical experience. Arthur Erickson, the world-renowned architect, himself a onetime novice at TBP, fondly remembered it as a "kindergarten" for aspiring professionals in the field of architecture and engineering.

Charles Edward Pratt, a principal at TBP, was a friend of Peter's who always maintained that an individual must "practice what [they] preach and not just teach." Peter believed in this approach and felt that an artificial distancing of the academic space from the pursuit of active professional practice resulted in at best *ad hoc* technical solutions and at worst a myopic understanding of practical realities. Peter belonged to a subset of University faculty members who were keen to blur these siloed conceptualizations of the "real" and "academic" worlds.

In a tribute to Peter, long-time colleague and friend David Covo reminisced on Peter's understanding of "how to work the bureaucracy." Drawing on the work of religious scholar James Carse, Covo explained how Peter understood the bureaucracy and the world at large as a game.

Carse had observed that games were of two types: finite and infinite. Both games had their unique sets of rules identified by participants. In a finite game, the intention is to win, while in an infinite game the intention is to keep the game going. If an infinite game was tending towards resolution then participants changed the rules in a way to ensure that the game continued. Peter's genius, Covo suggested, was that he understood the rules of both finite and infinite professional game playing so well that he deployed his intuition, knowledge, experience and alert thinking to ensure the outcomes of "the ball in play" or "winning the game" were achieved, usually the latter where bureaucrats were concerned. Peter Oberlander was strategic and tactical as a professional, able to convert setbacks, losses and unexpected outcomes into productive outcomes.

Regardless of the opposition, Oberlander worked around restrictions with enduring support from Frederic Lasserre who believed in his pragmatic approach to knowledge and action. He navigated and negotiated the worlds of academia and private practice deftly, creating new linkages and networks. This practical skill of keeping the ball in play was a critical form of practical knowledge that Peter transferred to the more alert of his students who saw him in action both in academic and public life.

This was the background to the sabbatical Peter took in 1955. It provided some space in which he could complete his academic credentials at Harvard and start a community planning consultancy that could function one step removed from his academic role.

In his doctoral studies, he hoped to contribute to planning thought by drawing on his decade-long educational and professional experiences in America, Britain and Canada. In reflecting on his role in federal government agencies focused on housing and planning in postwar Canada and experiences in community planning experiments in British Columbia, he hoped to identify what plagued Canadian housing and community planning initiatives at the time and what if anything could be done about it.

Peter and Cornelia Oberlander moved to the Eastern Seaboard to commence the residency required for the doctorate. Cornelia recalls it vividly.

> We lived in New York, because I was doing the Philadelphia Airport in Philadelphia, and Peter liked to live in New York because he was close to his mother. We lived in New York at 855 East 86 Street. That was at the Carl Schurz Park. The houses were built by the Astors in the nineteenth century. On Mondays, Peter would either go to the New York Public Library to work or else he would go to Boston. For the PhD, we had to be in residence at Harvard. We had a horrible apartment in Brookline [Massachusetts]. It had a drafting table, and I would do all the drawings. His thesis was the Town of Danvers. I have that in slides. This was partial fulfillment. You had to be sure you understood town planning. So he chose Danvers on route 128 in Boston. The final destination on that route was the town of Danvers. I did all the drawings. Peter had lovely slides of everything on the projector. A student came up to me and said, "No wonder Peter passed — he had a wife who could draw."

As is so often the case with those who attempt to complete a graduate degree in mid-career, Peter found the PhD dissertation a significant challenge. He began the project in August 1955. His committee included Arthur Maass, author of *Muddy Waters: the Army Engineers and the Nation's Rivers,* an exposé of water resource management, and *Area and Power: A Theory of Local Government,* which is a very fine exploration of how power is allocated in a modern democracy. Peter's thesis supervisor, Reginald Issacs, described by Cornelia as a "stickler," had a number of tedious criticisms of the dissertation when Oberlander submitted it in December 1956, and it was not until February 1957 that it was accepted.

A mid-career doctoral thesis can often provide an intellectual pivot towards the future, and this was certainly the case with Peter, notwithstanding his struggles with his supervisor. His topic was "Community Planning and Housing: An Aspect of Canadian Federalism." He later summarized the main findings and recommendations of his thesis in an article published in Queen's Quarterly with the jazzier title of "Community Planning and Housing: Step-Children of Canadian Federalism."

The thesis constituted the first comprehensive examination of the role of planning and housing in the historical context of Canada as an outcome of federal and provincial policy joined by local administration. It documented the fact that, unlike most settlements in "older" parts of the world which grew up more or less organically out of the confluence of human activities, Canadian settlements were very often the product of broader policy. The focus of such policies was often military (as with the establishment of the Fortress of Louisbourg or Halifax) colonial, (New Westminster) or commercial (Hudson's Bay Company lands and railway lands in Western Canada). The important underlying point was that, far from being an emanation of local initiative, most Canadian settlements arose from forces beyond the local community and these forces often involved what we more recently have called "senior" governments.

The drafters of Canada's constitution, the British North America Act, were clearly more concerned with the allocation of powers between the federal and provincial governments than with the needs of the new country's settlements. In deference to the principle of subsidiarity upon which that allocation was based, the founding fathers of Confederation allocated "residual powers" (those not specifically mentioned in the constitution) to the provinces rather than the federal government. In addition, the provinces were granted most of the important specific powers related to settlement, including property and civil rights, and municipal institutions.

A number of the powers assigned to the federal government, such as the regulation of ports (and, by extension, airports), and money and banking, had important implications for the development of cities and towns, but these were not recognized at the time. Oberlander's thesis drew the connections between these apparently unrelated powers and settlements and argued that the building of cities would only be successful if undertaken as a collaborative process that brought together the interests and engagement of all three orders of government.

The stresses and strains of the development of Canada as a modern economic, social, and political entity only made this need more urgent. The remarkable national mobilization required to fight World War II following the Great Depression rapidly accelerated the process. A particular area of focus was housing, where the federal government intervened directly to undertake the construction of homes for workers in industries that sprang up almost overnight to supply the material needed by Canada and its allies as the industrial strength of continental Europe was converted to the enemy cause.

Looking at Canada's human settlement needs from the perspective of the mid-1950s, Peter Oberlander suggested in his thesis what we would now call a "work around" rather than a more radical restructuring of Confederation to reflect the country's modern urban nature. He proposed the creation of "urban development boards" with representatives of all three levels of government which would be responsible for settlement planning and the allocation of resources within each province. The work of such boards would be augmented by a system of "grants in aid" for planning, modelled on the financial assistance for low-rent housing provided by the federal government under the *National Housing Act*.

The recommendations had all of the hallmarks of Peter's work: task-focused, based on collaboration rather than institutional change, and with a central role for planning. It would be 15 years before Oberlander would have an opportunity to test them in practice.

Community Planning Consultants

Back from his doctoral sojourn at Harvard at the Christmas recess in 1956, Oberlander began to collaborate on projects through a private planning practice.

Reginald Cave was a British citizen and a trained engineer from the University College London where he served in Britain's Royal Air Force as a pilot during World War II. He had established a small consulting practice, R.J. Cave & Company, Consulting Engineers, in downtown Vancouver in the same premises as Thompson Berwick and Pratt and partners. Peter and Reginald established Community Planning Consultants as its principals. Since they had existing commitments at the university for Peter and at the engineering practice for Reginald, they decided to hire a staff member who would manage the day-to-day running of the office. They found this person in a young Japanese-Canadian, Robert Furukawa. Furukawa warmly recalls their first meeting in Vancouver that transformed his professional and personal life:

> On a cold winter afternoon, I entered 1553 Robson Street, in the West End of Vancouver. The simple two-storey building housed the architects Thompson Berwick and Pratt upstairs and Reginald J. Cave & Co. Engineers downstairs. My appointment was to meet Engineer/Planner Reginald Cave, so I entered the

downstairs offices and was immediately greeted by a sweet smiling secretary/receptionist (Geraldine Baxter) who showed me in to meet Reginald. He greeted me with a hint of a smile and said, "Hi, the Professor will be here in few minutes." Little did I know that I would be using this same statement over and over again for the next 20 years!

Peter Oberlander, Reginald Cave, and Robert Furukawa had diverse ethnic and social backgrounds, and had their roots in their personal experiences of World War II. As a Jewish immigrant to England and then as an enemy alien in a Canadian internment camp, Peter bore the scars of having been a stateless person as a young adult. As a pilot in the British Royal Air Force, Reginald Cave had witnessed first-hand, devastation and killings in the war. He had suffered great personal loss in England and had eventually emigrated to Canada. Furukawa's family was of Japanese descent and had lived in Canada for two generations. In a shameful chapter in Canadian history, when Japan entered World War II, the Canadian government detained and dispossessed the vast majority of people of Japanese origin in British Columbia and sent them to internment camps inland from the Pacific in the West Kootenays. Overnight they lost everything they had consolidated over two generations.

After the war, the Furukawa family moved to Southern Alberta where beginning afresh was a tough struggle for a long time. Cornelia candidly recalls that being of Japanese descent, Furukawa struggled to find work when he moved back to British Columbia. "Peter took him under his wing and taught him. He recognized how good Robert was at drawing. He taught him planning on the job." Thus, while the legacy of the war for these three men was mostly a story of suffering, personal loss, humiliation and many dehumanizing moments, they came out of it with a burning desire to contribute to a better world.

Furukawa never got over his fascination with Peter Oberlander's approach to life. At Oberlander's memorial service he recalled, "We were driving over the Burrard Street Bridge, going from our office in the West End to Peter's home in Point Grey. Peter straddled both driving lanes on the bridge. I said, 'Peter, why are you doing this?' He replied, 'So that no one will get ahead of me.'"

Community Planning Consultants Ltd. was engaged in urban and regional planning projects throughout Western Canada and other parts of the world. This tiny but dynamic planning practice managed a diverse portfolio of projects including regional studies, new towns, industrial parks, municipal, recreation and resort plans, housing plans and special studies. The focus of their projects was communities of people, the environment and human activity within the region. Their concept of planning at different levels ranging from the region to communities guided their efforts in developing cutting-edge solutions in uncertain times that threw up a diversity of challenges.

Community Planning Consultants Ltd. was founded on a specific understanding of what planning meant. For Peter, Reginald and Robert, planning was "the active pursuit of goals and objectives shaped by a continuous process of decision-making systems." It was definitely not an academic exercise because to be relevant and meaningful a planning idea had to be thought through to ensure its implementation into action. Following a modernist paradigm of planning, they sought to make their planning practice, "comprehensive in a sense that it encompassed the totality of influencing factors."

For CPC's principals, planning as a profession had a responsibility to identify specific goals and outcomes that could be translated into objectives that, in turn, could shape actions in real time. Under the watchful eye of Peter, Reginald and Robert, CPC emerged as a practice founded on "interdisciplinary teamwork and harmonious decision-making on a collaborative basis." The trio clearly articulated their role not only in terms of providing technical expertise to their clientele, but also outlining a comprehensive set of services such as site planning, landscaping, managing plan implementation processes, overall project coordination, development supervision and continuous ongoing reviews. In addition to their role as planning consultants, they served as strategic advisors to their clients. The firm pursued a dynamic planning practice for two decades before being merged with Thompson, Berwick, Pratt & Partners, architects, engineers and planners in 1977.

Planning for Leisure: Kona

As tensions built up in the Pacific region in the years leading up to World War II, Hawaii's strategic location was recognized by the American military. In early 1941, the Pacific Fleet was relocated to Pearl Harbour from San Diego, and it was the Japanese attack on the fleet there on December 7 that year that brought the United States into the war.

Gradually, Hawaii emerged as a place for rest and recuperation for the wounded military personnel involved in the Pacific Theatre of World War II (and later, the Korean War and the Vietnam War). The vast expanse of virgin beaches such as Waikiki created an atmosphere of calm and healing for many wounded soldiers. They invited their families and friends to spend time with them in Hawaii as they recuperated. This brought many American visitors to Hawaii who enjoyed the scenic views, landscapes and benign climate it offered.

After World War II, a cash-strapped Britain turned to its colonies to collect revenues and resources to rebuild the British economy and its devastated cities. Grosvenor Laing Land Corporation was one such British corporation that looked for possibilities for revenue generation through land development opportunities.

In the early nineteenth century, King Kamehameha had united the various clans into a single Kingdom of Hawaii. His successors ruled until ousted by Euro-American private interests in 1893, and Hawaii was annexed by the United States in 1898. It had plenty of undeveloped volcanic lands held in the ownership of American and British land trusts. The economy was dominated by the sugar industry. Popular uprisings against the influence of the sugar lobbies resulted in Hawaii being granted statehood in 1959. Statehood prompted a move by the newly formed administration to create a general plan to undertake orderly development in Hawaii.

Land was a central resource for this initiative. The best stretches of land along the coast were owned by the Bernice. P. Bishop Estate charitable trust and the Campbell Estate Trust. Bernice Pauahi Bishop was a Hawaiian princess, philanthropist and direct descendant of King Kamehameha. She was married to an American businessman, Charles Bishop. Vast amounts of land in the state of Hawaii were held by the Bernice Pauahi Bishop Estate Trustees. Two-thirds of these lands were located on the "Big Island" of Hawaii, including Kona which had the single largest land area. Before her untimely death in 1883, Bernice Bishop willed her entire estate in a trust to build educational facilities (known as "Kamehameha schools") for Hawaiian children to improve the situation of the declining native Hawaiian community. The Trust sought expert advice help to provide them with a framework for a meaningful development of the Kona lands.

Robert Furukawa described the stranglehold the Bishop Estate had on developable land.

After Hawaii became the 50th state of the USA on August 21, 1959 (from 1898, the Islands were protected as a US territory), the State undertook to prepare a general plan of Hawaii immediately. This was vitally important to protect the very limited Island land resource, potable water, and the fragile ecology and landscape. The Bishop Estate held nearly 10 per cent of all Hawaii lands. Their holdings on Oahu in downtown Honolulu and Waikiki were highly valued properties. The Bishop Trust was an eleemosynary form of trust for the support and benefit of the schools of Kamehameha. The lands in trust were all bequeathed by Princess Bernice P. Bishop, the great grandniece of King Kamehameha, never to be sold!

The Bishop Estate Trustees, led by Atherton Richards, took their responsibilities very seriously. Furukawa recalls the comment from Senator Herbert Jackson, the head of the development corporation: "...the State encountered Bishop lands everywhere they went! They tried to push the Trustees but learned that NO ONE pushes Atherton Richards!"

In an effort to find a solution, the trustees of the Bernice P. Bishop Estate Trust collaborated with Grosvenor Laing Land Corporation of Vancouver to organize a week-long planning seminar at Kona. Peter Oberlander was invited as one of the planning expert participants to attend this seminar.

Through the week-long discussions, Peter suggested that Hawaii, given its historical trajectory and picturesque tropical setting, could be developed as a recreational economy. He suggested the idea of Kona, particularly the Trust's lands at Keauhou Bay, as a "Community for Leisure." Atherton Richards, himself a member of a Hawaiian pioneer family, was captivated by this idea. Furukawa later recollected

> Peter was the one that caught Atherton's attention. I recall him saying, "this young Canadian professor was the only one who expressed respect for Keauhou as the birthplace of King Kamehameha and advanced the concept of a 'Community for Leisure' by saying that this was a place where Hawaiian nobility lived, and leisure was part of their way of Kona life."

Six months later after many deliberations among the trustees, CPC received a letter from Atherton Richards at their Robson Street office. Richards noted that the "Canadian professor" had first mooted the idea of the community for leisure in the week-long discussions. As the birthplace of King Kamehameha, the Kona lands were of special importance for the Bernice P. Bishop Estate Trust that was governed by the wishes of Bernice Bishop herself. The trustees found that the "community for leisure idea was synonymous with the Kona way of life" and, therefore, befitting these precious lands. Peter was invited with his team to visit Hawaii to prepare a plan for the north and south Keauhou Kona Lands. Through implementation of such a plan the trustees hoped to give practical meaning to the new concept of a community for leisure.

In 1966, CPC began the work on planning the transformation of the volcanic Keaukou Kona lands to a "living and livable" Kona Hawaii Community to bring an appropriate new meaning to the birthplace of King Kamehameha. In the fall of 1967, CPC submitted a report to the Bernice P. Bishop Estate Trust outlining a plan for the Kona lands. The report addressed the need of the Trust to understand the total development potential and optimum utilization of the north and south Kona lands and suggested that a framework for this purpose be articulated through a comprehensive study. Within a year, CPC established an office in Honolulu for the Community of Leisure Project. This was the beginning of new relationships in Hawaii, including a partnership with a local landscape architect Robert Bush. The firm came to be called Oberlander, Bush & Cave. The recreation study for the Keaukou Kona Lands, Hawaii was submitted to the Bernice P. Bishop Estate Trust in 1970.

Robert Furukawa described the 400 acres of Keauhou Kona oceanfront lands formed by lava flows on either side of Keauhou Bay. The foreshore comprised 25-foot-high lava cliffs that dropped into the deep, blue ocean water. On this harsh landform with no beaches in sight, a golf course was built. It transformed the entire site. The lush green landscape provided breathtaking views with a backdrop of the sloping terrain of Mount Mauna Loa. Cornelia Oberlander's influence was evident in the planting of native trees and flowers which maintained the natural ecological relationships with the land. The transformation of the uninviting volcanic landscapes of Keauhou Kona into a living and livable region gave everlasting meaning to the birthplace of King Kamehameha — the final wish of his descendant Bernice Bishop.

Today, the Kamehameha Schools operate three campuses plus a number of pre-schools, with a total enrollment of more than 5,000. The Schools have the largest endowment of all secondary schools in the United States. The most recent estimate of its value exceeds $11 billion.

This project crystallized Peter Oberlander's approach to planning practice. First, the planning would be a continuing and dynamic process. Second, by suggesting a link between the administration and management of land and planning he sought to establish a new role for planning that would be powerful and effective. Third, planning could enable efficient and continuous returns from the land as an investment that could support provision of social services such as primary and secondary education. These concepts established the need for planning expertise as a mainstay in development projects, in turn generating demand for planning professionals with specific types of interdisciplinary knowledge and skills as opposed to only engineers or architect-planners.

Above all, however, the Kona project demonstrated the power of the concept of a continuum between ideas and action, of the principle that the one was useless without the other.

The futurist Joel Barker would later sum up the power of vision with action as follows: "Vision without action is merely a dream. Action without vision just passes the time. Vision with action can change the world." It was a concept that increasingly dominated the remainder of Peter Oberlander's life. In his eighties, Peter was centrally involved in the program for the UN Habitat World Urban Forum III, held in Vancouver in 2006. Its theme: "Our Future: Sustainable Cities — Turning Ideas into Action."

CHAPTER SEVEN:

A NEW TEAM AT
VANCOUVER CITY HALL

For most of the twenty years after World War 11, civic politics in Vancouver (and in British Columbia more broadly) was a class conflict between the socialists (the Co-operative Commonwealth Federation (CCF) or New Democratic Party (NDP) and its civic counterparts) and everybody else. The Non-Partisan Association (NPA) had been formed in 1937 for the express purpose of countering the "threat" presented by the CCF, which was finding fertile ground in the popular discontent arising from the Great Depression. NPA members had little in common more than a belief that the socialists ("Godless Socialists" as Social Credit Premier WAC Bennett would describe them) should be kept away from the levers of power at all costs.

The NPA believed that the cause of good civic government would be impaired if City Council were dominated by "party politics" rather than the best interests of the city, and its constitution dedicated the organization to improving civic government, supporting the best candidates for office and opposing the introduction of party politics. Not surprisingly, the "best candidates" most often came from, or enjoyed the support of, the downtown business and corporate community. This deliberate rejection of overt party organization in local government was the norm in many cities in Canada at the time, much to the mystification of many political scientists at academic institutions, for whom political parties are undeniably the essential glue that makes provincial and federal governmental systems work.

Former Vancouver Councillor Marguerite Ford recalls the early 1960s as a relatively simple time. "Vancouver was almost still a village in many ways. You could always find out what was going on." Anyone who had more than a passing interest in civic affairs could always join civic associations such as the Board of Trade or the Community Arts Council.

This folksy openness had begun to change, however. The city fathers (and they were all male, with the exception of the redoubtable Alderman Marianne Linnell) were concerned that Vancouver was stagnating, not "moving forward." Bill Rathie, elected as mayor in 1963, came into office with a reputation from the private sector of turning marginal companies around. The members of council were particularly concerned with retail competition from suburban shopping centres and the need to provide improved road access and parking downtown. They looked with envy at American cities, which were investing heavily in freeway infrastructure and the removal of "blighted" inner city areas through "urban renewal". With the assistance of some American planning consultants, council articulated some new policy directions, including promotion of a regional freeway system with a third crossing of Burrard Inlet, subsidy of office development in the downtown, publicly-led urban renewal and rezoning of land for light industry.

As Walter Hardwick recalled later,

> To many, these were overdue civic initiatives; to me and my students at the University of British Columbia, they were public interventions that fitted the obvious needs of a decade earlier; they were, in the 1960s, inappropriate, for the basic structure of the city, in functional terms, was changing rapidly. We were moving toward a "post-industrial society." In other words, the city government acted like a parent treating traumas of adolescence where, in actuality, a young adult was concerned.

The directions being considered by the city's leadership had grave implications for many citizens and their neighbourhoods. These citizens would have been very concerned about them — if they had known what was happening. But increasingly, the key decisions about planning, development and infrastructure were being taken behind closed doors at City Hall with the able assistance of the planning director-cum-City Manager, Gerald Sutton-Brown. They did not involve input from many sources, including the Vancouver Town Planning Commission, whose role was to advise City Council on planning issues in the city, to which Peter Oberlander had been appointed as a UBC representative in 1958, later serving as Chair.

In a gesture towards improving relations with community interests, Sutton-Brown created a Social Planning Department and appointed Maurice Egan, a former city councillor in Ottawa, to head it. One of his first hires was Darlene Marzari, a recent graduate of the London School of Economics. It would prove to be a fateful step, because Egan and Marzari found it impossible not to empathize with the communities that would be affected by the city's plans.

The key decisions being considered by the city were big. The plans for an inner city freeway network would link Highway 1 through the east side of the city to a waterfront freeway and, ultimately, to a third crossing to the North Shore, which in some schemes would involve a new "man-made" island east of Stanley Park. Coincidentally, the city was actively involved in the land-assembly stage of an urban renewal scheme in the Strathcona area east of downtown. The acquisition of property from the largely Chinese Canadian homeowners for Phase 3 of the urban renewal scheme would have, in the minds of city staff, the fortuitous by-product of producing a right-of-way for the freeway.

What became known as "the freeway debate" came to a head in 1967. By then, Bill Rathie had been replaced as mayor by Tom Campbell who Hardwick described as "a man with no clearly-articulated public position on civic development." On June 1, City Council gave notice that it intended to proceed with the component of the Vancouver Transportation Study that called for the first phase of the freeway system to be built through Chinatown.

Council reluctantly agreed to refer the decision to a public hearing on June 15, where it was revealed that no significant alternatives to the freeway had been considered and that there had been no evaluation of the proposal within the broader context of an overall transportation system, either at the city or the regional scale. When it became clear that the city council's decision had far-reaching ramifications that had not been fully considered, it decided to pause the process pending a further review of alternatives by consultants. The pause extended not only to the Chinatown freeway planning but also to planning for the Waterfront Freeway which had implications for the planning of major development proposals. There was further concern when City Manager Gerald Sutton-Brown refused to broaden the scope of the review of alternatives to be conducted by the consultants, highlighting the fact that the links were part of a larger system whose overall viability would be brought into question by a broader review. Mayor Campbell was scornful of the opponents, who he described as "Maoists, communists, pinkos, left-wingers, and hamburgers."

The forces lined up in favour of the freeway were formidable and included the downtown business community and, through their cost-sharing in the urban renewal land acquisition process, the federal and provincial governments. The most troubling aspect of the issue for those who questioned the wisdom of the freeway proposal was the absence of any overall plan for the city, particularly its transportation system, which would provide a context for such an important decision. Protests grew in the fall of 1967.

There was growing outrage in the Chinese community and the cause was joined by UBC students who marched in Chinatown in sympathy on October 19. A group of twelve professors signed a letter opposing the freeway and indicated their intent to attend the public hearing planned for later in the fall.

The public hearing on the freeway proposals was held on November 23, 1967 at City Hall. The time allotted was quickly used up by presentations supporting the proposal from the city's consultants and staff, and a second hearing was scheduled for two weeks later, December 7, at Eric Hamber Secondary School. The two hearings have been described as among the stormiest in Vancouver's history, which is saying a lot. Nearly all the presentations condemned the work the city and its consultants had done and were opposed to the proposal.

One of the exceptions was the presentation from the Town Planning Commission, of which Peter Oberlander had been elected the Chair in 1965. Although some members of the Commission felt that they should have been given more input to the decision by City Council, the advisory body had prepared a submission in support of the proposed freeway.

Oberlander discharged his duty as Chair of the Commission by reading its supportive brief, and then he resigned on the spot in protest. The crowd of 800 erupted in a standing ovation. In a question that summed up his core beliefs as a professional and a citizen, he asked,

> What kind of city do the people want? Planning is too serious a matter to leave solely to professional civic officials…The overall plan must come first, and the transportation fitted into it, not the other way around….The city must review its role in planning, it must take planning closer to the public.

The protests, culminating in Oberlander's resignation, punctured City Council's appetite for the freeway proposals, and in January 1968 it rescinded its June 1967 motion to proceed with them. The decision is now recognized as a watershed in Vancouver's history. By the time the freeway issue could be revisited, urban freeway plans were the subject of widespread opposition and revision in many North American cities. Most notable was the decision by Ontario Premier William Davis in 1971 to kill the Spadina Expressway in Toronto, saying, "Cities are for people, not cars."

Equally important, if not more so, was the way in which the experience summed up for many what was wrong at City Hall. As the freeway debate unfolded, and it became clear how little control over the city's affairs was being exercised by members of council, let alone the citizens, a group began to form the nucleus of a new political party. After initial meetings in private residences, including Walter Hardwick's on 49th Avenue and Peter and Cornelia Oberlander's on Olympic Street, the core group called a founding meeting of the new organization, to be called The Electors' Action Movement (TEAM) at the Grandview Community Centre on the evening of March 12, 1968. The chair of the meeting, Art Phillips, described TEAM as "not anti-NPA, not anti-NDP, but only for the whole city."

Phillips was elected President. The First Vice-President was the Teamsters' Union's Ed Lawson (later a Senator) and the Second Vice-President was Bill Bellman, founder of the super-sophisticated new "easy listening" radio station, CHQM. Walter Hardwick and Peter Oberlander became directors. TEAM was always open to participation from outside the boundaries of the City of Vancouver, and Don Lanskail, a lawyer from West Vancouver, who later became mayor of that municipality, had done the initial legal work to set up the organization (including suggesting its name) and became a Director.

At the meeting, Peter Oberlander outlined the deliberations of the Policy Committee which he had chaired. While he stressed that the new group's policies must emerge from the membership, he suggested they must encompass "human issues, economic issues, development and planning issues and governmental relations."

Art Phillips announced that the organization had established an office in the venerable Rogers Building at 470 Granville Street.

"TEAM had two wings," May Brown later explained. "One was devoted to figuring out how to fight an election, the other was on policy. Walter Hardwick led that group. I give him tremendous credit." Fifteen policy sub-committees prepared ideas for a consideration at policy conferences. "We had daylong policy meetings," Marguerite Ford recalled, "We had policies on *everything*. It was that agreement on policy that was fundamental to the cohesion of the group."

The scope of policies prepared and approved by TEAM was broad. Two key themes were that people elected under the TEAM banner would act in concert and be constructive. It was not sufficient to be opposed to freeways, for example, alternatives were necessary. So, a group led by Art Cowie and Bill McCreery prepared proposals for regional rapid transit and for a water-based transit crossing of Burrard Inlet that became the SeaBus.

TEAM's policies on city government included the restoration of City Council's authority, reorganization of the administration, provision of greater opportunities for public participation through neighbourhood planning processes, support for regional action on planning, transportation and housing, and coordination of planning and services for libraries, parks and schools at a neighbourhood scale. A key focus was on the use of the City's extensive land holdings; in the past, property had been sold to provide revenue to keep taxes down. TEAM proposed that land should be treated as an endowment to be leased, not sold, for an annual return to the City for civic purposes.

Not surprisingly, planning and development of the city was a major policy focus for TEAM. The organization supported retention of existing viable commercial and residential areas, provision of opportunities for mixed-use development and negotiation of a fair share of the profits generated by the City's development decisions for public benefit. One of the policies which would have the greatest impact was the proposal to redevelop the south and north shores of False Creek. This would lead to the conversion of an obsolescent industrial area and a waterway that was an open sewer into a neighbourhood of housing for a mix of incomes, marinas, new community facilities and public waterfront access as part of the goal of recouping public access to all of the City's 45-kilometres of waterfront.

TEAM's policies on parks and recreation reinforced the emphasis on providing better services for people by treating parks as activity centres rather than passive open space and by pursuing opportunities for integration of parks, recreation, schools and other City services. The best example of the eventual impact of these policies is the development of the Britannia Community Services centre, incorporating park space, K-12 education facilities, a branch library and a community centre and pool on a 17-hectare site jointly managed by representatives of the various City functions plus a community association.

In public education, TEAM espoused a child-based, individualized learning model to develop a wide range of competencies extending beyond straight academic accomplishment to include excellence in social and physical education designed to equip youth to participate effectively in a changing world. Decision-making was to be opened up to participation by teachers, students and community representatives.

Peter Oberlander later described the significance of the policy process undertaken by TEAM:

> Until 1968, everyone ran on an independent basis. But it never occurred to the electorate to ask what kinds of people comprised City Council. So there was no coherence, no cohesion because they didn't belong to a single party, and they had no platform. The important thing about TEAM in 1968 was to change that process to make it a political party, to create a platform, to get a lot of people to support joint policies and hang together through caucus, i.e., introducing the idea of a political system at the local level.

Later in the year, TEAM held a nominating meeting. Alan Emmott, the popular Reeve (Mayor) of Burnaby, had been recruited to run for Mayor of Vancouver under the TEAM banner. A key basis for his candidacy was the amalgamation of Burnaby and Vancouver. His nomination was approved by motion. Full slates of candidates for Council, the School Board and Parks Board were nominated. There was a deliberate strategy at work, as Oberlander recalled later: "We had to split our resources and learn how to do it, in order to set the stage for what was to come. It was a very deliberate choice. Walter suggested that we do this in stages and so we allocated each other's skills and resources."

In the elections later that year, Emmott failed to unseat Tom Campbell as mayor, but Art Phillips and Walter Hardwick of TEAM won two of the 10 seats on Council. Helen Boyce won a seat on the Parks Board.

TEAM had the most success in the elections for the School Board, for which Peter Oberlander was nominated. He remembered:

> I had always been interested in education. The School Board had been in a messed-up situation, and I decided to run for School Board along with Fritz Bowers [another UBC professor who would later become a member of Council and then City Manager] and Peter

Bullen. There were three of us, and we all got in. We topped the polls with more votes than Tom Campbell who never forgave me for that although he was elected as mayor.

The reform spirit in Vancouver was undoubtedly assisted by the winds of change which were beginning to blow in North America, prompted by resistance to US involvement in the Vietnam War, the assassinations of Martin Luther King and Robert F. Kennedy in the spring of 1968, and violent protests at the Democratic National Convention in Chicago.

At the federal level in Canada, in April 1968, the country was energized by the choice by the Liberal Party of Peter Oberlander's friend and Harvard colleague, Pierre Trudeau, as the leader to replace Lester B. Pearson. He won a majority government in June. His motto, "reason over passion," dovetailed nicely with the TEAM platform's emphasis on a comprehensive approach to civic governance, and his concern for individual rights collectively protected, as exemplified by the Charter of Rights and Freedoms, resonated with TEAM's emphasis on democracy and empowerment.

Once elected, the TEAM politicians gave life to the principle that they should work together on their common agenda. As Oberlander put it,

> We were able to have a caucus and for the first time we had an opportunity to coordinate policies across these levels. The idea of caucus between City Council, Parks Board and School Board was itself an innovation. We would meet every other week; I would read the council minutes, which I hadn't done before. We knew what other parts of the system were doing or plotting, It wasn't a revolt with barricades, but it was a radical change about how to do business, how to go from a small scale, a small town notion of housekeeping to a determined policy-based initiative of deliberate change based on consultation and debate.

At the School Board, Oberlander was immersed in a process to open up the school system and its governance to the community. Board meetings were held in local schools with an opportunity for the public to ask questions. Five local area assistant superintendents were put in place to bring the administration closer to neighbourhoods. Parent consultative committees were established in each school, along with a city-wide parent assembly. A wide range of school-community programs was established, including native home school coordinators, mothers and tots English programs and English as a second language programs operated by volunteers. Multicultural workers provided interpretation of school programs for various linguistic and cultural groups. Alternative school programs were established for gifted students, French immersion students and those with special mental or physical needs.

Peter Oberlander served as Chair of the Vancouver School Board in 1969-70. He considered running for City Council in 1970 but demurred because of his impending departure for Ottawa to serve in the Trudeau government as the first Secretary of the Ministry of State for Urban Affairs (see Chapter 8).

At the council level, the period between 1968 and 1972 was described by Paul Tennant, a UBC political science professor and TEAM activist, as

> Critical years in Vancouver politics, marked by half a dozen major political battles over urban renewal and redevelopment...In each case, the pattern was the same as in the great freeway debate. TEAM aldermen and the COPE (Committee of Progressive Electors) representative led the attack within council while citizen groups formed and fought within the community against the proposal. In each case, the mayor and almost all the NPA aldermen supported the developments, although as least two NPA council members sided with the citizen groups to provide an opposition majority on council. In each case, the citizens and the progressive members of council were victorious: the proposal was either stopped completely or postponed.

Although the election of 1970 produced relatively little in the way of change on Council, the Parks Board or the School Board, the muscle being exerted by TEAM was having a significant effect. This was evidenced in the election of 1972, in which the NPA did not even run a candidate for mayor, and TEAM swept into power with Art Phillips as mayor and eight seats on Council: the re-elected Walter Hardwick plus Fritz Bowers, William Gibson, Mike Harcourt, Geoff Massey, Darlene Marzari, Setty Pendakur and Jack Volrich. TEAM elected four members to the Parks Board and a majority to the School Board.

TEAM Councillors elected in 1972. Rear, left to right: Setty Pendakur, Walter Hardwick, Michael Harcourt, Geoffrey Massey. Front, Jack Volrich, Mayor Arthur Phillips, Darlene Marzari, Fritz Bowers. Absent: William Gibson.[17]

In his inaugural address to the incoming council on January 3, 1973, Mayor Phillips set the tone for the new administration. He graciously acknowledged the contributions of a number of departing long-serving members of council, including former Mayor Tom Campbell "whose flair for flamboyant statements will be hard to match."

Phillips set out the way in which the new administration proposed to implement its policy priorities. "We have said for some time that we intended to make City government more open — more responsive and accessible to the citizens. We intend to do this." He went on to propose the establishment of an information booth in the main lobby of City Hall, greater use of evening meetings for council, committees and public hearings and assignment of areas of the city to sitting aldermen "as a step in the direction of area representation," a question he proposed be studied by a council committee with participation by members of the Parks and School Boards. He added that he would ask Council to approve the hiring of a young man named Gordon Campbell as a Special Assistant in the Mayor's Office to respond to public enquiries and requests for help. Campbell would later be elected to city council, serving as an alderman and later mayor, Chair of the Greater Vancouver Regional District and President of the Union of British Columbia Municipalities before becoming Premier of British Columbia. With the by-then retired Walter Hardwick, in 1990 Campbell would lead the "Creating our Future" process at the Greater Vancouver Regional District that set the agenda for the Greater Vancouver region for a decade.

"We have said that we wanted the elected representatives to take charge." The Mayor continued, "We intend to do this too." The city administration would be "de-centralized," which would lead to the departure of Sutton-Brown and the provision of more independence to department heads and their staff. Phillips proposed a new standing committee structure and the assignment of key roles to members of council, including the non-TEAM members. In addition, he suggested that special committees be created to tackle problems such as the quaintly-named "skid road housing" in what is now known as the Downtown East Side and the downtown waterfront. The special committee on False Creek created by the previous council and chaired by Walter Hardwick was to be continued.

Phillips devoted particular attention to the City's participation in the Greater Vancouver Regional District, which he said would "be increasingly important to the future of Vancouver. The City Council must play a much more positive part in the development of the Greater Vancouver Regional District. All members of Council must be involved and fully acquainted with the activities of the Regional District. In the past, they were not." It was the basis for one commentator's later observation that "The GVRD works when the City of Vancouver takes it seriously — and vice versa."

In closing, Mayor Phillips reserved several items for his personal attention. One was the City's management of its own land, estimated at that time to be worth at least $60 million. "I do not believe that the City should continue its policy of selling off roughly $2 million worth of land a year in order to help finance capital programs. I do believe that the City could manage its land in such a way as to benefit the taxpayers of the city and also bring about more desirable development in the city." This proposal resulted in the creation of the Property Endowment Fund, to hold and lease City property for the benefit of present and future generations. The fund currently returns about $50 million per year to the City.

Reflecting on the recent election of the New Democratic Party to provincial office, Mayor Phillips outlined some matters for consideration with the new administration. Topping the list was "the Block 51/61/71 area in downtown Vancouver where the previous government had planned to build a 55-storey skyscraper." The result of Mayor Phillips' discussions with the new provincial administration was the Robson Square provincial court and office complex designed by Arthur Erickson with Cornelia Oberlander as the landscape architect, which would be completed in 1983.

Robson Square was first described as a skyscraper on its side, but in reality, it was a graceful and people-friendly addition to the downtown, reflecting a respectful urban presence for the province in contrast to the domineering edifice the previous administration had been pursuing. Erickson biographer Nicholas Olsberg would describe the design as follows:

> Arthur came in and said, "This won't be a corporate monument. Let's turn it on its side and let people walk all over it." And he anchored it in such a way with the courts — the law — at one end and the museum — the arts — at the other. The foundations of society. And underneath it all, the government offices quietly supporting their people. It's almost a spiritual progression.

It was prescient that Mayor Phillips would close his 1973 inaugural address by saying, "As Arthur Erickson once observed, 'North Americans have regarded their cities as places to work in and get out of, rather than places to live in and enjoy.' I think all that is changing."

TEAM functioned as a successful political party under Phillips, achieving electoral victories in the 1974 and 1976 elections. By 1979, Phillips had stepped down to seek a seat in the Parliament of Canada, and Jack Volrich succeeded him, running under the NPA banner. May Brown and Marguerite Ford brought new energy to the party in the late 1970s and made particularly important contributions at the regional level in parks and planning respectively. For his bid for the mayoralty in 1980, Mike Harcourt left TEAM to run successfully against Volrich as an independent. By 1982, TEAM had ceased to function as an effective party.

On May 20, 2010, a "TEAM Reunion" was held at the Museum of Vancouver to review TEAM's accomplishments from the perspective of nearly 40 years later. A number of achievements already mentioned here figured prominently in the discussion: False Creek, a transit-oriented transportation system, support for regionalism, a modernized city administration, a more open government and countless neighbourhood-specific improvements.

The meeting was addressed by Ray Spaxman, one of TEAM's early appointees as Director of Planning, who served from 1973 to 1989. He referred to the basic principles that underlay TEAM's more than 200 policies:

- Local politicians should be representative of every part of the city.
- Policies and processes should concentrate on people, not things, and focus on creating a better and more livable city.
- Municipal operations should be transparent, informative and encourage public involvement and discussion about changes planned for the city.
- Council should set out environmental, social and financial objectives and create the policies and plans to effect needed change.

Spaxman identified the redevelopment of False Creek among TEAM's most significant achievements:

> This was the time when the City initiated the complete revitalization of False Creek. It has changed from an industrial area of serious land, air and water pollution into what we tentatively conceived at the time, as a vibrant central city area oriented to and around a 200-acre area of accessible recreational water, walkways and parklands stitching together a ribbon of new neighbourhoods.

> False Creek was the first place anywhere in Canada to set and achieve the now enviable social goals of accommodating one-third low income, one-third mid-income and one-third higher income residences in a comprehensively designed inner city neighbourhood. It also achieved a high diversity of rental, subsidized, co-op and market housing of all types of occupancy and population profiles. The elementary school was built early. Bus service was provided before the place was completed to establish the public transit habit early in its development. It was the first place to follow the principles of planning promoted by Jane Jacobs, Christopher Alexander, Kevin Lynch and other notable design theorists.

Spaxman concluded his assessment by linking TEAM's early ideas to the concept of Vancouverism:

> While there are many theories (and credit-takers) about how the internationally renowned "Vancouverism" came about, I am convinced it was initiated by TEAM in the 70s. It was the combined abilities of Art Phillips and Walter Hardwick and their TEAM colleagues and those fundamental principles that TEAM articulated in its early days that shifted the nature of governance and planning in this city. They produced much of what we can admire about Vancouver today. It may be that those same humanistic principles need to be revisited today to deal with our current challenges.

The organization founded by Phillips, Hardwick, Peter Oberlander, and others had brought profound but peaceful change to a city that had seemed to teeter on the brink of social and physical disruption and decay. They had opened up its governance to the citizenry on the basis of fundamental principles of democratic control and rational, evidence-based decision-making. They had shown how people from the academy, the corporate sector and civil society can work constructively for the benefit of the community.

They had also put in place the basic framework of plans and ideas that could attract the constructive participation of other levels of government, working in support of community aspirations rather than in pursuit of their own agendas. Robson Square was - is - a graphic demonstration of the power of these ideas.

It would not be long before the federal government would be brought to the table constructively in projects such as Granville Island. In this, as with so many other examples of city building, Peter Oberlander would play a catalytic role.

CHAPTER EIGHT:

BETWEEN A ROCK AND A HARD PLACE: THE MINISTRY OF STATE FOR URBAN AFFAIRS

Peter Oberlander was fond of stating that the city is one of humanity's most beneficial and complex creations. It can be best understood as an organism, created and altered through the interplay of a vast array of human and natural influences. As with all organisms, different parts of the city play different roles in the success of the whole and the city grows and changes in response to stimuli.

To survive and prosper, the city must ensure that various basic functions are carried out, ranging from defence and life support through the basics of food and water and places to live and work through to the trading activities that allow a city to prosper — or not — through relationships with their hinterlands and other cities. Cities are the means by which humanity generates the surpluses of income, wealth and time that allow arts, culture, learning and technological progress to flourish.

Given the origins and basic organic nature of cities, which predate most of the constitutional institutions of the modern nation state, it would be hard to identify a subject matter in which terminology has created more confusion than urban policy. The constitution of Canada was created at a time when the focus of government was on extending governance and control over vast areas of unpopulated or underpopulated terrain and the treasure trove of natural resources which the colonizing powers assumed were theirs for the taking, notwithstanding the prior occupation of these lands and ownership of these resources by First Nations "from time immemorial."

The Fathers of Confederation conceived of Canada as a country in which responsibilities were to be divided between two orders of sovereign government on the principle of subsidiarity, which held that only matters related to the larger entity such as money and banking, interprovincial trade, and external relations would be assigned to the federal government, with the provinces assuming responsibility for matters of a local or regional nature.

As local government advocates and others like to point out, the constitution does not even mention cities or urban development. The closest it comes is to say that the provinces are responsible for "municipal institutions in the province." Perhaps equally important, given that cities are about land and people, is the assignment to the provinces of "civil and property rights within the province." To most observers for the first 100 years of Confederation, the equation was simple: "cities" equals "municipal institutions" equals "exclusive provincial jurisdiction."

Of course, it was never that simple. As Oberlander observed in his PhD thesis, central and colonial government had very often played a key role in the establishment and growth of cities, from the site selection and basic layouts for Halifax and Quebec City to the founding of the City of New Westminster by the Royal Engineers.

The rapid industrial development sparked by World War II and the urban development that followed its end in 1945 gave new urgency to federal and provincial interests in cities, including the establishment of the Wartime Housing Company and the enactment of the *National Housing Act* (1945) and the creation of the Lower Mainland Regional Planning Board in British Columbia (1949). By the end of the 1960s, more progressive provinces had embarked on provincially-led regional planning policies such as Ontario's Design for Development program, which sought to structure urban growth and expand the management capacity of local government through reorganization and the introduction of new regional government structures.

In its *Fourth Annual Review* in 1967, the Economic Council of Canada set out the challenges posed by urbanization for Canada's economy and society. It noted that Canada was among the most rapidly urbanizing countries in the world, with about 65 per cent of its population living in cities and sixty-one cities with a population of 100,000 or more.

The council saw no practical upper limit to the country's urbanization; 81 per cent of the population was forecast to be living in urban areas by 1980, adding to "the mounting collective requirements of the urban population." The council concluded,

> The dimensions of this challenge — of the need to provide adequately for urban housing, balanced transport systems, water supply and waste disposal, parks and recreation, the control of air pollution and many other urban services, all within the framework of efficient, orderly growth and an environment of improving quality — undoubtedly call for new and imaginative public policies involving all three levels of government, including new priorities in the allocation of resources.

The political implications for the federal government of a nation of cities were obvious.

The dying days of the Pearson administration saw a Federal-Provincial Conference on Housing and Urban Development on December 11 and 12 1967. Pearson had decided to step down (the formal announcement was to come on December 14) and various candidates — declared and undeclared — were vying to be his successor. On the night of December 11, the government very nearly fell from power on a confidence vote in the House of Commons, and an atmosphere of disarray permeated the conference.

The meeting was vividly described by Peter Oberlander's old friend Humphrey Carver in *Compassionate Landscape*. The first day was dominated by the provincial premiers "each making a formal statement, to display on the television screens of the nation, their most endearing style and territorial imperatives, like so many exotic birds displaying their plumage in some kind of sexual dance."

Although CMHC had put a considerable effort into preparing a series of proposed amendments to the *National Housing Act* for discussion, the minister responsible (John Nicholson) was not up to the task of presenting them. Pearson called on Paul Hellyer, the Minister of Transport, to speak about transport, after which Pearson introduced the idea, apparently hatched in his own office, of an intergovernmental council on urban development. One by one, the premiers politely but effectively strangled this idea to death. The conference was, Carver observed, a disaster, and "the beginning of about five years of stumbling and confusion in housing and urban affairs."

Hellyer had been a senior member of Pearson's cabinet and is still remembered, without much affection, for his determination as Minister of National

Defence to unify Canada's armed forces - the Army, Navy and Air Force - under a single command and uniform. He was a candidate to follow Pearson as the leader of the Liberal Party and Prime Minister, placing second after Pierre Trudeau on the first ballot before losing momentum. Trudeau not only won the leadership but went on to win a comfortable majority of the seats in the House of Commons in the general election held on June 25, 1968.

As was the tradition in those days, failed leadership candidates were given prominent roles in the government established by the victor. Hellyer served as Senior Minister (equivalent to Deputy Prime Minister), Minister of Transport and Minister responsible for Housing in the incoming Trudeau administration. He set up a Task Force on Housing and Urban Development and installed himself as Chair, a move that Carver suggests was an early and serious error. At UBC, Peter Oberlander's SCARP students were given class assignments preparing submissions to the Task Force.

Hellyer studiously avoided seeking the advice of the federal public servants in CMHC and elsewhere. He had a consummate faith in his own intellect, as evidenced by his lifelong belief that the earth was regularly visited by aliens who were responsible for many technological advances. In 1967, while Minister of National Defence (!), he attended a special ceremony to inaugurate an Unidentified Flying Object landing pad, a Centennial project of the Town of St. Paul, Alberta.

One of the somewhat startling side-effects of a Minister chairing a Task Force was the opportunity to make policy decisions on the run. When the Task Force visited Vancouver for a public meeting on November 7, 1968, they heard about the plight of Strathcona and Chinatown residents being forced from the homes they owned to make way for the urban renewal project which was financed by federal and provincial funds. The issue was conflated with the Freeway Debate, which a year earlier had culminated with Peter Oberlander's resignation as Chair of the Vancouver Town Planning Commission.

The Task Force was accompanied by Lloyd Axworthy as Hellyer's executive assistant who would later serve as Canada's Minister for Foreign Affairs in the government of Jean Chrétien and as the president of the University of Winnipeg. The young assistant was buttonholed by a spokesperson for the property owners, Shirley Chan, and a newly hired staff member in the City's Social Planning Department, Darlene Marzari, for a tour of the area affected and a chance to meet its residents. As a result, the next day the Minister issued an edict (by means of a telegram at least partially drafted by Chan and Marzari) freezing funding for urban renewal projects across Canada. It signalled a shift in emphasis from a top-down, bulldozer approach to urban renewal to one that supported rehabilitation of existing housing and neighbourhoods with the active involvement and consent of the affected residents.

Hellyer completed the Task Force report and, in a further strategic error, made it public in January 1969 before its recommendations had been considered by the federal cabinet. The report contained forty-seven recommendations, most of them focused on ways to improve the production of housing and based upon the then-controversial premise that public control, if not outright ownership, of land is essential. The report was particularly damning on the subject of public housing as it was then delivered in Canada, recommending that the program be suspended until its effects could be understood better. One recommendation that found wide support was that a federal ministry of housing and urban development be created.

When Hellyer finally presented his already-public recommendations to the federal cabinet in April 1969, they were rejected, and he had no choice but to resign from the government, with what Carver describes as "a roll of thunder and a flash of lightning."

While progress on the housing file continued, with the introduction of *National Housing Act* amendments later in 1969, the central question about the Task Force was, in Axworthy's retrospection, that "it was implicitly raising the basic question of whether a democratic system could survive in the kind of urban society that was being created in Canada."

Although they might not have agreed with Axworthy's characterization of the challenge posed by the Hellyer Task Force, officials in the Privy Council Office under Michael Pitfield were trying to devise ways in which the federal government could provide political leadership on complex problems, such as urban affairs, that had no clear jurisdictional home. The ultimate result was the establishment of Ministries of State under the *Government Organization Act*, which was passed in 1969. Although no specific responsibilities were assigned in this legislation, it provided that a Ministry of State could be created and supported by a secretariat and staff. As Pitfield later observed, the legislation was "not intended to be used to form permanent line departments." Ultimately, three ministries of state would be created by the Trudeau government: for Social Development, for Economic Development and for Urban Affairs.

Robert Andras, a car dealer from Port Arthur (now part of Thunder Bay as a result of the Ontario government's municipal reform initiatives), who had been elected in 1965, was appointed in July 1969 to assume Hellyer's former responsibilities as a Minister without Portfolio for housing, the first time housing had not been handled from the corner of the desk of a minister with a full set of other responsibilities. Andras commissioned an economics professor from Carleton University, Harvey Lithwick, to write a report "which would assist the federal government to determine what, if any, role it should play in urban affairs and the likely consequences of such a role."

Considerable political pressure to "do something about cities" was developing. Phil Givens, the former mayor of Toronto, had been elected in 1968 after hearing Trudeau speak lyrically about the role of cities as "dynamic centres of learning, creativity and culture" and believed that the new Prime Minister was "a kindred spirit" in the cause of greater federal support for cities. Once in Parliament, Givens seems to have chosen a path that would all but guarantee that his pleas for cities would fall on deaf ears with the key players in the Trudeau government: he irately criticized the government's inaction publicly and belittled the smaller provinces and their leaders because their populations were so insignificant compared to big places such as, well, Toronto. He resigned to run provincially in Ontario before the end of his term. Another Liberal caucus member, Perry Ryan, crossed the floor to join the opposition Conservatives over the same issue.

For their part, the Conservatives under Opposition Leader Robert Stanfield were also beginning to cultivate cities. In 1970, Stanfield made high-profile visits to Toronto and other cities and spoke to the Canadian Federation of Mayors and Municipalities about the need for a new federal ministry for urban affairs that would enable the federal government to, at a minimum, enhance its awareness of the impact on cities of its policies in areas such as employment and immigration. Stanfield appointed a caucus task force on urban affairs under veteran MP Alvin Hamilton.

Lithwick's report, *Urban Canada: Problems and Prospects,* was submitted in March 1970. It was supported by six monographs on the subjects of: urban poverty, housing, urban transport, the urban public economy, the urban future and alternative urban policies.

Taken together, the report and monographs were the most comprehensive description and analysis of Canada's urban problems that had yet been prepared. The analysis attempted to pinpoint those "urban" problems that were "of the city," in other words, the result of the process of urbanization and its interdependencies, in contrast to those that were "in the city" just because of the concentration of people in urban areas. In this framework, public transportation, for example, would be seen as a problem "of the city," while poverty would be a problem "in the city."

The language of Lithwick's report was academic and abstruse — Carver compared it to "reading a professional economist's validation of the propositions of Jesus Christ" — but it was clear enough that urbanization was a significant modern problem for Canada as a whole and a suitable subject for the attention of the federal government.

The main report contained a sweeping challenge:

> The roots of the urban problem lie in the very process of urbanization itself. This in turn is an essential dimension of national economic development. Solving the urban problem requires first and foremost a clear understanding of this relationship. Attempts to remove the symptoms alone have been and will continue to be as effective as pushing on a string. Any long-term solution must deal with the urbanization process. It must remove the inherent constraint of space which leads to the degenerative conditions associated with urbanization, while preserving the great benefits that are created by that process. To expect solutions on a scale that is far superceded [sic] by the magnitude of the problem is naïve. Yet this problem will be the one facing most Canadians in the decades to come. Dealing with it will not and cannot be simple. Alternatives are at hand that might provide the solution, but they require a new depth and breadth of vision and of commitment — nothing less than a national urban policy.

Later in the report, Lithwick summed up the options: "We have presented two broad alternatives. The first accepts the urban system and seeks to improve the required weaponry. The second seeks to choose its own battlefield." Leaving aside the metaphor that portrays urban policy as some kind of a war, anyone familiar with the political and constitutional realities of Canada in the 1960s could be forgiven for thinking that the time for choosing a new "battlefield" for urban policy was about 100 years past.

The creation of a Ministry of State for Urban Affairs was clearly signalled by the government in the fall of 1970.

It is not clear whether Harvey Lithwick or others made the wise decision that he would not be a suitable choice as the Ministry of State for Urban Affairs' first Secretary, although he obviously had a good deal to offer. One need look no further than his comprehensive report for evidence of this; although masterful in its sweep and scope, its propositions were nearly impenetrable and appear to have studiously avoided any ideas that could lead to concrete action. "Paralysis by analysis" would be the likely outcome.

So it was that the phone rang on the evening of Sunday, November 22, 1970 in Peter and Cornelia Oberlander's new home on Acadia Road in the University Endowment Lands residential community adjacent to UBC. Cornelia was cleaning up after serving dinner to Peter and their three children, then aged 10, 12 and 13. Cornelia remembers, "The voice on the phone said, 'This is your Prime Minister. I would like to speak to Professor Oberlander.' I put on my best Smith College voice and said I would get him." Trudeau offered Peter the new position of Secretary of the Ministry of State for Urban Affairs.

The appointment must have had some logic for Trudeau. He would have remembered Peter from Harvard, and they had enjoyed a skiing holiday in Europe when both were living in England. And there had been the encounter in Jean Sutherland Boggs' salon in Cambridge, Massachusetts in the mid-1940s, where Trudeau and Oberlander had debated whether federal governments in federated states had any role to play in the affairs of their nations' cities. The Prime Minister's assistant, Tim Porteous, had come across Oberlander's Harvard PhD thesis, "Community Planning and Housing: An Aspect of Canadian Federalism," in the Parliamentary Library and had brought it to Trudeau's attention. Clearly Peter had a comprehensive, rational view of urban policy in a federal context, and he seemed to be good at starting things.

Peter sought a leave of absence from UBC and accepted the position, starting in January 1971. He commuted between Vancouver and Ottawa for the remainder of the 1970-71 academic year. One of his last official acts was to preside over the graduation of the first PhDs from the School of Community and Regional Planning — and the first in Canada. At Community Planning Consultants, he instructed Robert Furukawa to "hold the fort and keep it going." Clearly, no bridges were being burned.

The purpose of the Ministry of State for Urban Affairs was set out in the Speech from the Throne on October 8, 1970:

> To foster coordination of the activities of all levels of government and contribute to sound urban growth and development, the Government proposes the re-organization of its urban activities under the direction of a Minister of State for Urban Affairs and Housing. The Government seeks, by making rational its efforts in these fields, and through consultation with those most directly concerned, to help Canadians reach and implement the decisions that will determine their urban future.

A week after the Speech, Peter Oberlander had gone to Ottawa for preliminary talks about the role and responsibilities of the Ministry. Two weeks after that, the October crisis occurred, a crisis that Ottawa treated as a direct challenge to the country's stability and power to govern itself. It would be July 1971 before the dust had settled enough for the proclamation establishing the Ministry to be debated and passed in the House of Commons.

One issue raised in the debate in the House was the selection of the Ministry of State mechanism, intended to be temporary in duration, for urban affairs. The leader of the New Democratic Party, T.C. Douglas, a former Premier of Saskatchewan, observed that "Housing and urban affairs are not a temporary matter." Perhaps the choice reflected the view of another Saskatchewan native in Ottawa, the mandarin Tom Shoyama who later stated that "Ottawa wasn't sure there was an urban crisis," reflecting an ambivalence that dogged the Ministry throughout its existence.

The Ministry was to develop policies for implementation within federal jurisdiction for three areas of focus:

- The ways in which the federal government, through its own programs, could have a beneficial influence on urbanization (it was estimated that there were 117 major such programs spread through twenty-seven different departments);
- Integration of urban policy with other federal policies and programs; and
- Fostering co-operative relationships on urban affairs with provinces and, through them, municipalities, and with the public and private organizations.

The Ministry's organizational structure reflected these areas of focus:

- An Assistant Secretary for Coordination and Development would look for opportunities for constructive engagement for "beneficial influence" "on the ground" through regional coordinators for each of the five major regions of Canada (British Columbia, the Prairie provinces, Ontario, Quebec and the Atlantic provinces) with the assistance of a "participation secretariat";
- An Assistant Secretary for Policy and Research would undertake the research and policy development work necessary for a more coherent approach to urban issues, both by influencing ongoing federal programs of relevance to urban development and by formulating urban policies for "integration" with other federal policies and programs; and
- The vesting, in the office of the Secretary, of responsibility for "fostering cooperative relationships" with provinces, municipalities and others, supported by a "Director of Bilateral and Multilateral Relations."

It was, perhaps, not accidental that the Ministry structure resembled a municipal planning department, with a "long-range planning" wing (Policy and Research) responsible for the official planning policies and the knowledge base, and a "current planning wing" (Coordination and Development) responsible for processing proposals and pursuing opportunities generated from outside the organization.

The role of Assistant Secretary for Coordination and Development went to André Saumier, an intelligent and literate public servant who, since being recruited to Ottawa from the Quebec government, had been involved in developing the Ministry of State concept in the Privy Council Office and was invited by Robert Andras to join the new Ministry. He would later go on to be President of the Montréal Stock Exchange. Harvey Lithwick was appointed Assistant Secretary for Research and Policy Development.

Oberlander and his new Ministry of State were between a rock — the Ottawa power structure — and a hard place — the provincial governments — from the start.

Official Ottawa at that time was a place of siloed departments and agencies whose senior officials' and ministers' power was defined by "clout" — how many programs, dollars and people you controlled. Ottawa's power and influence in the country was growing significantly as a result of generally positive economic growth that produced tax revenues that were more than enough for the federal government to discharge its responsibilities leaving it free — in the view of the provinces, anyway — to exploit its "spending power" by invading areas of provincial jurisdiction.

Official Ottawa at the time was still run by many of the people who had overseen the country's war effort and reconstruction with efficiency and bloody-mindedness, a mandarinate of men who lived north of the Green Belt established in Jacques Gréber's 1950 plan for the National Capital Region. If they were not themselves members of the Five Lakes Fishing Club, a weekend social club in the Gatineau region near Ottawa where little fishing ever got done, they knew people who were.

Oberlander had spent some time in Ottawa after the war and had been an avid follower of national affairs and federal politics since then, but he was by no means an "Ottawa man." Saumier, who had spent more time in Ottawa, later compared the traditional federal departments to "the Macedonian phalanx: irresistible when finally on the move, but ponderous and mindless."

As to the question of "clout," by definition, the Ministry of State for Urban Affairs had no programs, few dollars and relatively few staff. "Coordination" was a wussy term in Ottawa at that time. A "coordinator" was defined by one wag with Ottawa experience at that time as "Someone who gets between two people or agencies who would otherwise work together."

The "hard place" the Ministry confronted was the provincial governments collectively.

The future of Quebec — in or outside Canada — was the burning question, which had been accentuated by the October Crisis in the fall of 1970. The country looked to Pierre Trudeau to define a future where the two European founding peoples (French and English) and their cultures could prosper throughout the land or, failing that, to "put Quebec in its place."

Other provinces shared Quebec's resentment, to greater or lesser degree, of the apparent expansion of federal power into areas of provincial jurisdiction. Ontario, under Premier John Robarts, stepped forward to articulate the sovereign role of provinces; such a role was natural for the original Province of Upper Canada and the most populous and prosperous province in the federation. A case in point for Robarts with resonance today was the then recent successful effort by the federal government to bring about the introduction of Medicare, which he described, in his gravelly voice, as a "Machiavellian fraud."

Robarts assembled his fellow premiers at the Confederation of Tomorrow Conference in November 1967 to set out the basis for provincial priorities in an amended Constitution of Canada in which the federal and provincial governments would each have "disentangled" responsibilities and access to appropriate revenues sufficient to enable them to discharge them. The Government of Canada was not invited.

Notwithstanding the prickly relationship between Ontario and the federal government on constitutional matters, the fact remained that Ontario was the most urbanized province with the longest track record of managing urban growth through provincial policy. It was clear to Peter Oberlander that, if ever there were to be a suitable provincial partner — or adversary — for the federal government for a constructive approach to urban development, Ontario would be it. This was also evident to one of Oberlander's recent students, Ken Cameron, who had just finished a master's degree at SCARP where he had studied the role of senior governments in urban affairs.

It may be useful to describe in more detail the background to Ontario's approach to urban development at this time.

An Ontario commission of inquiry chaired by Lancelot Smith had just conducted a fundamental re-examination of the structure and financing of provincial, local and school government in that province. The Smith Committee report, submitted in August 1967, found that local government structure, in particular the absence of economies of scale due to the large number of small local governments, was an impediment to the efficient achievement of the two primary purposes of local government, to provide "access and service." Furthermore, the present structure represented an obstacle to the fulfillment of the Committee's mandate for producing "a tax and revenue system that is as simple, clear, equitable, efficient, adequate and as conducive to the sound growth of the province as can be devised." The Committee made a connection between the need for strong local government and the implementation of the province's long-standing objectives for regional economic development in its ten economic regions.

In November 1970, a few weeks before Trudeau's phone call to Oberlander, Ken Cameron started as a Research Officer in the provincial agency tasked with reforming local government, the Municipal Research Branch of the Department of Municipal Affairs. In the spring of that year, he had successfully defended his master's thesis "National Urban Growth Strategy in Canada," before an examining committee that had included Peter Oberlander and his thesis supervisor and mentor, Brahm Wiesman.

Ontario had promulgated the Toronto-Centred Region Plan in May 1970, setting out a growth management policy that was designed to provide for rapid growth within a context of affordable transportation, water and sewer services, and the protection of local communities. It suggested that urban growth be focused in two ways: through the structuring of development in existing communities along the shores of Lake Ontario (broadly to the east of Metropolitan Toronto) and through the stimulation of growth in more distant communities in the north of the region that were thought to have prospects for growth in housing and employment that was not dependent on commuting to the existing urban area. The two areas would be separated by a growth-shaping "parkway belt" intended to serve as protected green space as well as providing corridors for roads, hydro lines and other regional services, a dual function that perplexed many observers.

Under the leadership of Darcy McKeough, a dynamic young minister and former alderman from Chatham, Ontario, the Department of Municipal Affairs was conducting a raft of studies of local government organization prompted by the Smith Committee's findings. They would soon lead to a plethora of new, mainly two-tier, regional government systems, incorporating a reorganized and smaller number of local municipalities functioning within a new regional organization with important overall powers, particularly in planning. The new system was closely modelled on the highly successful system of metropolitan government established by the province for Toronto and its suburbs in 1954 and fine-tuned a couple of times thereafter.

Regional economic development was the responsibility of the Department of Treasury and Economics under the venerable veteran politician and seed merchant from Exeter, Charlie MacNaughton (whose aging bladder frequently prompted him to excuse himself from meetings to "drain the potatoes").

The bombshell hit on December 8, 1970 when Robarts announced his retirement from politics. Cameron had not been in Ontario long enough to have picked up on the signs that Robarts would be leaving, and he was dismayed. "Robarts just seemed to hold the whole system together," he recalled.

The leadership convention to replace Robarts was held in February 1971 in Toronto, and when the dust settled, William Davis, of whom it had been said that "you have to learn to take the bland with the bland," was elected leader, defeating McKeough and a number of other leading lights from the Robarts era.

The new Davis administration was presented with a report from a Committee on Government Productivity that had been appointed by Robarts in 1969. The report made a number of sweeping recommendations for the reorganization of the government through the creation of what would be dubbed "super ministers." Davis embraced these recommendations and, in the tradition of keeping your friends near and your enemies nearer, appointed his former rivals for the leadership to these positions.

Darcy McKeough was appointed to head the new Ministry of Treasury, Economics and Intergovernmental Affairs to take over responsibility for finance, economics, municipal affairs and intergovernmental relations, including provincial-municipal relations. Cameron was moved into the Intergovernmental Relations Secretariat, joining people who had provided support to Ontario's participation in constitutional negotiations and other heady aspects of the province's role in the federation. In the space of a few months, then, Oberlander and Cameron found themselves in key positions related to the federal government's new adventure in urban affairs. Cameron was forcefully introduced to two of the bedrock principles of Ontario's approach to federalism: resist, fiercely but constructively, federal incursion on provincial jurisdiction — and never, ever isolate Quebec.

Ontario and the other provinces were very skeptical about the Ministry of State for Urban Affairs. Many of them hewed to Trudeau's initial view that cities were entirely an area of provincial jurisdiction, and most had bought the concept advanced by Quebec and Ontario that all that was required to fix this (and virtually any other) problem would be for the federal government to turn over access to federal financial resources to the provinces. "Give us the money, and we will do the job."

In many provinces, it had been made clear to municipal affairs ministers, who were not high in the pecking order, that any realignment of responsibilities within Canada was the job of premiers and ministers of finance, not them. If realignment was not something the provinces could expect from MSUA, then the only other benefit the provinces could see from the agency would be to assist them in dealing with federal agencies with responsibilities that affected cities such as the Department of Transport or Citizenship and Immigration, which would bring the hard place back into contact with the rock. If this expectation was not fulfilled, the provinces thought, then MSUA was little more than "all talk and no money" with the potential to confuse Canadians further about who was responsible for what in their federal system.

The primary focus for "urban affairs" in most provinces was the ministry responsible for "local government" or "municipal affairs." Manitoba had a Minister of Urban Affairs (Saul Cherniack) as well as a Ministry of Municipal Affairs under Howard Pawley, and Quebec's Dr. Victor Goldbloom was Minister of Municipal Affairs and Minister of the Environment, but in nearly every case the primary responsibility of these men — and they were all men — was local government, narrowly construed. Ministers with these responsibilities did not stay in place very long; they were either on the way up (Pawley would become Premier of Manitoba) or on their way down, parked by premiers in a relatively junior portfolio pending a determination of their fate. Only in Ontario did relations with both the federal government and local government gain direct representation at a senior level in cabinet through the creation of the "Super ministry" of Treasury, Economics and Intergovernmental Affairs in 1972.

There was considerable camaraderie among the provincial ministers responsible for local government. They met annually in August for formal and informal interactions in one or other of the provincial capitals. At a social occasion connected with one such meeting, the delightful Dr. Goldbloom, a singer of some talent, regaled his colleagues with a rendition of the Whippenpoof Song, the signature number of a Yale a capella group made popular by Bob Hope and Bing Crosby in "The Road to Bali":

> We're poor little lambs who have lost our way
> Baa, baa, baa
> We're little black sheep who have gone astray
> Baa, baa, baa

The appreciative audience of provincial ministers were left to consider whether the song offered a commentary of any type on their situations within their governments or in the country as a whole.

Provincial officials had a pervasive attitude of superiority to local government. They never tired of reminding all who listened that local governments were constitutional "creatures of the provinces," even though a number of local governments predated Confederation and, in some cases, provinces and their colonial predecessors themselves.

It was true that a number of provinces had shown little interest in modernizing local government to enable it to provide effective governance in the twentieth century. The Smith Committee report in Ontario provided a clear picture of the impediments to the effectiveness of local government caused by the failure to modernize the structure and financial viability of municipalities to function as governments able to plan and provide for the democratic access and services needed by the province's growing urban population. A number of provinces, prompted in part perhaps by the pressure for more federal government involvement, embarked on government reform processes. These included Ontario (regional government and fiscal reform of local government), British Columbia (market value property assessment and regional districts) and Quebec (regional and urban *communautés*).

Some provincial officials were quite scornful of the motives of local government leaders in seeking a more formal approach to federal-provincial-municipal relations; in one briefing note to a minister, a senior Ontario staff member speculated that these leaders sought "to bask in the warm glow of national publicity" — as if no Ontario provincial politician or civil servant had ever succumbed to this temptation. In essence, many provincial officials thought that local politicians who pursued a national discussion about urban problems were just being uppity.

The other players in the piece were, of course, the municipalities, which the provinces were doing their best to keep hidden behind their skirts. Each province had one or more municipal association. In some provinces such as British Columbia, there was one municipal association in which all local governments were members, while in other provinces there could be several associations — rural vs. urban municipalities, counties vs. regions, etc. There was a national association — the Canadian Federation of Mayors and Municipalities (CFMM, now the Federation of Canadian Municipalities (FCM)), but its history had been controversial and not all of the 4,500 local governments then in the country were members. Added to this was the problem that the definitions of "cities" and "urban" then in use by Ottawa were intended to encompass an entity broader in geographic extent and in organic terms than "municipality" or "local government," which the constitution specifically allocated to provinces. (The agency that came closest to recognizing the organic nature of Canada's urban regions was Statistics Canada with its "Census Metropolitan Areas.") Notwithstanding these problems, there was no alternative to treating municipalities and their associations as the political voices of urban populations.

The CFMM as a national municipal organization with headquarters in Ottawa was a particular focus of provincial suspicions. These were exacerbated by the machinations of its Executive Director, Claude Langlois who Ken Cameron remembers as "the most devious and energetic schemer I ever knew. He was always looking around the next corner and herding his municipal cats into the same room."

The FCMM became a very strong organization under Langlois' management, producing a succession of knowledgeable, skilled, and wise leaders such as Mayor Ivor Dent of Edmonton, Mayor Marcel D'Amour of Hull, Mayor Des Newman of Whitby, and Mayor Allan O'Brien of Halifax. Langlois knew that the CFMM's weak point in purporting to represent Canada's local governments was the fact that not all 4,500 local governments in the country were CFMM members. He got around this by promoting establishment of an umbrella organization — the Joint Municipal Committee on Intergovernmental Relations (JMCIR), comprising the presidents of all the provincial and municipal associations in the country — to provide a coherent and credible voice. It was in some ways the predecessor of the Big City Mayors' Caucus, which Langlois and his successors would later use to good effect in providing a voice for Canada's cities in national affairs. The JMCIR had no staff, so it had to rely on the CFMM staff — Langlois — for assistance. "The JMCIR leadership were always careful to state that their agenda was not the CFMM agenda, but in my observation, there was never much of a difference between the two." Cameron says.

The ongoing machinations of the relationships between municipal organizations and the provinces were only one aspect of the dynamic environment in which the Ministry of State for Urban Affairs was established. In a retrospective, Peter Oberlander later compared the Ministry's early months "to building a boat, one plank at a time while running down a raging white-water river, dodging rocks and eddies while simultaneously laying the keel and frantically inserting oars where possible." To this description we could add the fact that, during this same period of time, Canada was dealing with the impact and aftermath of the October Crisis, which was the greatest threat to civil order the country had yet seen, and one in which the uses and limitations of federal power were a central dimension. Negotiations on the potential repatriation of Canada's constitution were also under way and would culminate in the Victoria Charter agreed between the prime minister and the premiers in 1971, only to fail due to the inability of the premiers to sell the proposal to their respective provincial governments.

This was the era of the intergovernmental conference in Canada, and it was widely believed that the potential for harmonization of urban policy lay in successful consultative meetings at the national level among representatives of the federal, provincial and local governments. Success in such endeavours was seen in Ottawa and across the country as the acid test of whether the Trudeau government's "Ministry of State" approach could bear fruit.

Darcy McKeough was recognized a key potential player in the process, not only because of Ontario's traditional leadership position among the provinces but also because McKeough's Treasury, Economics and Intergovernmental Affairs portfolio placed in his hands Ontario's approach to urbanization, local government reform and federal-provincial relations (including financial relations and constitutional issues).

McKeough was guided in his thinking by his respect for John Robarts' forcefully constructive view of the role of provinces in Confederation. In a speech during his bid for the party leadership that was ultimately won by Bill Davis, McKeough had said:

> We have heard some blustering talk in this leadership campaign about tough negotiations with Ottawa, about demanding a fuller accounting of federal assistance going to other parts of the country. I, too, will stand up for Ontario – but I will not pawn the Robarts mantle of statesmanship and reconciliation for a bigger fistful from the federal till.

McKeough responded with vigour to the challenge represented by the creation of the Ministry of State for Urban Affairs, avoiding the passive aggression shown by other provinces, many of whom showed a polite lack of enthusiasm and a leisurely approach, hoping that the whole thing eventually would go away (which it ultimately did).

The three municipal associations in Ontario formed a Municipal Liaison Committee to promote a unified approach; McKeough proposed that this group meet regularly with him as a Provincial-Municipal Liaison Committee and designated Ken Cameron as Provincial-Municipal Liaison Officer to facilitate the process. Cameron was able to organize a briefing for Oberlander and his staff with senior Ontario officials on the province's urban development policies.

The meeting took place in Toronto in January 1972. The Ontario contingent included Mary Mogford, the Secretary to the Cabinet and one of the province's top civil servants, which was an unprecedented role for a woman at that time. At the meeting, Cameron went to introduce Oberlander to Mogford. Before Cameron had had a chance to explain Mogford's position, Oberlander jumped to a conclusion and asked, "are you a secretary?" to which Mogford replied, "Yes, Dr. Oberlander, I am a secretary, the Secretary to the Cabinet."

Ontario showed in several ways that it was prepared to be a serious participant in tri-level consultations at the national level, perhaps drawing on McKeough's private school education (in his case at Ridley College), where one learned that one could not win the game by not playing. Ontario proposed that the conference agenda be coordinated by the Intergovernmental Conference Secretariat headed by Henry Davis, which had coordinated the constitutional discussions as well as a number of other federal-provincial meetings.

Senator Carl Goldenberg was recruited as a distinguished personage to chair the discussions. Goldenberg was well respected as a constitutional expert, but he had also led several commissions of inquiry into local government, notably in British Columbia in 1948 and in Metropolitan Toronto in 1965. Like many men at the time, Goldenberg was an inveterate pipe smoker. During one difficult meeting on the constitution, he was seen to be vigorously doing something with both hands below the table — cleaning his pipe as it turned out. Suddenly, the Ontario delegation opposite was rendered helpless by mirth: a junior staffer had passed a note speculating that Goldenberg was playing with himself.

Plans began to take shape for an initial national Tri-level Conference at the recently-completed Sheraton Centre in Toronto in November 1972.

At the federal level, the potential benefits and pitfalls of tri-level consultation were well recognized by the first Minister of State for Urban Affairs, Robert Andras. Oberlander later described him as providing "the stimulus for the Ministry's concept and its creation; intellectually, he made the most important and significant contribution to its initial operation." As a federal minister from Ontario and a man of some vision, Andras was well-equipped to interact with McKeough. In January 1972, however, Andras was replaced by Ron Basford from British Columbia, who was more engrossed in the progress of his political career in Ottawa, where influence was measured in terms of the dollars, people and programs a minister commanded. MSUA had relatively few of any of these.

McKeough continued to pursue his confident agenda. Also a pipe smoker, the "Minister of Everything" would work long hours in his office on the 7th floor of the Frost Building before striding across Queen's Park Crescent for evening sittings of the legislature. One evening he came steaming through the lobby with an armload of files and with a fully-stoked and lit pipe between his teeth. Before the security guard could warn him that the glass doors to the building were locked, McKeough had crashed pipe-first into them and the impact sent him sprawling back on the floor, surrounded by his files, pipe and wounded dignity.

A crash of a more serious nature was coming. On August 28, 1972, the *Globe and Mail* ran a story stating that, as Municipal Affairs Minister in 1969, McKeough had approved a subdivision in which he had a financial interest. It was later confirmed that the subdivision proposal had been submitted by a family company in which McKeough had no decision-making role and processed by the Ministry in a routine way without him having any knowledge or involvement. Nevertheless, McKeough recognized, "I had not done anything wrong, but a mistake had been made. I did not want the party or my leader to in any way be tarnished." In a move that seems curiously old-fashioned today, he concluded that the only honourable course of action was to submit his resignation, which he did on August 31, 1972. Davis accepted it and appointed the veteran Charles MacNaughton, McKeough's predecessor as Treasurer, to succeed him in the much larger portfolio of Treasury, Economics and Intergovernmental Affairs.

There was another ticking bomb on the road to a constructive relationship between the Ontario and federal governments in urban affairs. William Teron, an Ottawa-based developer and Trudeau confidant, who owned a significant amount of derelict industrial land on the Toronto waterfront, proposed to transfer his lands to the federal government at cost in return for an undertaking by Ottawa to create a new park there. The federal government decided to create a crown corporation with expropriation powers for this purpose, and the project, to be known as Harbourfront, was announced in the run-up to the federal election that would be held on October 30, 1972.

Ontario government officials were outraged. There had been no consultation with the province or, as far as could be determined, with the City of Toronto on an initiative that was intended to, and would, transform an important part of the core of the province's capital city. If this was intergovernmental co-operation in urban affairs, then Ontario wanted little to do with it.

The gambit typified for many the cynicism and complacency the Trudeau government brought to its 1972 election campaign, with its laughable slogan: "The land is strong." The land was not impressed; the Liberal majority was reduced to two seats.

It would be hard to imagine a more inauspicious context for the first formal meeting of the three levels of government November 20–21, 1972 (recognition of First Nations as governments was at that time far in the future). The federal government was in a state of shock from a near-death electoral experience. Its Minister of State for Urban Affairs was focused on Ottawa and had little patience with talking and meetings. Ontario's Minister was clearly in a caretaker mode, the Premier's office was expressing reservations about tri-level meetings as a potential federal incursion into provincial jurisdiction, and provincial officials were smouldering from the Harbourfront debacle.

Other provinces were only too happy to join in the general skepticism about the whole endeavour. Notwithstanding the able chairmanship provided by Goldenberg, who Oberlander described as "puckish," there was only a limited amount of good will to overcome the sheer mechanics of having a sensible discussion involving the federal government, ten provinces, and a dozen and a half municipal associations. The municipal representatives must have felt like children witnessing a domestic dispute between parents in which their welfare was an afterthought.

As was so often the case with Canadian intergovernmental meetings, the main outcome of the first national tri-level conference was a decision to meet again, this time in Edmonton, in October 1973. By then, Ontario's leadership on the issue had been energized by the appointment of John White as Treasurer and Minister of Economics and Intergovernmental Affairs. White had a master's degree in economics from the University of Western Ontario. He had chaired the Ontario legislature's Select Committee tasked with reviewing and making recommendations on the report of the Smith Committee inquiry into finance and government structure, and these had been taken into the heart of government policy.

The new Treasurer was a self-professed fan of Lewis Mumford, particularly his diagnosis of the ills of society resulting from excessive centralization and the concentration of power in ever larger and more complex institutions. At one of the first meetings of the Provincial-Municipal Liaison Committee, White stated,

"I want us to move power and money from the federal level to the provincial level to the municipal level."

White's approach played well with municipal leaders in Ontario, including Toronto's newly-elected "tiny perfect mayor," David Crombie, one of a wave of reform leaders (including Vancouver Mayor Art Phillips) elected in Canadian cities at that time. At a successful provincial-level tri-level conference held at Trent University in Peterborough in late May 1973, Crombie lauded White's approach, "Good on you, Mr. Minister," he said.

White cemented the province's political relationships with local government with his willingness to take a direct action on irritants and his use of the Provincial-Municipal Liaison Committee meetings to hold "line" ministers (and, more awkwardly, their deputy ministers) to account for centralizing initiatives that, in the past, had often been initiated by the province without even consulting local government. Having decided not to run for re-election, White relished the opportunity to use his remaining influence to do what he considered to be the right things. Ken Cameron served as White's executive assistant at this time and was astounded at the man's energy and refreshing vision of a new approach based on invigorating local government. At one point, White was described as "the best thing to happen to local government since [Robert] Baldwin [the architect of local government in Canada]."

There was, however, no escaping the reality that money was increasingly viewed as the currency by which progress in intergovernmental relations in urban affairs was being measured. This was, perhaps, not surprising, given the complexity of Canada's urban system and the length of time that would be needed to provide an agreed framework of urban policy that could realign public decisions towards better urban outcomes. Local government leadership, whose goal in establishing the Joint Municipal Committee on Intergovernmental Relations had originally been a seat at the table of constitutional negotiations, began to realize that significant jurisdictional change wasn't on, and started to look for changes in financial arrangements.

Given his Mumford-inspired mantra of decentralization, White was a natural ally for local government in seeking federal agreement to fiscal reform, which was also supported by Quebec and a number of other provinces. An early indication of the prospects came when White, as Treasurer, attended a federal-provincial meeting of finance ministers in Ottawa. The federal minister, John Turner, attended the meeting but did not appear to be present; he spent his time obsessively underlining, with pen and ruler, every line in his briefing book rather than engaging in serious conversation about the suggestions of the provinces for new fiscal arrangements. Finally, an exasperated White asked Turner, "Have you been given instructions to reject everything these men suggest?"

White put his own fiscal ideas on the table at the second national tri-level conference in Edmonton in October 1973. In what became known as "the Edmonton Commitment," he announced that Ontario would increase its transfers to local governments and agencies at the rate of growth of total provincial revenue and pass on to local governments the full benefit, "dollar for dollar," of any net gains in new unconditional tax sharing by the federal government.

The pressure at the Edmonton conference for change in fiscal arrangements was sufficient to produce agreement that a national Task Force study of public finance would be undertaken under the leadership of John Deutsch, the first chairman of the Economic Council of Canada and President of Queen's University. The study was to be completed in time for the consideration of its results at a further tri-level meeting scheduled for 1976, and the task force completed its report in February 1976, just prior to the untimely death of Dr. Deutsch.

Although the Task Force amassed a vast amount of data on expenditures and revenues of the three levels of government, the incidence of various taxation mechanisms and total debt, there was little in the way of penetrating analysis of this information. That task was undertaken in a report called "Puppets on a Shoestring: The Effects on Municipal Government of Canada's System of Public Finance" published by the CFMM in April of 1976. The report darkly stated that the Deutsch study foreshadowed "the decline and fall of municipal government as we now know it in Canada within five years." It demonstrated that, whatever "fiscal imbalance" existed between the responsibilities and revenues of provincial governments in relation to the federal government, it paled into insignificance beside the chronic imbalance under which local government across the country had laboured for many years.

The confirmation of the fiscal plight of local government dampened the enthusiasm among the provinces for further national tri-level meetings. They foresaw themselves as the ham in the sandwich in what were bound to be acrimonious discussions about money. The meeting scheduled for August 1976 in Winnipeg was cancelled and there the initiative ended.

Other tri-level meetings focused on the provincial level or on particular urban regions and made considerable progress in dealing with more local issues.

As of July 1972, for example, Oberlander was able to report to his Minister that there were active efforts under way to establish tri-level consultation and coordination mechanisms in Halifax, Quebec City, Winnipeg and Vancouver. In commenting on the establishment of a mechanism in Winnipeg in a letter to Manitoba's Deputy Minister of Municipal Affairs, Oberlander reiterated his lifelong belief that talking should be accompanied by tangible action: "The effectiveness of a tri-level arrangement would be enhanced if it were possible to announce one or more jointly sponsored projects at the same time as the consultative mechanism was declared."

But the grand dream of a realignment of responsibilities through intergovernmental negotiation was dead. In Ontario, John White's Edmonton Commitment was retained as a principle of provincial-municipal relations after he left politics in 1975 until the recession of the early 1980s when it was quietly buried.

Meanwhile, in Ottawa, the Ministry of State for Urban Affairs as an organization took shape, and Peter Oberlander was engaged in all the details, including the selection of office space, initially in an office complex at 333-335 River Road in Vanier (and later at the former La Salle Academy, a heritage building on Sussex Drive). Oberlander recruited David Zirnhelt as his executive assistant.

Oberlander and Zirnhelt had crossed paths when the latter was a graduate student in political science at UBC and active in student politics as president of the Alma Mater Society during the tumultuous events surrounding Jerry Rubin's visit to UBC in October 1968. He recalled being impressed with Oberlander's interest in reform of university governance, encouraging students' involvement as citizens with rights and responsibilities within the university. They also worked together on TEAM in Vancouver. Zirnhelt was aware that Oberlander was considered by the Trudeau government to be a leading thinker on urban matters, and he was not surprised to learn that Peter had been recruited as the first Secretary of the MSUA.

A self-described "country boy from the Cariboo," Zirnhelt was pleased to interrupt his graduate studies to join Oberlander in Ottawa, where he learned about the power and rewards of being an executive assistant when the assistant and principal have mutual respect and trust.

> He was always willing to get in touch with people who wanted advice or wanted to pass on information. And I think that's the first mark: to be open to the world and other citizens, and be accessible

and to develop a sense of camaraderie… The way he liked his office to be managed was that he wanted to remain in contact with people who were doing things in the world, including students, and people not so important yet. He was always willing to mentor people who had an interest in creating a better world.

Zirnhelt recalls Oberlander's patience with his "country boy" executive assistant, particularly when he drove Oberlander to three different hotels in Toronto before finding the one where the Secretary was to attend a meeting.

In late 1971, Zirnhelt left MSUA to complete his studies at UBC before returning to the Cariboo, where he became a cattle rancher and horse logger. In 1989, he was elected as an NDP MLA for Cariboo in a by-election, going on for re-election in 1991 and 1996. He served in the cabinets of NDP Premiers Mike Harcourt and Glen Clark.

Oberlander tapped the Ottawa bureaucracy for Zirnhelt's replacement in January 1972, hiring David Dunlop, from the sister Ministry of State for Science and Technology, who would serve Oberlander for the remainder of his time in Ottawa. Dunlop remembers Oberlander's attention to the physical layout of the Ministry's offices at 355 River Road in Vanier.

> "Oberlander orange" was the colour of the day. It was even in the halls and the elevators and there were holographics with the colour. It was also the era of bringing in plants…all over the place. It was refreshing. It was a fun place to go into because of the discussions, the people there, the characters who would come in.

Peter Oberlander liked signing everything with a very large fountain pen whose ink would take a long time to dry. He wanted to find a way make it dry faster. Dunlop had the old 1885 blotter of the Ottawa Journal, which his grandfather had founded. He loaned it to Peter while they worked together so that the Secretary could "very dramatically" roll the blotter over his signature.

After the Oberlander family established themselves in a rented home in Rockcliffe Park, the upscale neighbourhood near Rideau Hall and the Prime Minister's residence at 24 Sussex Drive, they held a cocktail party for senior staff and other important contacts. When André Saumier arrived, his wife mistook Peter in his white shirt and bow tie for the butler, and handed him her coat.

On a more serious level, Saumier made a significant contribution to the Ministry's focus on regional coordination to bring a federal urban perspective to projects on the ground in Canadian cities. As a former Deputy Secretary to the provincial cabinet in Quebec, the Ministry's Assistant Secretary for Research and Coordination was intimately familiar with the jurisdictional shoals through which the Ministry would have to navigate in Quebec and other provinces. Saumier recruited as regional coordinators a number of individuals who had courage and credibility, including Jean-Jacques Lemieux in Quebec, Michel Barcelo in Ontario and Cyril Rosenberg in British Columbia. These individuals were able to insert themselves into issues at the local and regional levels where one or more federal agencies could provide some leverage for outcomes that could be more consistent with good urban policies and planning than would otherwise have been the case.

In a retrospective written a decade after the demise of MSUA, Saumier described the life of these officials.

> Instantly dismissed as negligible by the federal departments whose programs they were supposed to reshape and deploy — without however paying for them — and immediately, declared **persona non grata** by the provinces, and forbidden any contact with their municipalities, the emissaries of the Ministry of State for Urban Affairs started to work.

Saumier listed a dozen or so accomplishments that resulted from the Ministry's coordination role, including the federal office building development on the Halifax waterfront, the Old Port in Montréal, Harbourfront in Toronto, railroad relocation in Regina and the stunning redevelopment of Granville Island in Vancouver.

One accomplishment that resulted from something not happening was the absence of a second major airport in the Toronto region. The failure of Montréal's second airport at Mirabel was at least partly due to the fact that Canada could no longer deny landing rights in Toronto to transoceanic flights, which, due to constraints at Malton, were thought not possible to accommodate without a second airport in southern Ontario. Federal transport officials thought that a location west of Toronto would be more in keeping with traffic trends as they then existed. The provincial government recognized the growth-shaping importance of this decision in relation to its strategy of promoting growth to the east in the Toronto-centred region. It argued for a location east of Toronto to be combined with a new community the provincial government was willing to establish at North Pickering. MSUA provided the perspective, not entirely welcomed by Transport Canada, that the urban development considerations as well as aviation concerns should have an influence. The consideration of this issue — and the expenditure of significant sums of money on planning and land acquisition — lasted long enough for it to become clear that modern technology would allow the expansion of Malton as a preferable option to a new site. A large and costly mistake had been avoided.

The Policy and Research Division, initially headed by Harvey Lithwick, had the woollier task of identifying the elements of federal responsibility that had the greatest impact on urbanization. Those who had read Lithwick's report might have expected that the Ministry would take on the reshaping of the whole urban system in Canada through a "national urban policy," but it became clear that the Ministry did not have the time, resources or clout to undertake such an endeavour. Instead, the Ministry sought through the use of analytical tools and strategic initiatives to influence Canada's urban system as it evolved within the prevailing economic, political and jurisdictional framework.

Some observers of the establishment of the Ministry were surprised that two of the top three positions went to academics, and it might have been assumed that, with this common background, Oberlander and Lithwick would get along. Such an assumption would have overlooked Oberlander's lifelong commitment to moving "from ideas to action" and its inconsistency with Lithwick's preoccupation with the concept of an "urban system" of almost infinite complexity.

Lithwick's initial appointments included a number of other academics, who may not have been sufficiently aware of the constraints to inquiry and expression that came with a role in government, contributing to a serious uprising among the research staff, which was only quelled by Oberlander's direct involvement. In any event, Lithwick lasted only about six months as Assistant Secretary and in September 1971 he was replaced by Jim MacNeill, a more seasoned federal public servant who had been working in the newly-minted Department of the Environment that had been created earlier that year under Jack Davis.

Three strategic initiatives undertaken by the Ministry dealt with federally-owned land, national housing legislation and railway relocation. All were clearly within federal jurisdiction and all could be seen to have significant impacts on the development of Canada's cities.

Oberlander later recalled the impetus for the policy on federally-owned urban land.

> To everyone's surprise, including the Prime Minister and his
> Cabinet, the federal overnment was and remains the single largest
> land owner in Canada, including within its major urban areas.
> Among the six largest cities, the federal crown, through nineteen
> different agencies, owned 200,000 acres of land in 1971-72, often
> strategic in their location and invaluable as an economic asset.
> Not only was the magnitude of that property interest startling to
> the Cabinet, but even more amazing was the fact that there was
> no single place in Ottawa that could tell us where it was, for what
> federal purpose it was owned or used, or what income or costs were
> involved in this substantial real estate.

Further inquiries revealed that there was no policy framework for the ownership, use or disposal of land within the federal government. The initial Memorandum to Cabinet on land management articulated the strategic role of land as a resource, with optimum social use as the objective of management. As Oberlander described the concept:

> Land was to be managed not by departments but by a central agency,
> and once land was in the inventory, it should never leave it again; it
> could be used and reused, under public and private initiatives and
> only in exceptional circumstances sold.

It was Vancouver Mayor Art Phillips' Property Endowment Fund writ large.

The Memorandum to Cabinet rapidly found favour, due in part to a pent-up feeling that the departments with responsibility for land assets were not moving particularly quickly to modernize their approach. André Saumier described it as that rare thing in government: a "good, fast crisis." The change in direction had a permanent impact on federal policy on land assets, leading, ultimately, to a systematic process of "shopping" surplus land around federal agencies, then with provincial and local governments, after which truly surplus lands were to be turned over for disposition to a new federal crown corporation, the Canada Lands Company.

The new process later also assisted the federal government in identifying crown lands in which First Nations may have an interest, permitting the resolution of those interests prior to any disposal as an alternative to the cumbersome and costly process of attempting to achieve such resolution after lands were transferred out of federal ownership.

The *National Housing Act* amendments introduced in 1973 were inspired by the change in direction taken by Paul Hellyer in 1968 when he abruptly terminated the urban renewal program that had generated such strong community opposition in Vancouver and Toronto. The *Act* authorized programs that supported the social component of housing and encouraged the participation of communities and citizens in neighbourhood improvement, residential rehabilitation, assisted home ownership and co-operative housing.

The value of these programs can perhaps be judged by the impact of their termination by the government in the mid-1990s by Prime Minister Jean Chrétien and Finance Minister Paul Martin as part of the war on the federal deficit. The loss of these programs is widely seen as being the origin of the problems of housing, poverty and homelessness that besiege Canadian cities to this day. We do not, perhaps, reflect often enough on the way in which program changes that are relatively small in financial terms can have a dramatic and negative impact out into the future.

The Ministry's focus on railway relocation reflected the fact that the centre of virtually every Canadian city was built around railway terminals, yards and intermodal facilities which, by the 1960s, had begun to be obsolete. Passenger rail was in decline and the competitive position of rail freight was being eroded by trucking. Land-intensive railway-based activities were increasingly being accommodated in new facilities on the outskirts of cities close to regional and intercity truck routes. Working with the Ministry of Transport, the MSUA sought to stimulate the replotting and reuse of the large tracts of land occupied by obsolete rail facilities. The purpose of the *Railway Relocation and Crossing Act* was described in the initial announcement as follows:

> Ridding urban areas of grade crossings, railway sheds, warehouses, shunting-yards and other rail paraphernalia, often underused and obsolete, which create certain congestion and evident pollution in populated urban centres. These proposals...enable such areas to be transformed into better habitats of neighbourhood improvement, parks and open spaces, producing a better environment precisely where it is most needed."

Not surprisingly for an initiative with Oberlander's hand in it, the *Act* provided funding for the preparation, at the city level, of a plan for rail relocation and urban redevelopment as an initial stage. Later stages could entail funding for the relocation of facilities and the use of federal resources to acquire lands necessary to the implementation of a relocation scheme. The Act had limited success because, according to Oberlander, "the provinces were sceptical and effectively stymied any local interest, despite strong and sustained local demand in Regina, Winnipeg, Kamloops and elsewhere."

Chemistry in the relationship between a Ministry and its Minister is key to any successful agenda for change, and here the experience of MSUA is decidedly mixed. In retrospect, the prospects for success of the Ministry of State concept might have been greater if MSUA had been the responsibility of a seasoned federal minister. Although the founding minister, Robert Andras, was capable and intelligent (and would later hold more senior portfolios such as Manpower and Immigration and Treasury Board before leaving politics in 1979), his appointment as Minister of State for Urban Affairs seemed a small step above Minister without Portfolio in the Ottawa power hierarchy.

Oberlander and Andras worked well together in the critical six-month period in which the new Ministry was established. Oberlander later reflected that Andras "clearly provided the stimulus for the Ministry's concept and its creation; intellectually, he made the most important and significant contribution to its initial operation and deserves considerable credit for its success."

In January 1972, Andras essentially traded jobs with Ron Basford who had had what Oberlander described as "an important but incomplete career at the Department of Consumer and Corporate Affairs" (which included the still-born conversion of Canada to the metric system of measurements). The move to Urban Affairs was not seen by Basford or anyone else as a step up in the government, and one associate described him at this time as "grumpy." Oberlander and Basford both hailed from Vancouver and had a number of common experiences upon which to draw, but the chemistry between them was never right and soon became toxic.

Basford recruited Ian Clark from the Treasury Board Secretariat planning unit to be his executive assistant. Clark was another Vancouverite (and schoolmate of Ken Cameron) and a Rhodes Scholar and Harvard graduate. Clark's mandate, as Basford described it to him, was to bring some order to the "three-ring circus" created by three competing egos in his portfolio: Oberlander, the newbie, as

Secretary of the Ministry of State for Urban Affairs, Herbert Hignett, the veteran head of CMHC which still believed that it had earned the role of being the federal focal point for urban matters and resented the creation of the Ministry, and the redoubtable Douglas Fullerton, Chairman of the National Capital Commission who was building a strong profile amid the Ottawa elite for projects such as the Rideau Canal Skateway.

When Cameron became Executive Assistant to John White, the two former schoolmates, building on a relationship established in Miss Thorburn's Grade 2 class at Lord Kitchener School in 1952, would conspire to facilitate communication between White and Basford, discussing when "your guy" might be available to talk on the phone to "my guy."

Chroniclers of the MSUA story have described its evolution in three stages: coordination of federal policy, funding of urban initiatives and partnering with cities directly on projects, noting that the resistance from the provinces grew at each stage until the Ministry's demise in 1979. For most of Basford's time the Ministry was in the first stage, which involved establishing coordination mechanisms and consultation processes with the provinces.

Basford believed that success for the Ministry — and for him politically — lay in achieving tangible results, and he had little patience with the apparently endless policy and research discussions that dominated life at MSUA at that time. As his students at UBC had noted, one of Oberlander's habits was to repeat his favourite aphorisms (at SCARP it was "The city is here to stay"), old chestnuts which, while informative, tended to get tedious after a while. At MSUA, Oberlander was fond of describing the urban system as a "seamless web" of interdependence, and Basford converted this into a nickname for his deputy minister. "Here comes the Seamless Web" he would say, or "What does the Seamless Web think of this idea?"

Basford's insistence on tangible results that would benefit his career would seem to have fit well with Oberlander's lifelong commitment to converting "ideas to action," but the fact remained that at this early stage the Ministry's role was primarily to achieve success through others.

Thus, for example, while an achievement as important as the recasting of the government's policy on its land holdings reflected exactly how the Ministry was intended to work, it lacked the profile and association with the Ministry and its Minister that were crucial to Basford's view of success. Another factor may have been that, in a parliamentary system, deputy ministers are appointed by, and accountable to, the Prime Minister not the Minister. Oberlander was known to have a long-standing personal relationship with Prime Minister Trudeau that might have been unsettling to Basford at a critical point in his career.

One thing on which Oberlander and Basford could agree was the need to exploit the urban potential of Granville Island, a former sand bar in False Creek in Vancouver on which industrial land had been created by landfill in the early twentieth century. Originally called Industrial Island, Granville Island had a number of industrial functions that were coming to an end. The TEAM group on Vancouver City Council saw the potential for the repurposing of the island as well as False Creek and its surrounding lands for the development of housing, commerce and marine recreation facilities.

In 1972, Basford and Oberlander sponsored an order-in-council transferring Granville Island from the National Harbours Board to CMHC, setting the stage for a planning process that built upon and celebrated its industrial architecture and created spaces that defied conventional logic by permitting automobiles and pedestrians to coexist. Today, Granville Island is one of the most popular spaces in the Vancouver region and among its top ten tourist attractions, and one that shares only with Gastown the quality of being truly urban. Ron Basford Park on Granville Island commemorates this achievement.

Ron Basford Park, Granville Island[18]

After the federal election in mid-1974, Basford was replaced by Barnett Danson, former Parliamentary Secretary to Prime Minister Trudeau, as Minister of State for Urban Affairs. Danson was an early enthusiast for a more conscious federal role in urban affairs, having sponsored seminars on the subject in his Toronto-area riding before his appointment to cabinet. Oberlander described him as "the most enthusiastic and urban-centred MSUA Minister. As a member representing urban Toronto and Ontario generally, his creative skill and energies helped the Ministry maintain and accelerate its initial momentum during political complexities and frustrations."

By the time Danson arrived in the Ministry, Oberlander had already decided to return to academic life at UBC at the end of his three-year secondment. Being a private man in respect to such matters, he never publicly stated his reasons and, although the Ministry acknowledged his vision and passion, his departure was not widely lamented.

Although Oberlander could reflect with satisfaction on the establishment of the Ministry and a number of successes that would have enduring impact, the ongoing challenges within Ottawa and the continuing passive aggression shown by the provinces foretold a difficult road ahead. The election of the Parti Québécois as the provincial government in Quebec in November 1976 would put new stresses on the viability of federalism as a fundamental of governance. Increasingly, Ottawa saw a need to ensure that it could not be characterized as intruding on the jurisdiction of the provinces. For those in the federal government who continued to be uncomfortable with a federal role in urban affairs (which may have included the Prime Minister), the Ministry increasingly seemed to be a liability.

It was at this point that the activities of Peter Oberlander and the Ministry of State for Urban Affairs intersected with some broader developments in humanity's efforts to govern its affairs for its enduring survival. While at the newly formed Department of the Environment prior to joining the Ministry, Jim MacNeill had become involved in the growing field of international co-operation on environmental matters, including Canada's preparations for the first United Nations conference on the human environment that was to be convened in Stockholm in June 1972. His request that he be allowed to continue in this role after his transfer to Urban Affairs, in November 1971, proved to be fortuitous.

MacNeill continued to attend the meetings of the 58-member Preparatory Committee for the conference and served as a special advisor to Maurice Strong, the Canadian visionary about the future of humanity and the UN's Secretary-General of the Stockholm Conference. Oberlander had taken an interest in the Stockholm conference very early in his tenure as Secretary, offering the Ministry's assistance to Strong in a letter dated February 8, 1971 in which he complained about Ottawa's "endless snow and below zero temperatures." Reflecting his lifelong interest in international co-operation for a better future, Oberlander stated that Canada had a "special role" to play in the UN's emerging interest in the human environment.

Maurice Strong at the United Nations Conference on
the Human Environment, Stockholm 1972[19]

In 2012, MacNeill recalled,

Stockholm was mainly concerned with environmental pollution
in its many forms, but human settlements had been added to its
agenda in belated recognition of the South's concerns about the
tens of millions who were rushing annually to existing cities and
towns and spreading slums that were swamped by poverty, squalor
and disease. After joining the Ministry, I continued to attend the
PrepCom meetings and added the work of the subcommittee
on human settlements to my other duties. Our discussions
confirmed both the frightening dimensions of the South's human
settlements crisis and the fact that we had neither the time nor
the resources to address it effectively in Stockholm. During the
final PrepCom before Stockholm, a few of us from a number of
like-minded countries came to the view that the issues of human
settlements justified their very own conference. When I got back to
Ottawa, Peter quickly came on board. Together, we persuaded our
Minister Ron Basford and just weeks before leaving for Stockholm,
he requested Cabinet to authorize the Canadian delegation to
propose that a UN Conference on Human Settlements be held in

1975 (it was later changed to 1976) and that Canada offer to host it. Cabinet agreed.

Peter Oberlander was unable to attend the Stockholm Conference due to other commitments related to the first National Tri-level Conference a few weeks earlier, but he recognized its implications for his future and that of the Ministry. Stockholm is now widely recognized as the beginning of the international effort to reshape humanity's relationship with the natural environment. It provided the foundation for concepts such as sustainable development, defined by the Bruntdland report in 1987 as "development that meets the needs of the present without compromising the ability of future generations to meet their own needs," and for future landmark events such as the Earth Summit in Rio de Janiero in 1992.

During the Stockholm Conference, MacNeill led the negotiations in the committee concerned with human settlements. He was joined by the only other person from the Ministry in the Canadian delegation, a brilliant professional from André Saumier's staff named Michel Lincourt. Together with their Scandinavian, Dutch, Australian, Indian and other like-minded colleagues, they drafted an appropriate resolution and soon had enough countries signed on to secure its passage. Subsequently, the conference adopted what became known as the "Canadian initiative". They asked Victor Goldbloom, the Quebec Minister of the Environment, who was a member of the Canadian delegation, to present the resolution to the Plenary.

Although the decision to select Vancouver as the venue for the conference was driven by the availability of appropriate hotel space, Basford was delighted with this choice and flew with MacNeill to New York in November 1973 to invite the UN General Assembly to hold Habitat in Vancouver in May 1976.

The initiative to host the Habitat Conference gave a boost to the flagging credibility of the MSUA as an enduring influence on federal domestic policy. This was ironic, because the whole debate within Canada had been whether urban affairs were anything other than "matters of a purely local or private nature" which were assigned to the provinces under the constitution. MSUA had demonstrated that federal responsibilities had an important impact — for good or ill — on Canada's cities, but its mandate had, to use Oberlander's words, been a sacrifice "offered up upon the altar of federal-provincial relations."

In promoting international attention to the human, economic and environmental challenges of and within urban settlements, the federal government, with its unquestioned authority over Canada's role on the international scene, provided itself with a broader focus of action than it enjoyed within the country's borders. Recognition of this potential gave impetus to Canada's efforts through its international development programs and its support, some years later, for the International Institute for Sustainable Development in Winnipeg and the International Centre for Sustainable Cities in Vancouver to export the country's expertise in building good cities.

But the die was cast. The MSUA's last Minister, André Ouellett, and its last Secretary, William Teron, were fairly obviously focused on facilitating a graceful retreat from an explicit policy focus on urban affairs by the federal government. In November 1978, it was announced that the organization would be wound up on March 31, 1979.

The impact of the MSUA experiment was summarized in 1985 by one of its architects, the late Michael Pitfield, as follows:

> ...its credibility and effectiveness developed surprisingly quickly. It contributed substantially to the shaping of policies and programs indirectly involving urban affairs. It played an increasingly important consultation role in the budget formulation. Most significantly, it began to define the objectives and shape the policies of federal involvement in housing and in urban development. Priorities were better defined and programs reoriented, laying a basis for new instruments of policy that permitted reductions in expenditures with increased impact in a difficult economic environment.

> Nevertheless, the public image of MSUA continued under a cloud. As the government's leadership of federal-provincial relations became increasingly controversial, MSUA appeared more and more of a liability because it was a constant forum for attack. As the 70s came to an end, the Trudeau government came to look upon MSUA first, as a front for a retreat to show the public federal sensitivity to provincial demands and, ultimately as a piece of the government apparatus to sacrifice in order to demonstrate federal sensitivity to popular concern with "Big Government." As the 1979

general election came down upon it, the Trudeau government declared victory and wound up the Ministry of State for Urban Affairs. From my own perspective, it was wound up just as it was beginning to succeed."

That was, of course, not the end of the matter. Largely through the continued efforts of the Canadian Federation of Mayors and Municipalities, renamed the Federation of Canadian Municipalities in 1976, local government kept the focus on the need for the federal government to play a conscious and constructive role in the country's cities. "A New Deal for Cities" became Finance Minister Paul Martin's rallying cry in his assault on the leadership of Jean Chrétien in the early 2000s and centrepiece of his term as Prime Minister from 2003 to 2006.

The ebb and flow of conscious engagement by the federal government in urban affairs would continue for some time to come against the backdrop of the growing political strength of cities that flowed from their growing electoral importance. Led by forceful mayors with considerable leadership skills, Canada's cities were increasingly recognized by both the federal government and the provinces as partners in nation-building.

CHAPTER NINE:

GOING GLOBAL

Canada's decision to host the 1976 Habitat conference had strong roots in the country's long-standing tradition, solidified in the Pearson era, of engagement with the world in collective security, peacekeeping, and international development assistance. The country's experience in two world wars and in what President John F. Kennedy described as "a hard and bitter peace" had forged a recognition that, if for no other reason than self-interest, Canada had to be engaged in the global search for peace, prosperity and social justice. In this context, it was logical that Canada strongly support the involvement of the United Nations in the challenges surrounding the human environment and human settlements.

The roots of Peter Oberlander's interest in global action to set a social foundation for peace, security and justice were equally deep:

> I had always been interested in the UN. My father already worked for the League of Nations, so I had some sense of what was happening. The League of Nations survived in various tentacles. One of them was International Labour Organization (ILO). And ILO officers sought refuge in 1942 at McGill. So as I walked to the School of Architecture building, I passed by ILO, dropped in to say hello. I knew from the beginning some of the ILO enterprises across the world.
>
> I became good friends with Ernest Weissmann, a Dubrovnik-raised Yugoslav who came to New York to build the Yugoslav pavilion at the International World's Fair. He stayed and later he began to work in reconstruction; he was very involved in the early rebuilding of

Central Europe. The winter of 1945-46 was bitterly cold, it was the worst winter Europe ever had, because it was destroyed. The question was: what can you do to house millions of refugees literally overnight? He and a man called Ben Reiner invented a very simple program, the first housing program of the UN, which was shipping blankets. That's where my connection comes from.

Weissmann then moved to New York and, by 1952, he had hired me as a consultant. The focus was housing, building and planning, not human settlements yet. It was the UN Housing, Building and Planning Centre, housed on the 36th floor of the UN building in New York.

A global perspective had also been a major theme in Oberlander's years as the Director of the UBC School of Community and Regional Planning. Peter's involvement with international development planning began with the Colombo Plan, an agreement signed between the seven Commonwealth nations in 1950: Canada, Australia, Sri Lanka, India, New Zealand and Pakistan. It was a co-operative venture of self and mutual help for economic and social development between these nations. The Colombo Plan Program at UBC was initiated to enable an exchange of planning professionals from the former British colonies in South Asia, South East Asia and Africa to "expand their practical experience by a wider academic knowledge and theoretical point of view."

It was during this time that the American-educated nationalist leader, Kwame Nkrumah, became the first Prime Minister of the Gold Coast, a western sub-region of the former kingdom of Ghana that was colonized by the British. Simultaneously, the World Bank initiated its first economic development mission to western Africa. Within a few years, the Gold Coast achieved independence from Britain to create the Republic of Ghana. With Kwame Nkrumah as Prime Minister, Ghana signed an agreement with the International Bank for Reconstruction and Development, a wing of the World Bank within the UN. As part of this program of mutual co-operation, Peter was involved in assisting the government of Ghana in developing an Institute of Community Planning along the lines of SCARP at Accra.

Peter had vivid recollections of his experience in creating a development plan for Accra, Ghana. Kwame Nkrumah was a man of great insight who had put together a plan for development as suggested by the terms of the agreement with the World Bank. He needed assistance in terms of implementing the plan that encompassed public services, health, education and transportation. Nkrumah requested expertise from member nations in the areas of housing, building and planning. Ghana had inherited the British legislative system and showed a willingness to follow the British model of planning in a way that it could address Ghanaian needs. The UN put together a team to work in Ghana. Being part of the UN program on housing, Peter was appointed to the team.

The UN expert team quickly realized that it was futile to give Ghana advice on housing, building and planning because of the vastly different cultural, political, social and economic context in Ghana at the time. A non-western culture, multi-lingual societies, tribal factionalism and a lack of western legal systems proved challenging barriers.

On the other hand, the UN team's handicap was lack of local knowledge and a language for communication with the communities, government officers, and newly established education institutions. So they struck upon the idea of creating a new breed of Ghanaian "barefoot planners" because they realized the need for contextually relevant planning. In order to provide a common language of communication, Nkrumah proposed the use of the English language, deftly avoiding the difficult problem of selecting one of Ghana's numerous languages over the others. In this way, planning could proceed as a process of transferring expertise from the UN team to Ghanaian nationals.

After Kwame Nkrumah took over as Prime Minister, he initiated an ambitious nation-wide education plan to ensure universal access to education at various levels. A graduate from the University of Pennsylvania himself, Nkrumah encouraged primary, middle-school, secondary, higher education, and teacher training programs. With independence in 1957, education policies became law.

The UN bureau of technical assistance operations appointed Peter to advise the UN on the problems involved in establishing a regional training centre in community and development planning in Ghana. UBC sanctioned Peter's leave for six weeks travel to Ghana for this purpose in 1959. After touring the city of Accra, meeting with government officials and agencies, surveying the Ghanaian educational setup, Peter developed a detailed report on the existing conditions and his recommendations. By the winter of 1961, based on Peter's recommendations the national government and the UN agreed in principle to establish the Institute of Community Planning. In a few months, a formal agreement was signed between UBC, the bureau of technical assistance operations of the UN and the state of Ghana to establish the Institute near the capital city of Accra.

Back in Canada, UBC had already established an exchange program under the Colombo Plan for civil servants from South East Asia, South Asia, and Africa, either working in the departments of town and city planning or as future planners to participate in a special course in community planning and urban development. Having successfully conducted this program a year earlier for Indonesian town planners, UBC invited Ghanaian students for such training to Vancouver in the fall of 1959. This training was not offered as a degree program but as an exposure to a broader set of ideas about community planning. These planners returned to Ghana and became important change agents in their homeland. But UBC's efforts didn't end there.

At UBC, Norman MacKenzie announced not only the signing of the agreements but also the appointment of Alan Armstrong, a senior advisor on community planning at CMHC and professor in planning at UBC's Schools of Architecture and Community and Regional Planning, as the Director of the Institute of Community Planning in Ghana. The Institute's objective was to build on existing capacities of local students as planning assistants who would work on development planning projects in partnerships between the Ghanaian state and communities. Eventually it was hoped that the Institute could emerge as a regional hub for training junior planning staff from Ghana and other countries located in the western African sub-region.

With the Institute's inauguration due in the fall of 1961, preparations to welcome the first cohort of planning students were well underway. Peter accompanied Armstrong to Accra, to help him make arrangements for establishing the institution. The agreement was based on the assumption that Canadians would hand off to Ghanaians in the process of establishing the Institute. UBC would supervise the operations of the Institute for a period of three years, Armstrong would be Director for a year and Oberlander would be a consultant and advisor to the Institute for that period. Eventually, Brahm Wiesman would take on the role of guiding the Institute in Ghana.

Under the leadership of Norman MacKenzie, an overseas student service committee was established at UBC in the summer of 1961. The Committee was chaired by Dr. Cyril Belshaw, associate professor of Anthropology and director of the Regional Training Centre for the United Nations Fellows at UBC. Thirty graduate students were shortlisted for paid teaching assignments in primary and secondary schools in Ghana for a period of 18 months. In addition, two home economists were recruited to advise the Ghanaian government on public health and nutritional problems at the local level.

These efforts were streamlined by a conference held in Montréal that involved the Canadian National Commission for UNESCO and Canadian universities. From these discussions emerged the idea of a national coordinating committee to recruit students for service in underdeveloped countries. This marked the beginning of Canadian university-level and federal aid programs across the globe and was the precursor of the international program of the Association of Universities and Colleges of Canada (AUCC).

The program attracted the support of Maurice Strong who had joined the Pearson government as deputy minister responsible for "external aid," a role that morphed into the Canadian International Development Agency (CIDA). Strong initiated a separate federal diploma program for students from Indonesia, Philippines and India to promote an exchange of ideas around the modernization agenda for "developing" societies. The School of Community and Regional Planning was also involved in housing some of the students invited to Canada through this exchange.

In 1961, Peter was appointed by the United Nations Technical Assistance Administration to a mission to assist the government of Trinidad and Tobago. His task was to advise the prime minister's office through the town and regional planning division on what would be an appropriate planning organization for the specific geopolitical conditions in that country.

The theme that ran through all of these activities was capacity-building, the idea that the focus of Canada's international aid efforts should be the development of the ability of nationals in the recipient countries to take the responsibility for planning and building better cities and societies. It was a manifestation of the philosophy, which Oberlander had helped CMHC present to the Massey Commission, that great cities could only be built in any country by people trained in that country for this purpose.

In a 1961 essay titled "Planning Education in Newly Independent Countries," Peter Oberlander summed up this philosophy as follows:

> In spite of various efforts to adapt educational programs available at American universities to the needs of overseas students, the establishment of an appropriate teaching and training program

"at home" will prove more satisfactory for the student and provide important and lasting by-products. The export of planning teachers would help establish or support indigenous institutions and speed the process of helping new countries to plan for themselves the sort of development that will achieve their own social and economic goals.

As the Oberlander family settled back into life in Vancouver in 1974, Peter resumed his post as Director of SCARP, which Brahm Wiesman had been filling in an acting capacity. He also ran unsuccessfully as a Liberal candidate in the federal election held on July 8 of that year.

Although Peter had no official involvement in the preparations for the forthcoming UN Conference on Human Settlements, he used his position and international reputation to raise awareness and help Vancouver get prepared for the meeting. As the months went by, he became more and more concerned that insufficient progress was being made in organizing the Vancouver meeting. Always preferring to speak to the organ grinder rather than the monkey, he attempted repeatedly to reach the Minister, Barney Danson, on the phone to register his concerns. He most often ended up talking to Danson's assistant, Charles Kelly who had been tasked by Danson with keeping Oberlander off his back. Given Oberlander's dogged determination and passion for the cause, Kelly had his hands full.

In the meantime, a considerable effort was being expended by Oberlander's successor at MSUA, Jim MacNeill, and others, to bring about the conference. Environmental management, particularly its international dimensions, had been a focus of MacNeill's career until then, and it would prove to be so for the remainder of his life. The importance of human settlements in this context had become evident. As he later recalled,

> During the 1960s and 1970s thoughtful people everywhere were convinced that we were living at a juncture in history in which decisions made and unmade would be crucial to our future on this earth and, in response, governments planned a series of special UN conferences to explore those issues of greatest concern and the possibilities for addressing them. Stockholm on the environment in 1972 was followed in 1974 by Bucharest on population growth, Rome on food supplies, and Caracas on the uses of the sea and in

1975 by Mexico City on the role and status of women. A conference on human settlements and urban affairs was seen by many as a synthesis of them all since it was in communities large and small that people played out their daily lives and in the process made the trillions of individual decisions which over time determined the future state of our planet.

At a practical level, the road to a successful United Nations conference on human settlements ran through some challenging terrain, both intellectual and political in nature.

Navigating the intellectual terrain entailed the need to define the scope of the subject of human settlements, involving as it does the "trillions of decisions" that MacNeill described. If the conference focused on everything, it would achieve nothing. Recognizing the need for early definition of the subject matter and the apparent inability of the United Nations to fulfill this need, the Ministry organized a seminar at the University of British Columbia in May 1973, to which twenty international experts were invited. The meeting was chaired by Barbara Ward, Lady Jackson, founding president of the International Institute for Environment and Development in London, UK and the author, among other works, of *Only One Earth,* the unofficial theme book of the Stockholm Conference.

The report on the UBC seminar "Human Settlements: Crisis and Opportunity" was substantially written by Ward and became the guide for the development of the content of the conference. The six themes identified in the report were: human needs in settlements, the role of settlements in national development, environmental quality in settlements, special problems in human settlements, managing human settlements and international co-operation. Ward's report noted that, while many international issues required separate consideration of the "developed" and "developing" worlds, human settlement problems were a common issue for all of humanity. Her subsequent book, *The Home of Man,* published in 1976 with an introduction by Enrique Penalosa, by then the Secretary-General of the Habitat conference, provided a clear description of the many-faceted challenges that urbanization posed for humanity.

The political terrain initially was in Ottawa and the United Nations in New York. The first critical decisions concerned the date and the venue for the conference. The challenge of coordination with other UN activities that related in some way to human settlements and the sheer magnitude of the organizational task resulted in a decision to shift the date of conference back one year to late May and early June 1976.

Toronto, Montréal, and Vancouver were the only cities considered capable of hosting such a meeting, and a search for the necessary hotel rooms led to the selection of Vancouver by default, a decision that would not displease Minister Basford, with his Vancouver political base, or Oberlander. Canada's proposals for the time and venue were presented by Basford and MacNeill to the UN General Assembly in November 1973. Shortly thereafter, Secretary-General Kurt Waldheim accepted Maurice Strong's recommendation that Enrique Penalosa be appointed as Secretary-General of the conference.

In Ottawa, the typically Canadian tendency to assign one task to many (why designate one leader when half a dozen will do?) was clearly not working. The burgeoning job of coordinating the efforts of a multitude of federal agencies not to mention provincial and municipal governments and non-governmental organizations was outstripping the distributed model of responsibility that the government had initially selected, involving MSUA, CMHC and External Affairs among others.

The magnitude of the stakes involved for Canada's reputation was highlighted by a major dust-up over whether representatives of the Palestine Liberation Organization, a body considered by many to be a terrorist organization that was nonetheless recognized by the UN in November 1974, should be allowed to enter Canada to attend a UN conference on crime scheduled to take place in Toronto in September 1975. In essence, it was a conflict between domestic politics (with a provincial election due in Ontario) and the UN principle that host nations cannot dictate who can and cannot attend official UN functions. For a time, the whole Habitat conference was in jeopardy, until Canada agreed, just before the Habitat preparatory committee meeting in New York in August 1974, that attendance at the Toronto conference would be governed by UN rules. It would not be the last time that the politics of the Israeli-Palestinian conflict would threaten the potential for a successful conference.

After some further deliberations, in October, the federal cabinet appointed MacNeill as Canada's Commissioner General for the 1976 Conference on Human Settlements, with full access to key decision-makers and the necessary resources.

The arrangements in Vancouver were to be overseen by Hugh Keenleyside as Associate Commissioner General. After a career as a Canadian diplomat and the head of the UN's Technical Assistance Agency, Keenleyside had "retired" to British Columbia in 1959 and had served as the first Chair of the newly-nationalized provincial electrical utility now known as BC Hydro.

The Israeli-Palestinian issue reared its head again in November 1975 when the UN General Assembly passed a resolution condemning Zionism as a form of racism, which prompted the Vancouver City Council to adopt a resolution revoking its invitation to host the conference. Only after concerted efforts by the then-minister of Urban Affairs Barney Danson, MacNeill, Keenleyside and others was the council persuaded to walk back their resolution.

The Vancouver conference was designed from the outset to be a UN meeting like no other. In making their preparations, member countries were persuaded to produce films on their experiences and aspirations for human settlements, and these are a powerful record to this day. Then in addition to the formal meetings, which were to be held in a downtown Vancouver hotel, the federal government encouraged and supported the creation of a parallel conference for members of the public and non-governmental organizations at the former naval air base at Jericho Beach on the west side of the city, which was made available through the good offices of Park Board Commissioner May Brown. There, under the inspired leadership of Alan Clapp, a derelict airplane hangar was converted to a celebration of all things urban, including "the longest bar in the world" made from a slab of British Columbia Douglas fir. After Barney Danson met Clapp, he said, "That guy is either a genius or the craziest guy in the world."

Bill Reid Mural at Habitat Forum 1976[20]

Within Canada, the federal government supported a program of demonstration projects to showcase Canadian expertise in human settlement planning and development. Included in its recommendations to the conference was the creation of a new international organization to spur action on human settlements, which was to become the Centre for Human Settlements at UBC and a major legacy of the meeting.

Media attention to the events in Vancouver was enhanced by the "Vancouver Symposium" organized by Barbara Ward during the week before the formal meetings. It featured some high-profile people, such as the futurist Buckminster Fuller as well as Mother Teresa, who evoked the human and moral dimensions of global inequities. The seminars and exhibitions of the "counter-conference" at Jericho were carried to the formal meetings downtown on live screens and through demonstrations that drew national and international attention, as when Margaret Trudeau, the Canadian Prime Minister's young wife, carried a bucket of water from Jericho to downtown to symbolize the importance of action to provide access to clean water as a basic human right.

The intended substantive output of the formal meetings was contained in what came to be known as the "Vancouver Declaration on Human Settlements" and its associated "Vancouver Action Plan" containing sixty-four recommendations for national action. Under the chairmanship of Barney Danson, the discussions went relatively smoothly; he was even able to arrange for Barbara Ward to present the "Fourteen Points" approved during the previous week's symposium, even though she did not represent a national government and was not formally permitted to address the gathering.

But then the UN members who had sponsored the resolution equating Zionism with racism broke their agreement to keep that issue out of the discussion and introduced provisions making oblique reference to the infamous resolution. Despite the best efforts of the Canadians and others to keep the Israeli-Palestinian issue from derailing the work that had been done, the meeting dissolved in procedural disarray.

Looking back in 2012, MacNeill recalled that, notwithstanding the rancour that had attended the conclusion of the formal conference, much had been accomplished since the initial focus on human settlements had been put forward at Stockholm:

Nations had for the very first time put the issues of rapid urbanization, exploding cities and human settlements on the global agenda. They had also agreed on a process to keep it there, a process that led to Habitat II in Istanbul in 1996 [and later Habitat III 2016], along with regional meetings and mini-habitats every five years. Habitat and its NGO Forum had energized the media and stimulated the development of civil society bodies and research institutes devoted to the issues. Governments had approved the first global action plan for human settlements, with sixty-four recommendations for national action and several programs for international co-operation. And they had established both a Fund and a new Habitat program and Secretariat, centered in Nairobi alongside UNEP, to facilitate the process, monitor progress and exchange information.

Prime Minister Pierre Trudeau and UN Secretary General Kurt Waldheim[22]

Although Peter Oberlander had had no official role in the Habitat 76 meetings, he had done a considerable amount to exploit and leverage the opportunities they had presented. In a series of papers published in a book entitled *Canada: An Urban Agenda*, prompted by the 1975 joint conference of the Community Planning Association of Canada and the American Society of Planning Officials (of which he was President), he demonstrated his penchant for using milestones to record progress. In the book's preface, he asked, "Could we put together an agenda for a discussion of more appropriate urban policies with 1976, perhaps, as a hinge in the unfolding process of change?"

Oberlander played a key role in establishing the Centre for Human Settlements at the University of British Columbia as a legacy of the Habitat Conference. He became the first director of the Centre, responsible to an interdisciplinary Board of Management chaired by the Dean of Graduate Studies. The Centre was created to further the goals of the Habitat conference by providing a research focus for issues relating to human settlement. One of the main functions of the Centre was to provide access to the audio-visual reference library of video tapes of the 240 presentations contributed by the 140 nations participating in the 1976 conference.

Turning over the Habitat 1976 papers to UBC: Front row (left to right) Hon. Ron Basford (Minister of Justice), UBC President Douglas Kenny, Hon. Barnett Danson (Minister of State for Urban Affairs). Back row: Hon. Hugh Curtis (B.C. Minister of Municipal Affairs and Housing), Enrique Penalosa (Conference Secretary General)[22]

This was the genesis of Peter Oberlander's role, described by one participant as "the Forrest Gump of human settlements," someone who seemed to be ubiquitous as the advocate for the spirit of Habitat during the coming decades.

Such an advocate would be sorely needed, as things turned out. The impetus for action on human settlements coming from the 1972 Stockholm conference had resulted in the establishment, in January 1975, of the United Nations Habitat and Human Settlements Foundation (UNHHSF), the first official UN body dedicated to urbanization. Then under the umbrella of the United Nations Environment Programme (UNEP), its task was to assist national programs relating to human settlements through the provision of capital and technical assistance, particularly in developing countries. The UNHHSF was given an initial budget of $4 million US for a total period of four years.

The Vancouver conference resulted in the creation, in December 1977, of the United Nations Commission on Human Settlements — an intergovernmental body — and the United Nations Centre for Human Settlements (commonly referred to as "Habitat"), which functioned as the executive secretariat of the Commission. Between 1980 and 1990 Peter Oberlander served on the Canadian delegations to the annual meetings of the UN Commission on Human Settlements, based in Nairobi, Kenya.

Habitat was also mandated to manage the UNHHSF funds. From 1978 to 1996, with meagre financial and political support, Habitat struggled to prevent and to ameliorate problems stemming from massive urban growth, particularly in developing countries.

By the early 1980s, it was clear that the energy and commitment to the environment and human settlements that had been generated by the Stockholm and Vancouver conferences were flagging. On a global basis, it was clear that the price of the economic development that was taking place was the degradation of the natural environment and the well-being of many of the world's people. The United Nations asked Norway's Prime Minister, Gro Harlem Brundtland, to create an organization independent of the UN to focus on environmental and developmental problems and solutions.

In 1987, the Brundtland Commission, whose formal name was the World Commission on Environment and Development, issued its report, *Our Common Future*, which reformulated the focus of international action around the concept of sustainable development, meaning "development that meets the needs of the present without compromising the ability of future generations to meet their own needs." Cornelia Oberlander remembers Peter handing her the report, saying, "This report will change your work."

Sustainable development became the energizing concept behind the UN Conference on Environment and Development — best known as the Earth Summit — held in Rio de Janeiro, Brazil, in 1992, twenty years after Stockholm, of which Maurice Strong was the Secretary-General. By then, the federal Liberal government had been replaced by Brian Mulroney's Conservatives who had a remarkable green streak exemplified by strong ministers of the environment, notably Lucien Bouchard and Jean Charest. Responding to the international challenge to respond to the Agenda 21 action plan that would result from Rio, Canada produced an extensive action plan for sustainable development.

The only initiative from Canada's Agenda 21 that would survive the change in government when the Liberals under Jean Chrétien formed government in 1993 was the establishment of an "international centre for sustainable cities" in Vancouver. It was spearheaded by Bob Wenman, the only MP from Western Canada who supported Environment Minister Jean Charest's unsuccessful bid for the Conservative party leadership to succeed Mulroney. With Alan Artibise, a former director of SCARP, as its initial CEO, this organization promoted practical, scalable projects to demonstrate urban sustainability (including social, economic and environmental components) in Eastern Europe, Southeast Asia, Africa and China.

The approach of the International Centre for Sustainable Cities ("Sustainable Cities International") was to identify a local sustainability problem such as solid waste management in a place where there was interest among the representatives of government, the private sector, and civil society in finding a solution. Successful solutions were then "scaled up" to be applied on a broader basis, and "scaled out" to apply the lessons learned to other areas of sustainability.

Peter Oberlander served as one of the federal representatives on the board of the Centre for a number of years and Ken Cameron was a director for its entire life from 1992 to 2012.

After the 1992 Rio summit, UN Habitat found new energy in the prospect of organizing a Habitat II conference to take place in Istanbul in June 1996 to assess two decades of progress since Habitat I in Vancouver and to set fresh goals for the new millennium. The overriding objective of the conference, as described by UN Habitat, was "to increase world awareness of the problems and potentials of human settlements as important inputs to social progress and economic growth, and to commit the world's leaders to making cities, towns and villages healthy, safe, just and sustainable." It was a marked shift in emphasis from the view of urbanization as a negative force to be mitigated or reversed that had prevailed at the Vancouver meeting.

Canada and British Columbia had a strong presence at Habitat II, coordinated by Canada Mortgage and Housing after the demise of MSUA. Peter Oberlander was appointed Special Assistant to Dr. Wally N'Dow, Secretary-General for the conference. Included in the Canadian delegation were Michael Harcourt, who had recently stepped down as Premier of British Columbia, and Darlene Marzari, Minister of Municipal Affairs and Housing. Harcourt later characterized the urbanization trends presented at the Istanbul conference as an "urban tsunami," which provided a focus for his considerable contributions to the cause of sustainable cities at the national and international levels in the period after he left politics.

Although Habitat II was a success, the organization was in serious difficulty as a result of financial and administrative problems. After N'Dow's departure, Darshan Johal, a graduate of SCARP who had spent a career in UN organizations, was appointed Acting Director of Habitat in 1997. In a visit with Johal at the Habitat office in Nairobi, Oberlander exhorted his former student to take action to reform the organization. When Johal demurred, saying he was only Acting Director, Oberlander said, "Exactly. You're the Acting Director; therefore, you must *act!*"

Oberlander and Johal met frequently throughout their respective careers. A few weeks before Oberlander's death, Johal recounted one of their more memorable moments:

> I showed him a photo in which Imelda Marcos was entertaining the delegates at the 1981 session of our Commission. Peter recognized several delegates and, of course, himself sitting in the back. Then he reminded me that one evening I had danced with Imelda Marcos in Manila.
>
> I explained how it had happened. The First Lady had grabbed my hand and dragged me to the dance floor, despite my protesting that I did not know how to dance. "Anyone who can walk can dance," she said. "But, Madam, I might step on your toes and spoil your

shoes." "Don't worry about the shoes. I have many others," she said with a wink.

Peter was obviously enjoying the story. I concluded by telling him what transpired in Nairobi upon my return. The Turkish Ambassador happened to be at the airport. He came running to me in great excitement and kept saying, "So it's true, it's true. I can tell from the glow on your face that you danced with Imelda Marcos." Setting aside diplomatic protocol, I put my hand on His Excellency's shoulder and calmly said, "But Mr. Ambassador, you should have seen the glow on *her* face!" Peter clapped his hands and roared with laughter.

After the appointment of Anna Tibaijuka as Executive Director in 2000, the centrepiece of UN Habitat's international action program became its biennial World Urban Forums, the first of which was planned for Nairobi in 2002. These meetings were intended to be all-inclusive in terms of attendance, overcoming the artificial divide between the official meeting of governments and the participants from civil society that had characterized the 1976 conference.

As part of its preparations for the Earth Summit planned for Johannesburg for 2002, thirty years after Stockholm, Environment Canada held a series of consultation meetings across the country to seek input to Canada's national position. The Vancouver meeting was held at the Waterfront Centre Hotel. Peter Oberlander, Ken Cameron and Nola Kate Seymoar (CEO of the Vancouver-based International Centre for Sustainable Cities) found themselves seated next to each other at the open-square table designed to facilitate dialogue.

Inspired by Oberlander's propensity to exploit milestones, they began riffing on the themes: Stockholm 1972 + 30 = Johannesburg 1992, the World Urban Forum planned for 2004 in Barcelona with no venue then set for 2006, and Habitat (Vancouver) 1976 + 30 = 2006. Thus, the idea of Canada hosting the 2006 World Urban Forum in Vancouver was born.

The idea fitted neatly with the feeling that it was time for Vancouver (and Canada) to step out on the world stage, having hosted the highly successful Expo 86 and being in the final stages of bidding for the 2010 Winter Olympic Games, which it would win in July 2003. It would be an opportunity to showcase the Vancouver region's growing achievements in urban sustainability, building on its ground-breaking Livable Region plans and the somewhat ephemeral urban quality known as "Vancouverism."

In the coming weeks, the idea got legs. Oberlander secured the support of Stephen Owen, MP for Vancouver Quadra and Minister of Western Diversification in the Chrétien government, while Cameron and Seymoar worked their contacts locally, nationally and internationally. The idea was not well-received in official Ottawa, where the rather vague benefits of another international meeting paled in relation to the time and money that would have to be spent.

An invitation from Canada to host the 2006 World Urban Forum in Vancouver was not in Prime Minister Chrétien's Johannesburg speech when he left Ottawa in August 2002, but the lengthy trip, including a stopover in Switzerland, offered some opportunities for those outside the bureaucracy to have some further influence. When he got to the conference in Johannesburg at the end of August, Chrétien extended the invitation –— not once, but twice: first to a business group and then to the plenary session.

Prime Minister Jean Chrétien and UN Secretary-General Kofi
Annan at Johannesburg Summit September 2002[23]

The plan for Vancouver in 2006 gave added importance to Canada's participation in the Second World Urban Forum in Barcelona in September 2004. The Canadian delegation, led by the Minister for CMHC, Joe Fontana, included Owen and Oberlander as well as Cameron and Seymoar. The Canadians were pleased to see that the Barcelona organizers had exerted a considerable effort to make the event open and inclusive of non-governmental interests and to emphasize networking and dialogue. They were determined to build on these aspects in Vancouver.

Back in Canada, extensive consultations and discussions got underway for World Urban Forum III to be held at the Vancouver Convention Centre on June 19-23, 2006. National and regional advisory committees were established, a series of background papers was commissioned and published, and an experiment in simultaneous electronic consultation named the "Habitat Jam" was organized. Charles Kelly, who had been Barney Danson's executive assistant at MSUA and was by then a local businessman, was appointed Commissioner General. He was ably assisted by Phil Heard, an unflappable wizard at organization and crisis management and veteran event manager.

Oberlander, Seymoar and Cameron were determined to ensure that the World Urban Forum leave a legacy in Vancouver, something that would recognize the region's leadership and perpetuate the cause of international co-operation for urban sustainability. As a contribution to the knowledge base of the conference, they worked through the International Centre for Sustainable Cities to produce "From Ideas to Action: 70 Actionable Ideas for the World Urban Forum 3."

It was all going swimmingly until the Liberal government of Paul Martin lost a vote of confidence in the House of Commons on November 28, 2005, forcing a winter general election on January 23, 2006 that resulted in a minority government under Conservative leader Stephen Harper. It was evident to anyone who had been paying the slightest attention that UN conferences, the UN, cities, sustainability and global human challenges would be among the things in which the new government would be the least interested.

And it proved to be so. The conference was, as Mary Tyler Moore would say, "not awful," but the Prime Minister and his senior ministers studiously avoided it, and it was clear that the prospects for any continuing interest in urban sustainability on the part of Canada's national government — let alone a legacy for the Vancouver region — were slim to nil.

In spite of the disappointment felt by many, Peter could take some satisfaction in bringing the world's attention on human settlements back to Vancouver and Canada, the stage upon which he had done so much to demonstrate the importance of great settlements to the future of humanity. In the cover story of the first issue of UN Habitat's magazine, *Urban World*, published a few weeks before his death, Oberlander set out his view of the role of the city in the future.

> The city is humanity's greatest achievement. It needs care and stewardship to bring its historic role into the new century...It is an enduring artifact, a resilient organism. The city is fragile, yet robust, a global partner in social, economic and environmental progress.

> The city's historic role is deeply embedded in most languages, carrying within its Latin roots "civitas" yielding to "civilization." The Greeks gave us "polis," we thrive in metropolitan communities. Recently, and on a global scale, all of us proclaim citizenship as allegiance to a nation state; we acquire and change citizenship ceremonially...City states preceded the creation of nation states and have endured...The city is an instrument of change. It is our only hope for the global survival of an expanding population that will have to share limited resources on a finite globe.

At a ceremony in Washington, DC on October 3, 2009, World Habitat Day, Peter Oberlander was posthumously awarded the UN Habitat 2009 Scroll of Honour "for his lifetime of promoting the urban agenda around the world."

CHAPTER TEN:

TIKUN OLAM: REPAIRING THE WORLD

"To take no part in the running of the community's affairs is to be either a beast or a god!" — Aristotle

During one of many sessions going through Peter's papers searching for material for this book, Cornelia Oberlander turned to Ken Cameron and said, "Have you heard the phrase *tikun olam?*" Not for the first time in Cameron's conversations with either of the Oberlanders, he had to confess he had no idea what she was talking about. "They were his last words to me. It's a Hebrew expression that, roughly translated, means repairing or healing the world," she said. "I think it sums up Peter's life very well."

Why would Peter dedicate his life to healing the world and to pursuing that mission as a Canadian? Given his treatment, not only by the Nazis in Austria but also by Britain and Canada, it would not have been surprising had he devoted himself to wealth accumulation, religious study, pottery any other calling that would have allowed him to turn inward and heal the wounds that been inflicted on him. That he did not do so seems to be attributable to a deep desire to contribute to a better future, not only for himself and later his family but also for all of humanity. As Cornelia put it after his death, "The indignity of being interned most likely shaped Peter's direction to work for the betterment of humanity."

"Citizenship" seems to be the term that best sums up Peter's motivations. It is a word to which most dictionaries (including Dictionary.com, cited here) ascribe two meanings, both of them relevant to an understanding of his life.

The first meaning is "the state of being vested with the rights, privileges, and duties of a citizen." From the perspective of this meaning of the term, Peter experienced the full gamut of formal citizenship status, from his youth in a comfortable middle-class family who had been citizens of Austria for 400 years through the complete erasure of that status as a result of their forceful ejection from that country. Whatever citizenship status Peter had had on landing in Britain was stripped through his internment, and he arrived in Canada without any documentation of his birth, nationality or educational attainment. From his "complex and ambivalent" welcome to Canada, Peter developed a deep commitment to the country as proud citizen.

For the last 10 years of life, he was a Citizenship Court Judge, inducting new immigrants to citizenship and informing them of their rights and responsibilities. These included the following **rights**: to vote, to be a candidate, to enter, remain in or leave Canada, to earn a living and reside anywhere in the country, to the protection of official language rights in English and French and to apply for and hold a Canadian passport. With these rights, and equally important in Peter's mind, were the **responsibilities**: to obey Canada's laws, to vote, to respect the rights of others, to respect private and public property and to care for Canada's heritage.

Not having these rights and responsibilities is inconceivable to native-born Canadians, and not having some sort of citizenship is something experienced only by refugees. Given Peter's experience, citizenship in its formal meaning was deeply significant.

The second meaning of "citizenship" is "the character of an individual viewed as a member of society; behavior in terms of the duties, obligations, and functions of a citizen, as in an 'award for good citizenship," It is this second meaning that infuses Oberlander's life as presented in this book. As with most people with a record of achievement, Peter played many roles. Not only was citizenship a theme in all of them, nearly all of them also had a global dimension. He was a perpetual educator, a dedicated public servant, a skilled practitioner, a lifelong partner, a liberal Jew and a caring and engaged parent.

He saw himself primarily as an educator, and he viewed the School of Community and Regional Planning at UBC as his most important legacy. He believed that the contributions of the school's graduates in a variety of roles and settings throughout the world represented the greatest amplification of his values and perspectives. In 2006, the Canadian Institute of Planners selected him for the President's award. The citation stated, "Your lifetime dedication to the education of planners and to the needs of community on a global scale are unmatched by any Canadian."

In addition to his association with UBC, Peter had significant involvements with Simon Fraser University, Langara College, and the Hebrew University of Jerusalem. His educational philosophy emphasized the need for a kind of "contextual integrity," insisting initially that planning in Canadian cities be undertaken by planners trained in Canada, and later that locally-appropriate planning education be provided in other countries such as Ghana.

Public service was never far from Peter Oberlander's mind, whether it was serving as the Chair of the Vancouver School Board or offering himself for election to the House of Commons. His role as the first Secretary of the Ministry of State for Urban Affairs gave him the opportunity to apply his thinking and practice to the thorny problem of providing effective national governance for a federated nation of cities.

Oberlander's role as a planning practitioner was permeated by his insistence that ideas be translated into action, whether it was in providing a strategic vision for postwar West Vancouver or bringing to life the idea of a "community for leisure" in Kona. These physical and local planning exercises were always placed within the context of the broader region and the imperatives of global change. Equally important, they were conceived with implementation in mind.

Peter's partnership with Cornelia — "56 wonderful years minus 7 days and never a dull moment," as she put it — was simultaneously highly traditional and intensely modern. She was fond of mentioning the number of meals she had made for him — "143,000 meals in 63 years of marriage minus seven days." — and the fact that he couldn't boil an egg. Peter's mother had told Cornelia that carrying bags of groceries was beneath his dignity. He tended to introduce her at social events as "Mrs. Oberlander," and he described her magnificent landscape design contribution to the plan for the sacred lands at Keauhou, Kona (it would later earn her an honorary degree) as "landscaping by Cornelia Oberlander." "Friends always wondered how we could build two houses and still be together," she recalled. And yet they were collaborators and partners in a working relationship of equals.

Cornelia Hahn Oberlander and H. Peter Oberlander
at the Einstein Tower, Potsdam, 2005[24]

As their two equally distinguished careers developed, they drew on each other's strengths. When the children were young, Peter and Cornelia would have dinner with them as a family then work together into the wee small hours after they were in bed. As she later observed, "There wasn't a professional proposal that left this house that we weren't both completely satisfied with."

They each received honorary degrees from UBC (Cornelia's was first, and there were to be half a dozen from other institutions) and were inducted into the Order of Canada. The recognition for Cornelia continued after Peter's death as she carried on into her 90s as Peter would have expected. Among other honours, she received the Sir Geoffrey Jellicoe Award of the International Federation of Landscape Architects, and she was the inaugural recipient of the Canadian Governor General's Award in Landscape Architecture. In 2017, she was promoted to Companion of the Order of Canada, the highest echelon in Canada's honour system. There is not a great deal to be gained by speculating on which of these two people had the greater ability or the more distinguished career, but Cornelia would not come second in any such analysis.

The lives of Peter Oberlander and Rabbi Philip Bregman of Temple Sholom were intertwined for more than 30 years. They shared a love of Judaism and an attachment to Israel. The Oberlander family played a key role in the development of the Temple from the early years when its rented premises on 10ᵗʰ Avenue were fire-bombed on January 26, 1985 in a chilling reminder that Vancouver was not immune to violent anti-Semitism. It continued with the Oberlanders' contribution to Richard Henriquez's design of the new building on Oak Street in a prominent location with a wide frontage that rejected the European tradition that synagogues should be tucked away on secondary streets to be less of a target. Peter and Cornelia started the Temple's first religious classes in their home.

Bregman and Oberlander were both firmly on the liberal side of Jewish tradition, but Oberlander's German liberal approach was not as conservative as the philosophy that Bregman had absorbed by Rabbi Gunther Plaut at Toronto's Holy Blossom Temple. They had vigorous discussions. As a Citizenship Court Judge, Peter inducted Bregman's American wife as a citizen of Canada, describing Canada and the United States to her as "two countries separated by a common language." Both men subscribed to the Book of Isaiah's outward-looking notion of Judaism as *Or LaGoyim*, a light to the nations.

As parents, Peter and Cornelia reflected the formality of their European upbringing, with its emphasis on hard work, good behaviour and education as a preparation for a constructive life. But there was also fun. "Peter was a loving father who, in the early years, came home to play with Judy, Tim, and Wendy after dinner," Cornelia remembers. "He was even punctual at 6:30 p.m. sharp to assist the children with their dinner. We worked hard but we also played hard. We skied almost every weekend in the winter. In the summer, Peter loved to swim in the icy water at Saturna [Island] and also we swam with the Mergansers in the Queen Charlottes [Haida Gwai]. Above all Peter opened our eyes to the beauty of the world with his awareness of good design."

At Peter's funeral, Judy Oberlander said:

> Many of us will remember two of his favourite mantras: *L'dor v' dor*, translated from Hebrew as "from generation to generation," and the Latin expression *Carpe Diem*, "seize the day." Here lies the opportunity of sharing knowledge, experiences and leadership responsibilities from one generation to another, and at the same time to seize the opportunities which life presents each and

every day. With great style, Peter did both. Despite unbelievable challenges at different stages of his life, he always looked at the sunny side of life.

Such an outlook is indispensable for anyone who seeks to contribute as a citizen to a better future.

It was only in the late nineteenth century that the concept of citizenship expanded from the locality where one was born to the new nation states, particularly in Europe. The development of western democracies supported the tendency for the residents of a country to be regarded as citizens with rights and responsibilities rather than subjects whose lives were subject to the whim of a royal order. Like ethnicity or religious identity, however, citizenship has been a two-edged sword, an instrument of both inclusion and exclusion.

The twentieth century trends of global conflict, mass migration, and economic integration tended to blur the relatively simple concept of citizenship as a belonging to a single nation state. With the economic and social integration of Europe after World War II came the creation of rights to live, work and play within a broader territory without formal internal borders. The recognition of humanity's collective peril in a time of potentially catastrophic nuclear conflict and environmental degradation has led to efforts to create international institutions, under the umbrella of the United Nations and other bodies, designed to protect the future of the human race collectively as well as individually.

From the perspective of the first quarter of the twenty-first century one cannot, however, avoid the somewhat darker trends that have accompanied the effort to secure what the Brundtland Commission described as "our common future." Nativism, ethnic and religious extremism, economic protectionism and old-fashioned parochialism are powerful influences on the world as it is and on what it may come to be. There always seems to be a body of thought that would prefer to build a wall rather than a bridge.

In this context, Canada may have developed a concept of citizenship that is unique and useful. The University of Toronto's Mark Kingwell summarized it well: "Justice is long and hard work, never-ending, the work of citizens. In our increasingly networked and decentralized lives, we may only rarely consider citizenship the most important fact about us. Metaphysically speaking, it's probably not. 'Canadian' is not an identity; it's a relationship."

If Canadians have indeed redefined citizenship as a relationship, it is at least in part because we have been able to learn from people whose life experience reflects the progression of the concept of citizenship in the past century. Often that experience includes severe hardships resulting from humanity's attempts to reconcile atavistic instincts with the imperatives of a crowded planet, to reach a holistic and personal peace. Such people have been able to blend the particularism of their ethnic, religious and national origins with a sense of responsibility to humanity as a whole, recognizing that we are the first species able to cause — or to avert — our own destruction.

Peter Oberlander was such a person. He showed the way towards a better future for the human family. For him, the key to that future was — and remains — better cities.

APPENDIX A:

LIST OF PERSONS INTERVIEWED

Angeles, Leanora
Ben-Natan, Daniel
Bregman, Philip
Clark, Ian
Damaz, Ala
Dodek, Irene
Dorcey, Anthony
Dunlop, David
Enemark, Tex
Fallick, Arthur
Ford, Marguerite
Furukawa, Robert
Gerson, Martin
Ginnell, Kevin
Gurstein, Penny
Harcourt, Mike
Hein, Scot
Hogan, John
Johal, Darshan
Kelly, Charles
Knight, Nancy, and the members of
the UBC President's Committee on
Campus Enhancement
Laquian, Prod
MacNeill, James

Massey, Geoffrey
Miller, Frieda
Newbrun, Eva
Oberlander, Cornelia
Oberlander, George
Oberlander, Wendy
Owen, Stephen
Pendakur, Setty
Rees, William
Saumier, André
Schwinhamer, Steven
Seymoar, Nola Kate
Siedler, Penelope
Smith, Patrick
Sullivan, Sam
Swain, Harry
Van Ginkel, Blanche
Verhayden, Maggie
Weller, Karen
Zirnhelt, David

APPENDIX B:

MAJOR REFERENCES

Publications

Cameron, Ken. "Some Puppets: Some Shoestrings! The Changing Intergovernmental Context," in *Urban Affairs: Back on the Policy Agenda*, eds. Caroline Andrew, Katherine A. Graham and Susan D. Phillips. Montréal and Kingston: McGill-Queen's University Press, 2002.

Carver, Humphrey. *Compassionate Landscape*. Toronto, The University of Toronto Press, 1975.

Damer, Eric and Rosengarten, Herbert. *UBC: The First Hundred Years*. Vancouver: The University of British Columbia, 2009.

Herrington, Susan. *Cornelia Hahn Oberlander: Making the Modern Landscape*. Charlottesville and London: University of Virginia Press.

Hoffman, Paul. *The Viennese: Splendor, Twilight and Exile*. New York: Doubleday, 1988.

Lithwick, N.H. *Urban Canada: Problems and Prospects*. Ottawa: Central Mortgage and Housing, 1970.

McDougal, A.K. *John P. Robarts: His Life and Government*. Toronto: University of Toronto Press, 1986

McKeough, Darcy. *The Duke of Kent*. Toronto: ECW Press, 2016.

Menes Kahn, Bonnie. *Cosmopolitan Culture: The Gilt-Edged Dream of a Tolerant City*. New York: Atheneum, 1987.

Mumford, Eric. *The CIAM Discourse on Urbanism, 1928-1960.* Cambridge, Mass.: MIT Press, 2000.

Oberlander, H. Peter (ed.). *Canada: An Urban Agenda.* Ottawa: Community Planning Press and ASPO Press, 1976.

Oberlander, H. Peter and Fallick, Arthur. *The Ministry of State for Urban Affairs: A Courageous Experiment in Public Administration.* Vancouver: The Centre for Human Settlements, University of British Columbia, 1987.

Oberlander, H. Peter and Newbrun, Eva. *Houser: The Life and Work of Catherine Bauer.* Vancouver: UBC Press, 1999.

Oberlander, H. Peter. "Housing and Community Planning: Step-Children of Canadian Federalism. *Queen's Quarterly* (1957) pp. 663-672.

O'Neill, Helen. *A Singular Vision: Harry Seidler.* Sydney: HarperCollins Australia, 2013.

Spicer, Zachary. "The Reluctant Urbanist: Pierre Trudeau and the Creation of the Ministry of State for Urban Affairs." *International Journal of Canadian Studies* 44 (2011), 185–199.

Spicer, Zachary. "The Rise and Fall of The Ministry of State For Urban Affairs: A Re-Evaluation." *Canadian Political Science Review,* Vol. 5, No. 2, 2011, 117-126.

Stinson, Cathy. *Love Every Leaf: The Life of Landscape Architect Cornelia Hahn Oberlander.* Toronto: Tundra Books, 2008.

Waite, P.B. *The Lord of Point Grey: Larry MacKenzie of UBC.* Vancouver: UBC Press, 1987.

Ward, Barbara. *The Home of Man.* Toronto: McClelland and Stewart, 1976.

Research Works

Oberlander, H. Peter. *Housing and Community Planning: An Aspect of Canadian Federalism.* Thesis submitted in partial fulfillment of the requirements of a Doctor of Philosophy in City and Regional Planning, Harvard University, 1956.

Film and Video Resources

Oberlander, Wendy. "Nothing to be Written Here." 1996 (copy on deposit at Vancouver Holocaust Education Centre)

School of Community and Regional Planning, University of British Columbia. Interview with Peter and Cornelia Oberlander: December 2008

Online Resource

"Enemy Aliens: the Internment of Jewish Refugees in Canada, 1940-43" Vancouver: Vancouver Holocaust Education Centre, 2012.

APPENDIX C:

ABBREVIATIONS AND ACRONYMS

AUCC	Association of Universities and Colleges of Canada
CFMM	Canadian Federation of Mayors and Municipalities
CIDA	Canadian International Development Agency
CMHC	Central (now Canada) Mortgage and Housing Corporation
FCM	Federation of Canadian Municipalities (new name for the Canadian Federation of Mayors and Municipalities as of 1976)
GSD	Harvard University Graduate School of Design
HABITAT	United Nations Human Settlements Program
ICSC	International Centre for Sustainable Cities (also known as Sustainable Cities International)
LMRPB	Lower Mainland Regional Planning Board
MSUA	Ministry of State for Urban Affairs
SCARP	University of British Columbia School of Community and Regional Planning
UBC	University of British Columbia
UNESCO	United Nations Economic, Social and Cultural Organization

APPENDIX D
PHOTO CREDITS

1. University of British Columbia Archives, [UBC 41.1/1848.2].
2. University of Victoria.
3. Judy Oberlander.
4. City of Vienna https://www.wien.gv.at/english/history/overview/ringstrasse.html .
5. Wikipedia.
6. https://commons.wikimedia.org/wiki/File:Votivkirche_Maximilianplatz_ Wien_1900.jpg.
7. Wikimedia File Bundesarchiv Bild 183-1987-0922-500, Wien, Heldenplatz, Rede Adolf Hitler.jpg.
8. Google Images: https://upload.wikimedia.org/wikipedia/commons/8/86/HMS_ Sobieski_FL8900.jpg.
9. Courtesy of the Oberlander family, Vancouver Holocaust Education Centre Collections. Photo: Jessica Bushey.
10. McGill University Archives, RG 76 / PR036824.
11. By Max Dupain - National Library of Australia, Public Domain, https://commons. wikimedia.org/w/index.php?curid=16543848.
12. University of British Columbia Archives, [UBC 5.1.4551].
13. The Ubyssey, October 25, 1968.
14. University of British Columbia Archives, Photo by Jim Banham [UBC 41.1.197].
15. 19461000 Bartholomew Map.
16. http://www.historicplaces.ca/hpimages/Thumbnails/44587_Large.jpg.
17. Vancouver Sun.
18. https://granvilleisland.com/directory/ron-basford-park.
19. https://lifesite-cache.s3.amazonaws.com/images/made/images/remote/https_s3.ama-zonaws.com/lifesite/6-Strong-at-Stockholm_1_810_500_55_s_c1.jpg.
20. https://commonground.ca/habitat-76/, photo by Walter Quan.
21. https://www.unmultimedia.org/s/photo/detail/186/0186517.html.
22. H. Peter Oberlander papers.
23. http://www.un.org/events/wssd/photos/020904sgphotos.htm.
24. Judy Oberlander.
25. Angela Walkinshaw.

INDEX